WARRINGTON REFLECTIONS

Janice Hayes

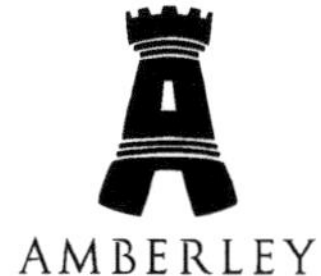

AMBERLEY

First published 2023

Amberley Publishing
The Hill, Stroud, Gloucestershire, GL5 4EP
www.amberley-books.com

Copyright © Janice Hayes and Culture Warrington, 2023

The right of Janice Hayes to be identified as the Author
of this work has been asserted in accordance with the
Copyrights, Designs and Patents Act 1988.

ISBN 978 1 3981 0532 4 (print)
ISBN 978 1 3981 0533 1 (ebook)

British Library Cataloguing in Publication Data.
A catalogue record for this book is available from the
British Library.

Typesetting by SJmagic DESIGN SERVICES, India.
Printed in Great Britain.

Introduction

Warrington as we find it today is an enterprising and progressive town ... with unlimited scope for development. The town has altered considerably during the last few decades ... but the town still possesses many places of great antiquity.

This extract from *The Warrington Guardian's Directory and History of Warrington and its Environs* may have been written in 1908 but it also echoes similar changes witnessed by present-day Warringtonians.

Many of these changes were also witnessed in towns and cities across the country; others were the result of planned local development following Warrington's designation as a New Town in 1968 which ended a period of post-war stagnation. Town centre renewal had been halted whilst planners and conservationists debated the rival claims of traffic, people and historic buildings. Pressing issues like the regeneration of the derelict Second World War military sites of Risley Munitions Factory, Padgate RAF Camp and Burtonwood US Army Air Base sat alongside the broader issue of making Warrington a successful regional growth point.

Two agencies were to realise the master plan for the new town by 1991. Warrington New Town Development Corporation (WNTDC) was to develop the new areas of Birchwood, Padgate and Westbrook on the derelict sites together with Pewterspear to the south of the Manchester Ship Canal. Each area was to have an infrastructure of roads, employment sites, shopping centres, housing, schools and community facilities. Warrington Borough Council was responsible for the regeneration of the town centre and areas of the old borough. The Second World War had brought an end to 1930s proposals to regenerate the Old Market Area which survived until the creation of Golden Square in the 1980s when many of the town's old buildings disappeared in the long-running conflict between progress and conservation.

The geography of Warrington also changed with the local government reform of 1974 which brought parts of old Lancashire and Cheshire within the borough boundaries. Some traditional villages like Grappenhall, Thelwall and Appleton outwardly retained their rural character whilst new districts at Padgate, Birchwood, Westbrook and Chapelford have emerged. The population of the town also swelled and by the early twenty-first century included new residents from the contemporary global society.

The late twentieth-century nationwide decline in heavy industries saw Warrington cease to be a 'Town of Many Industries', where the majority of the workforce toiled in factories which dominated the townscape and created pollution which hung over the town like a pall. By the twenty-first century the workforce was mostly concentrated in the distribution centres or business parks on the outskirts of the town and the old factory sites had found new uses as retail centres or as housing estates.

For the factory workers of Cockhedge and iron and steel workers of Bewsey living alongside the factory was a necessity, but with the growth of the town's public transport network in the early twentieth century wealthier Warringtonians moved away from the town into new suburbs south of the new Manchester Ship Canal, where streets of new villas sprang up while the age of private car ownership saw yet more housing estates pop up around the town.

As the era of the horseless carriage gave way to the age of the motor, Warrington felt a particular impact because of the strategic importance of its bridge as a vital node on the national transport network. Although nearby motorways siphoned off some of the through traffic, the rise in local commuter traffic and family car journeys inevitably placed a strain on the local infrastructure. Whole areas of the town were transformed by the creation of ring roads and distributor roads designed to relieve traffic congestion. By the late twentieth century a network of motorways, expressways, local distributor roads and the old highways had linked the town centre with established villages and New Town Development areas.

Warringtonians' daily life has also changed almost beyond recognition with the disappearance of traditional family-run businesses like butchers, grocers and corner shops. In their place have come nationwide chain stores, supermarkets, coffee shops and out-of-town retail parks.

Warrington's townscape continues to evolve. In September 2022 plans were submitted to demolish the disused Unilever site at Bank Quay, finally ending two centuries of Warrington's soap-making industry and removing the most prominent reminder of Warrington's industrial past. Simultaneously preparations began for the demolition of Fiddler's Ferry power station and its distinctive cooling towers which had dominated the town's skyline for a more modest half century. Meanwhile New Town House was bulldozed into history and another major redevelopment of the neighbouring Cockhedge Centre was announced.

Warringtonians past and present have given the town its unique character and many of them look out at us curiously from the official photographs, picture postcards and informal snapshots to help us reflect how Warrington has changed through time. Whole areas of the townscape have altered so drastically that it is often hard to mirror past and present views, and key vantage points have themselves disappeared.

The districts which make up the present town each deserve a separate volume to reflect their changing built environment, but the town's professional and amateur photographers have left the largest legacy showing the transformation of central Warrington. *Warrington Reflections* invites the reader to take a time-walk through the town's constantly evolving landscape and pause to look out for the remaining reminders of the past whilst navigating the latest developments.

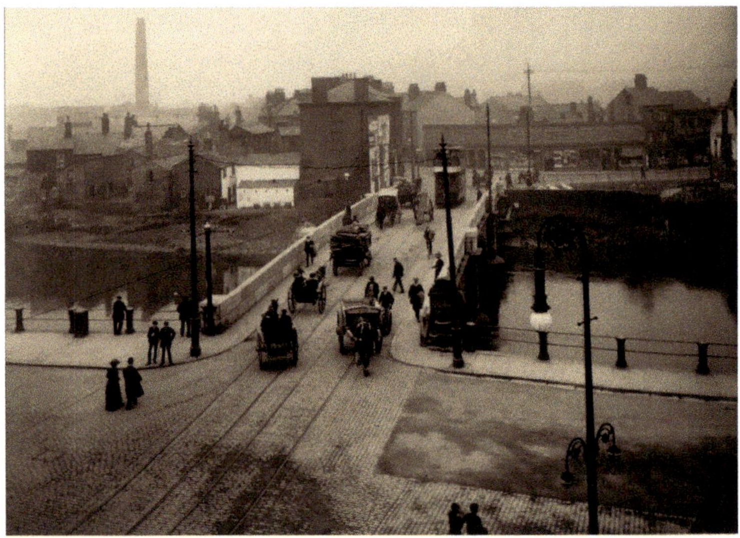

This view from the old Academy building over Warrington Bridge was impossible to replicate in the present day as the building was moved to a neighbouring adjacent site in the 1980s!

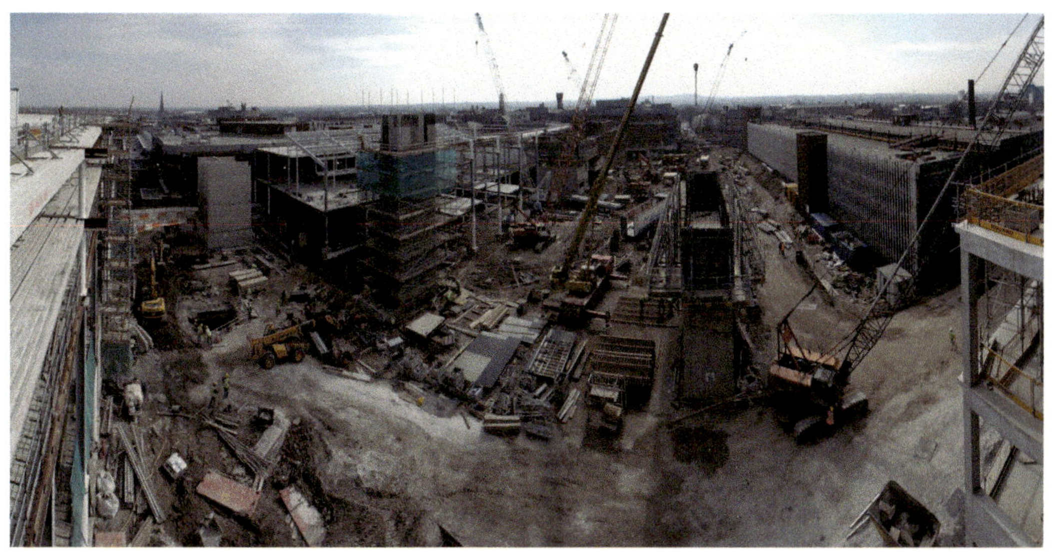

Construction of the second phase of Golden Square as Midland Way takes shape (left) and Legh Street car park (right) awaits demolition.

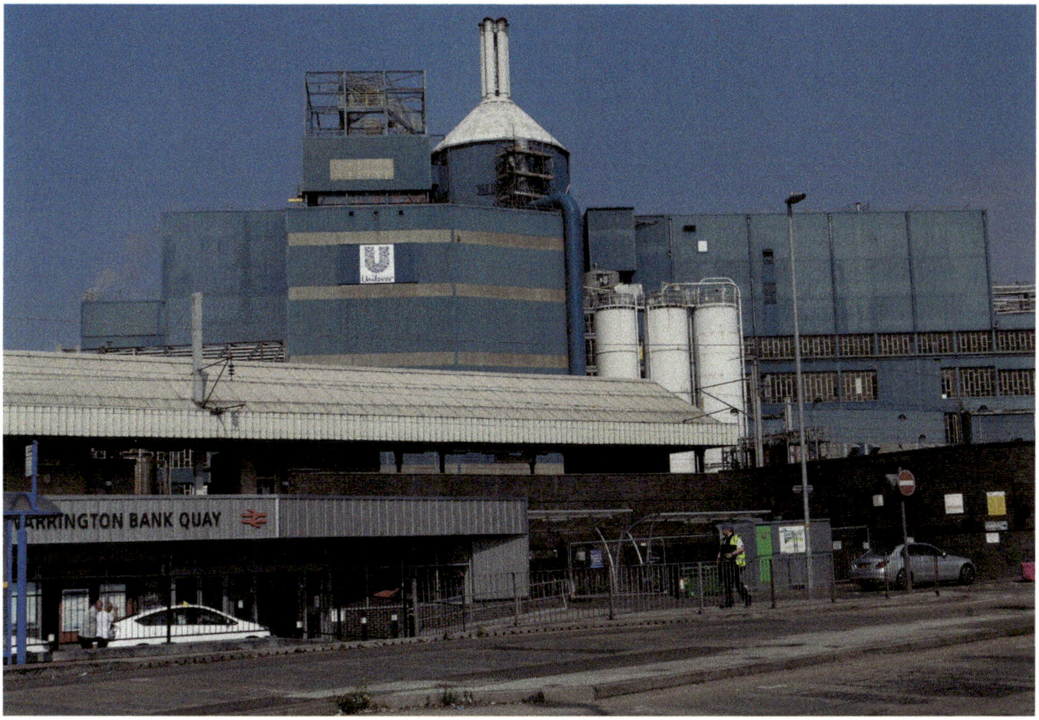

Travellers arriving at Warrington's Bank Quay station used to be greeted by the smell of soap from the former Crosfield's/Unilever works but by 2023 both will have disappeared forever.

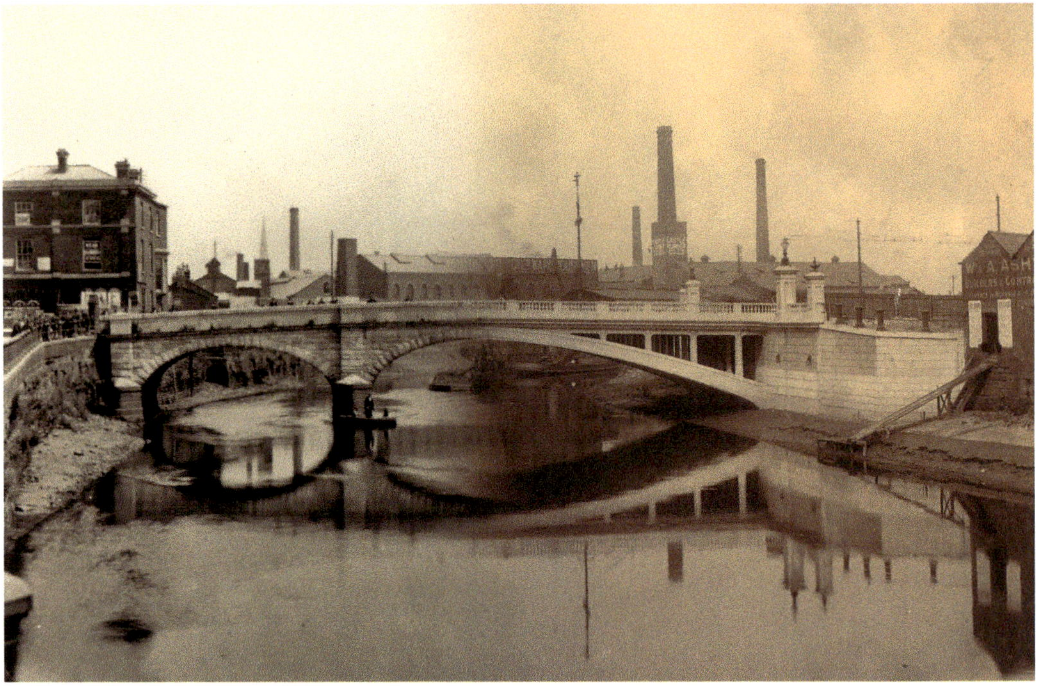

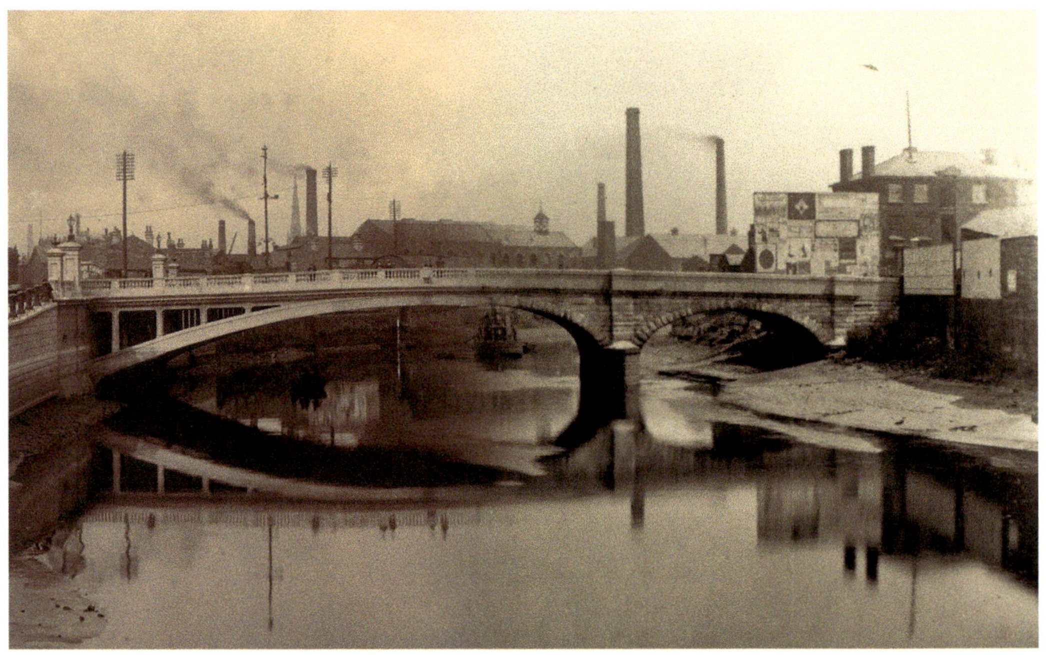

Location has been crucial to Warrington's prosperity throughout its history. From earliest times people came to Warrington to cross over the River Mersey – first by the ancient ford at Latchford and later by bridge. In 1837 a sturdy three-arched stone bridge, named after the new Queen Victoria, was opened (seen in the earlier photograph, above left). By 1900 the 20-foot-wide bridge had proved inadequate for the increasing volume of road traffic and an 85-foot-wide replacement was built.

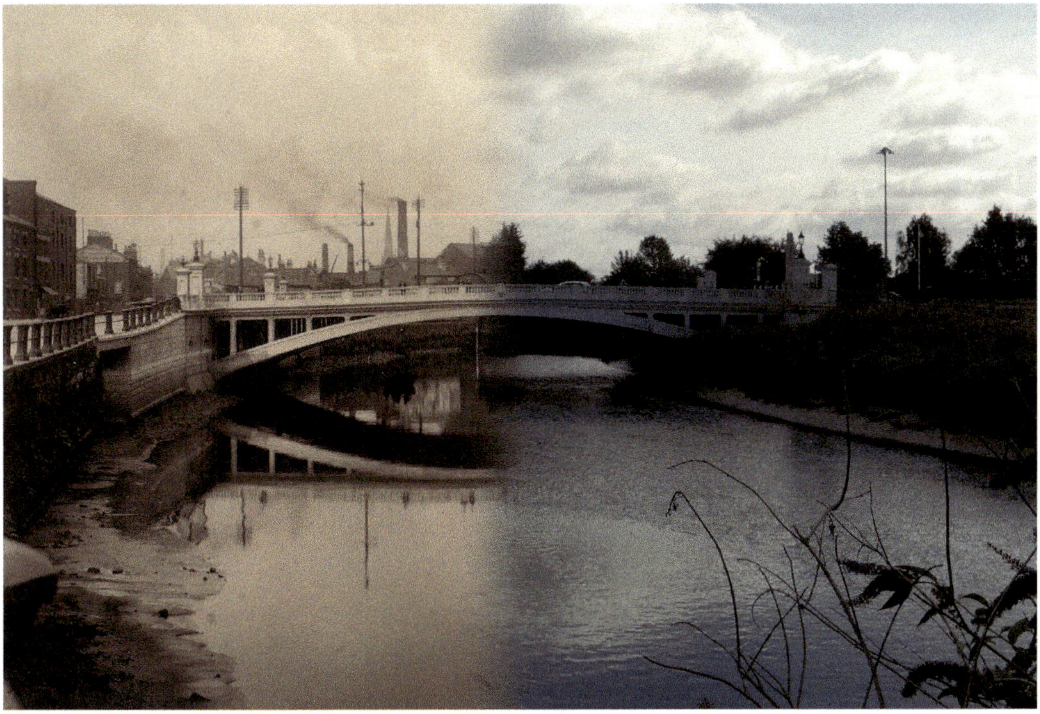

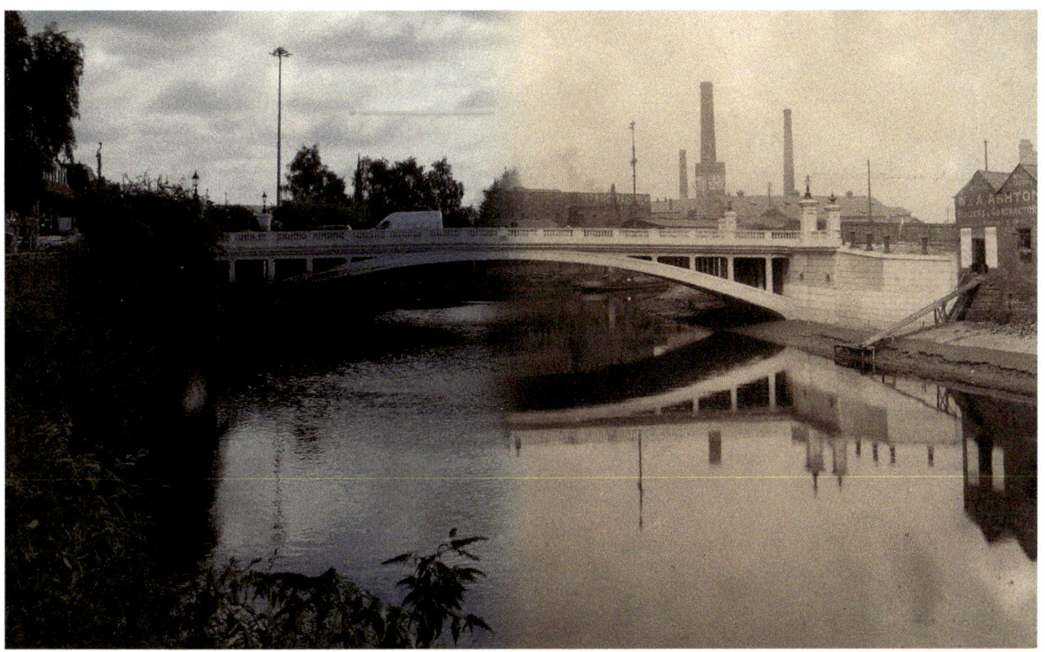

A much wider single-span reinforced concrete bridge, designed by local engineer John James Webster, was built between 1911 and 1915 with a second crossing added in the 1990s. Webster's bridge is still in use today but river traffic rarely passes beneath it. The industry which lined the Mersey's banks has disappeared and today nature is beginning to reclaim the riverside with even an occasional seal spotted nearby.

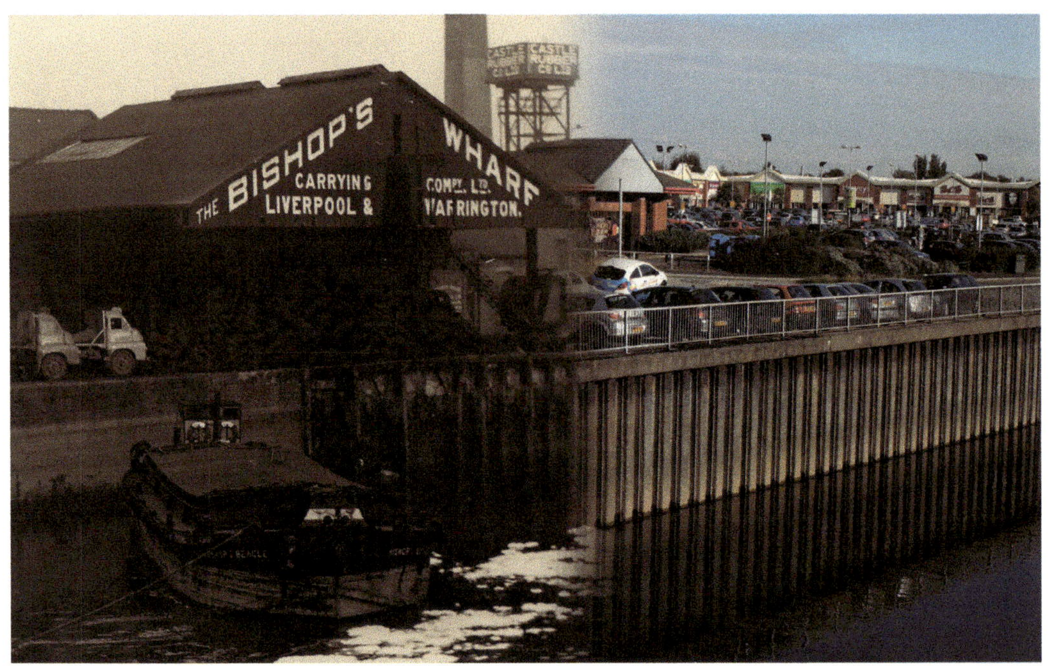

By the nineteenth century the River Mersey was a major transport highway serving the town's industries. Although most activity was concentrated at Bank Quay a second dock developed at Bishop's Wharf serving mainly local tanneries and paper mills. By the late 1950s many of the tanneries had closed and the riverboats soon disappeared. A new retail park has replaced Bishop's Wharf which has been demolished, although the fast food outlet echoes the warehouse's design.

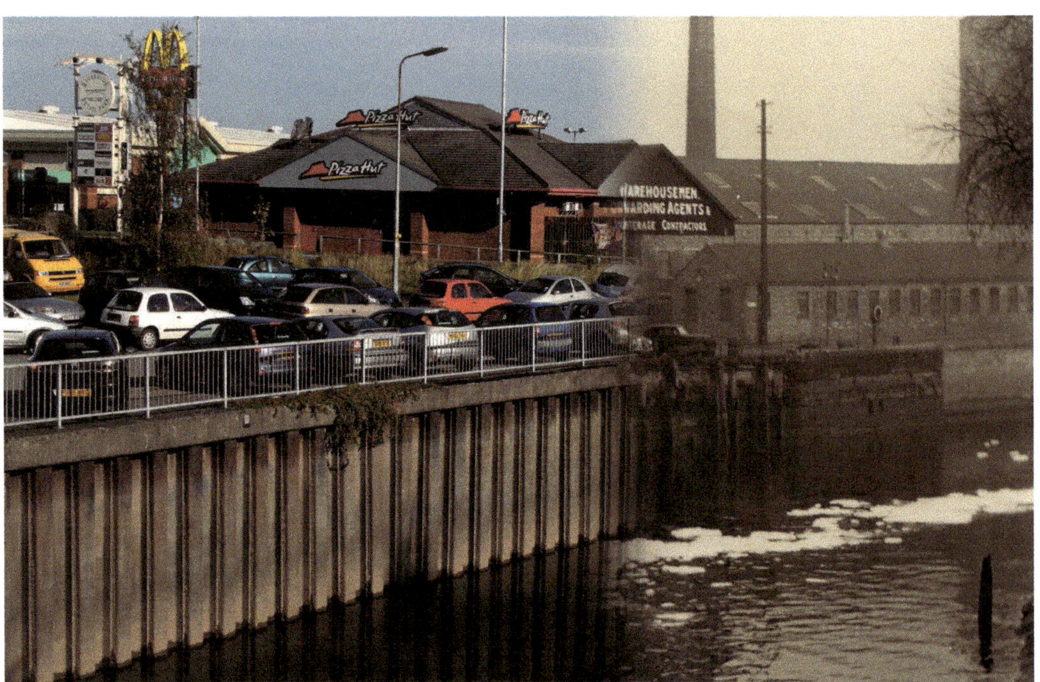

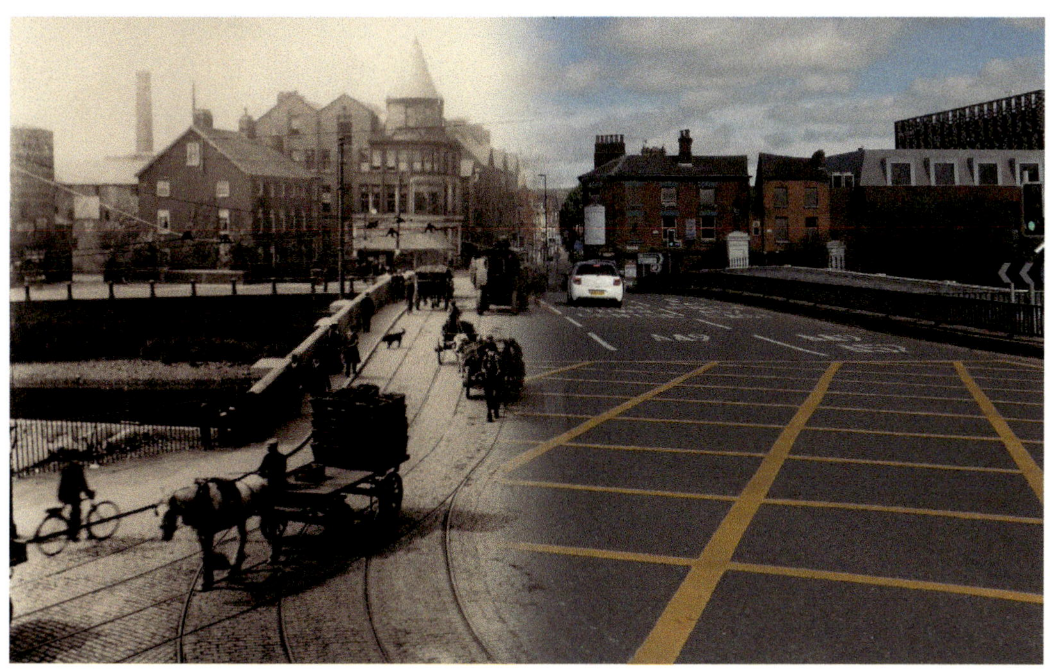

Early on a Sunday morning in 2022 Warrington Bridge is eerily empty of traffic. Rush hour on the old Victoria Bridge in 1910 seems hardly busier but there were already signs that it was too narrow to cope with increasing traffic. The properties on the near right are now the site of the war memorial and few of the buildings at Bridge Foot have survived into the twenty-first century.

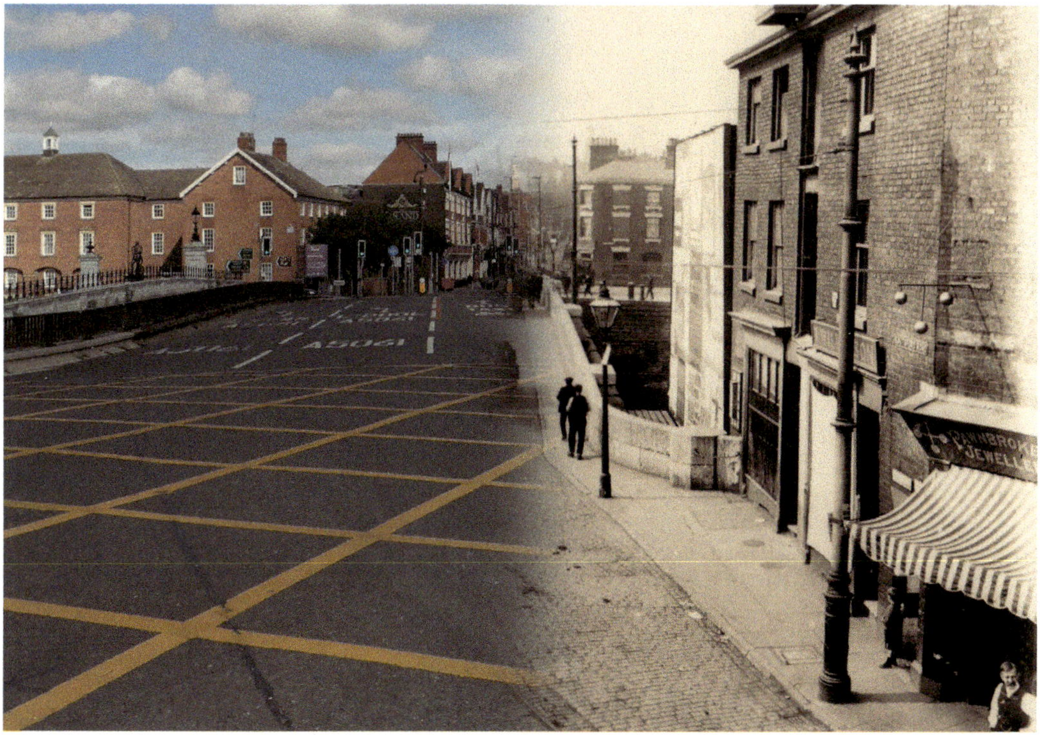

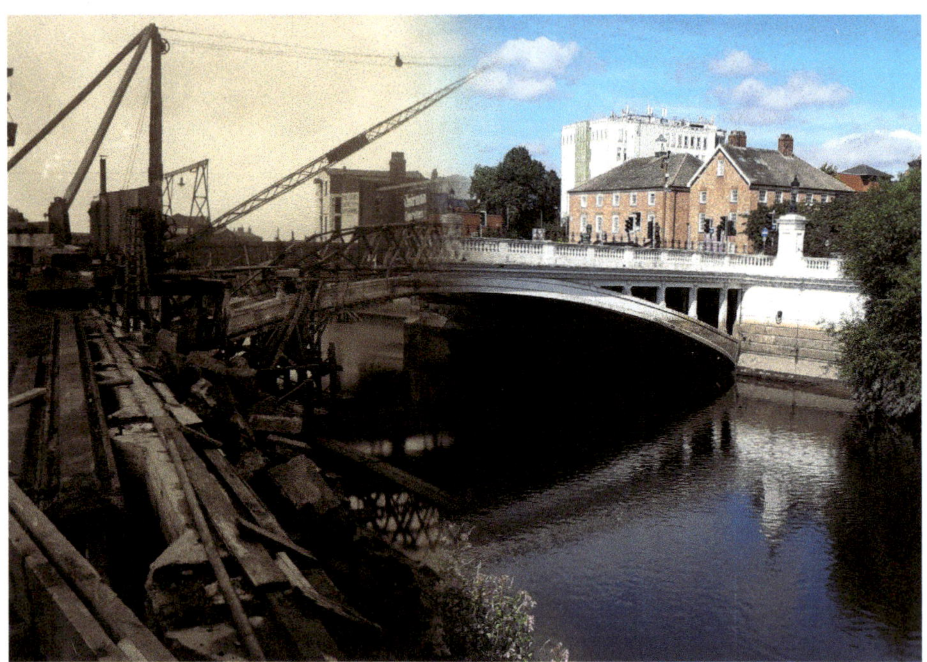

The first half of Webster's new bridge opened in July 1913 and by March 1914 the Victoria Bridge had been demolished as work began on the section nearest to Bishop's Wharf. The older view shows the scale of the building work and the modern view reveals the delicate silhouette of Webster's design. In 1914 the prominent feature on the skyline is the conical roof of Tower Buildings to the right while in 2022 the bulky grey telephone exchange is dominant.

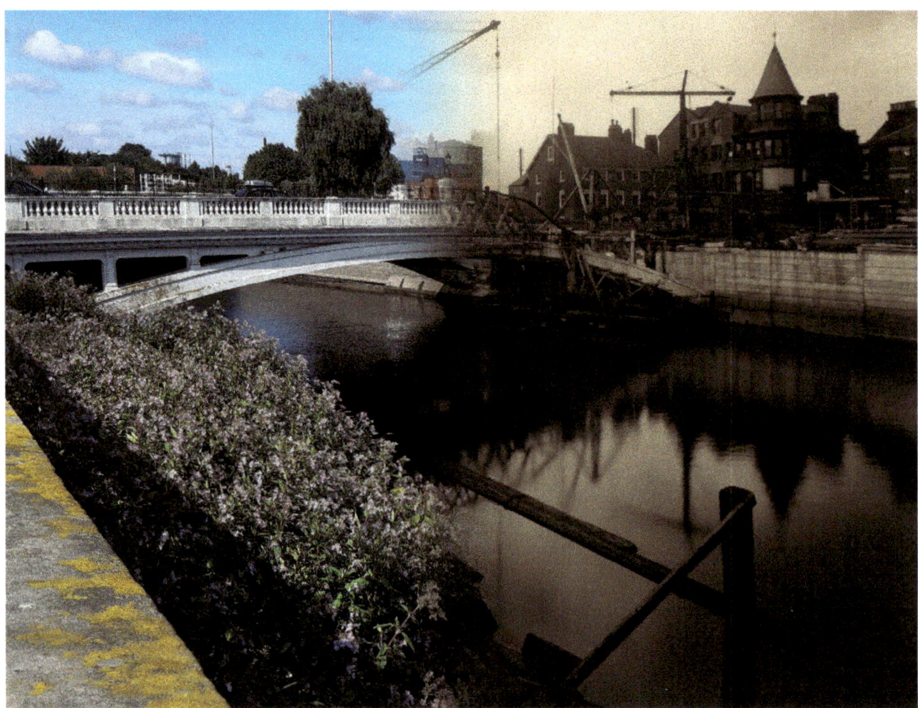

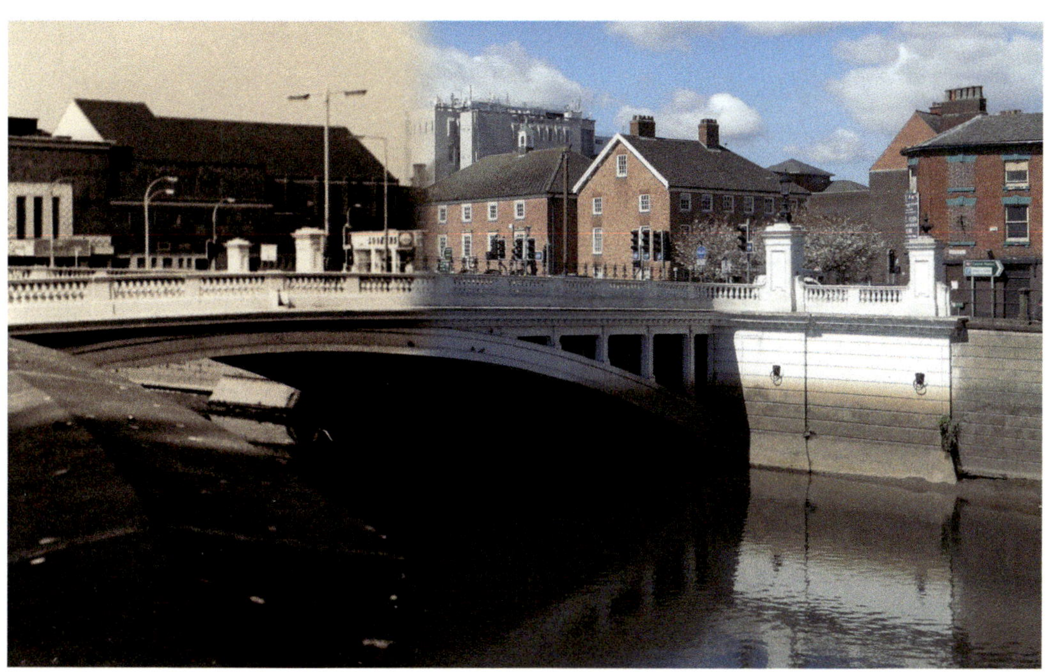

The backdrop of Bridge Foot had changed by the date of the earlier photograph which, probably dates from the 1960s. Rising above the bridge's carriageway on the left is the substantial shape of the Ritz cinema. To its right is the original old Academy building which was championed by conservationists because of its association with acclaimed scientist Joseph Priestley in the eighteenth century. Meanwhile planners were beginning to see its position as a barrier to improving the traffic flow at Bridge Foot.

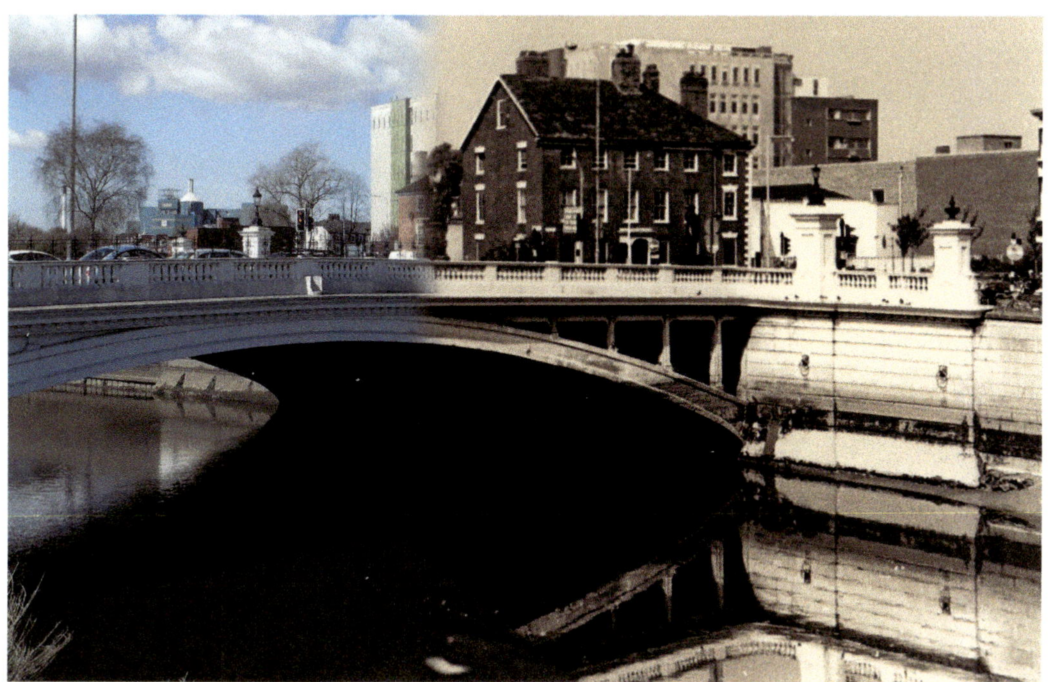

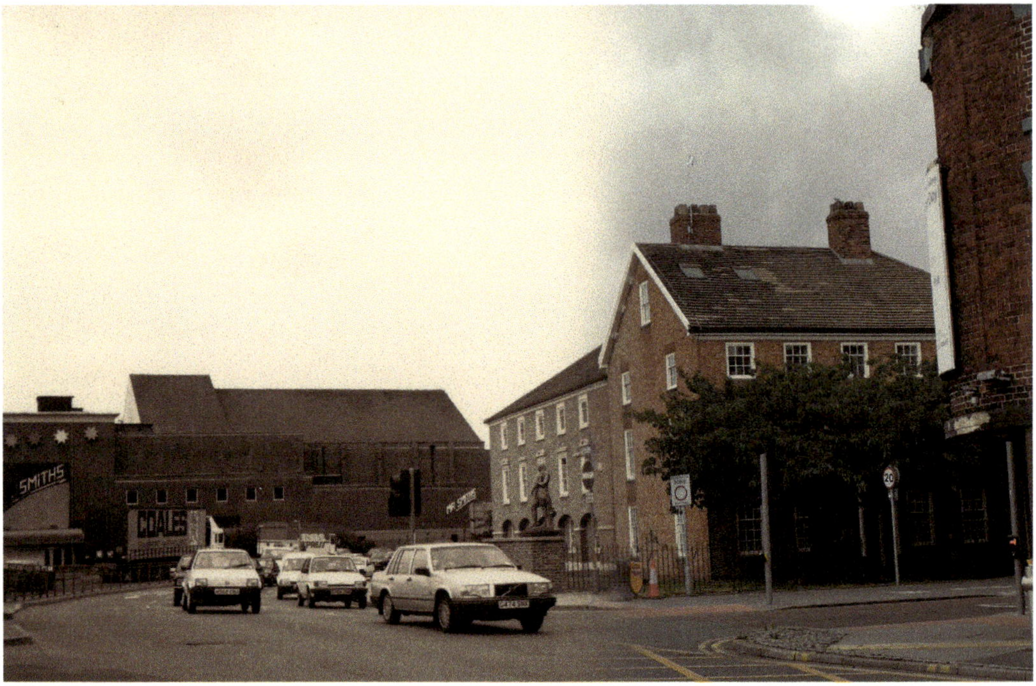

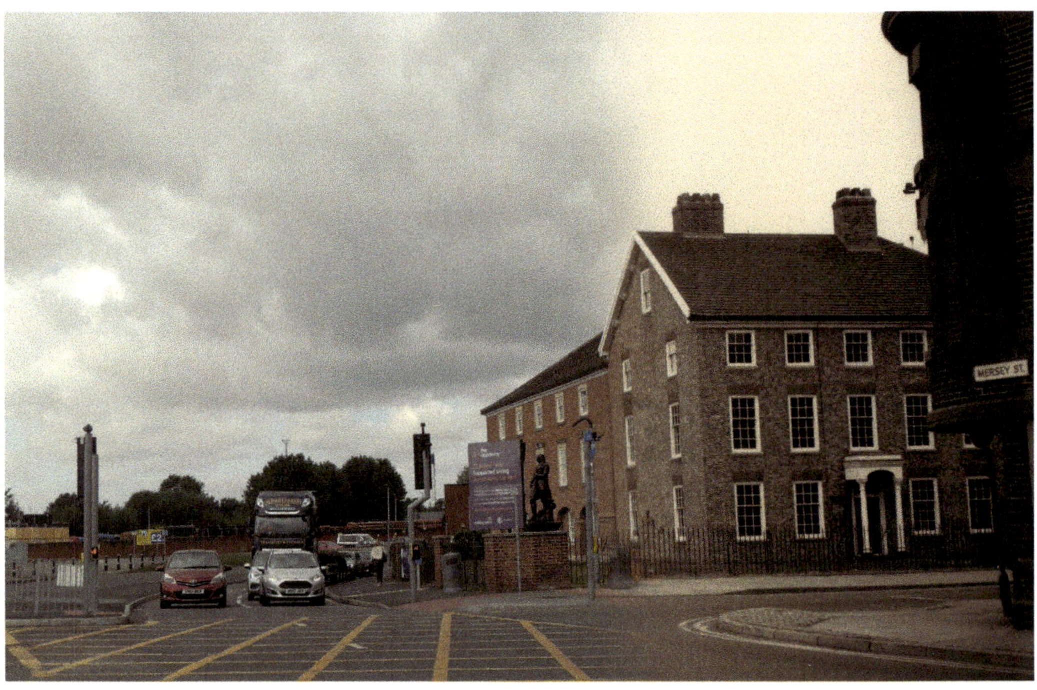

On 22 May 1981 a remarkable feat of civil engineering allowed the widening of Bridge Foot and apparently saved the historic Warrington Academy. Contractors Pynford's sliced the building from its foundations and winched it to the adjacent site of the former Tower Buildings. By the 1990s image the Academy building had been replaced by a replica. The Ritz cinema had become Mr Smith's but was destroyed by fire in the early hours of 15 April 2015.

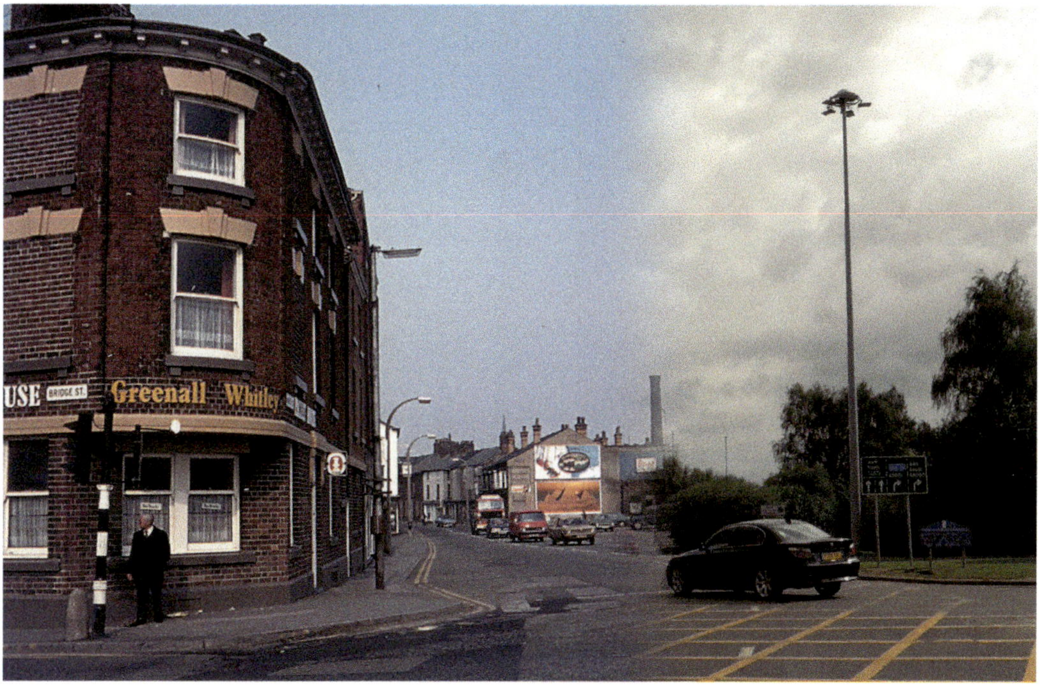

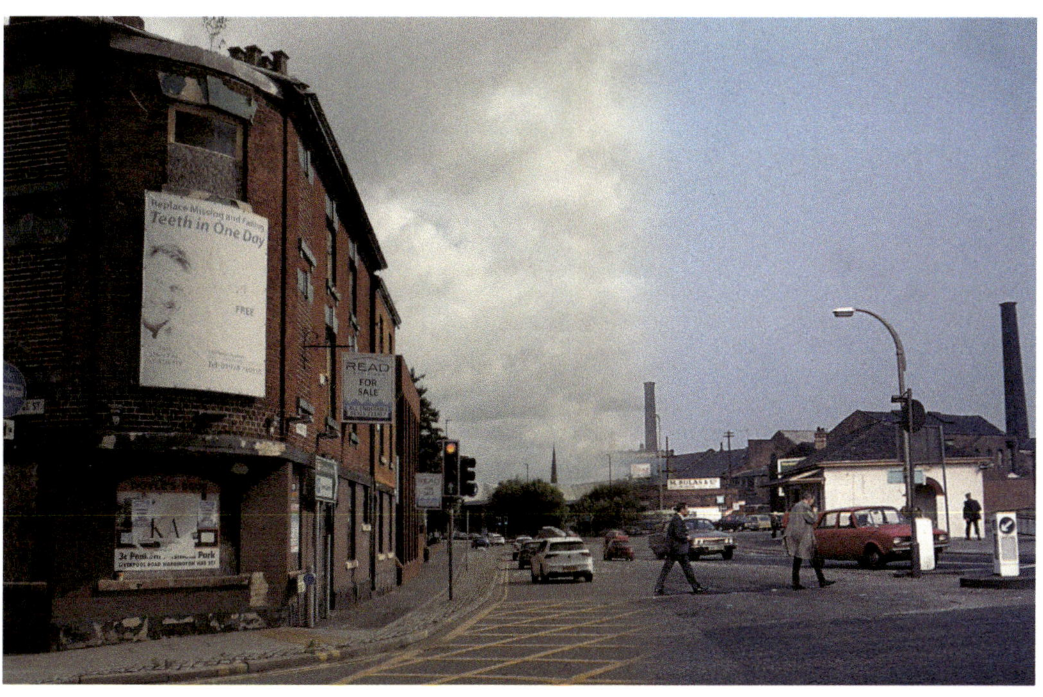

The Packet House pub (left of both images) identifies this as a view down Mersey Street from near the Academy. By 2022 the former pub seemed to be in terminal decline. The buildings to the right have been demolished since the 1990s image which shows Mersey Street curving to the left creating a traffic bottleneck. The shops and old tannery chimneys were cleared away creating a post-industrial landscape which became the approach to the second river crossing.

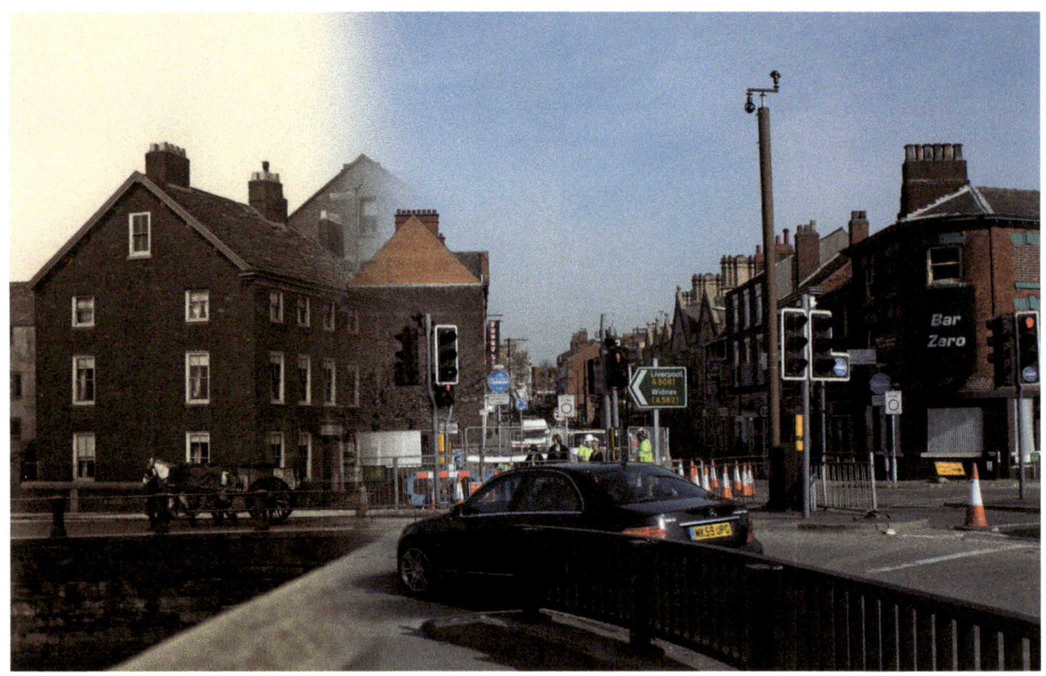

Travellers crossing Warrington Bridge were funnelled down Bridge Street to the town centre. In the thirteenth century Warrington's lords of the manor, the Boteler family, had built the bridge as a route to their lucrative market and with it a 'New Street', later appropriately known as Bridge Street. The early 1900s view shows the winding route to Market Gate and the distinctive Tower Building which was demolished to make way for the old Academy.

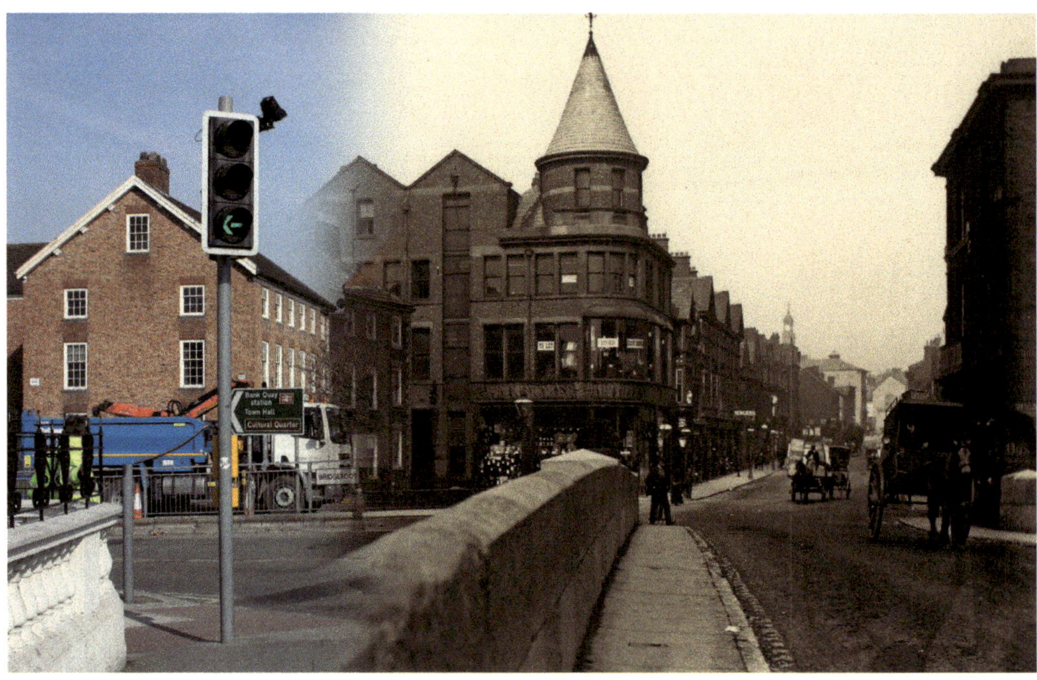

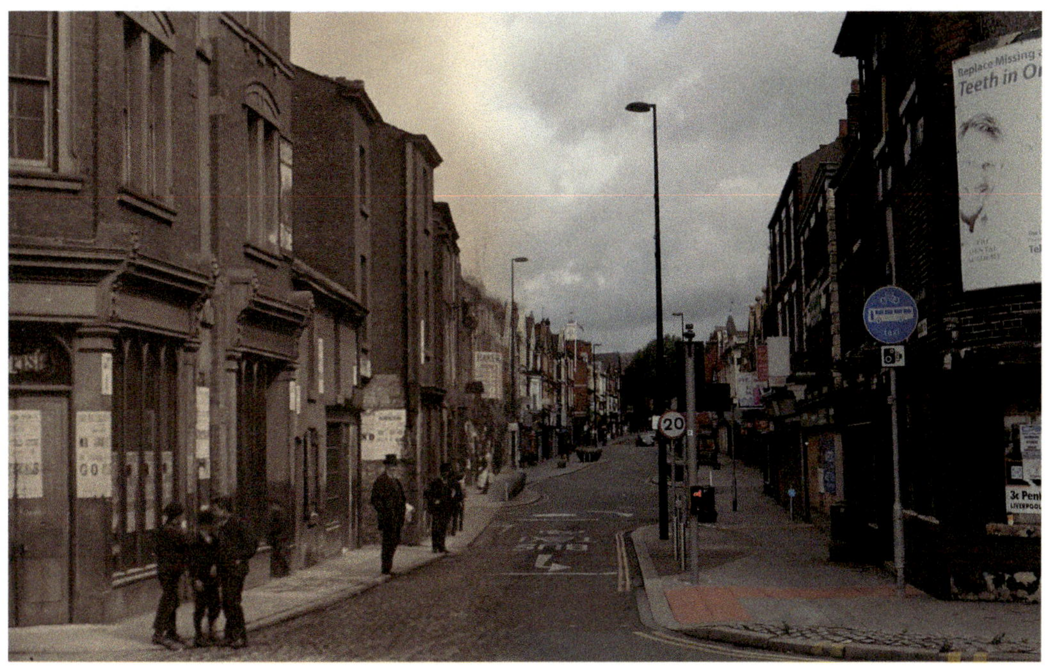

This view down Bridge Street from Bridge Foot beside the Packet House pub (right) shows how much the streetscape has changed. From the 1880s the council undertook the complete rebuilding of the west side of Bridge Street (adjoining Sankey Street) allowing the street to be widened to around 60 feet to cope with the growing volume of traffic. Redevelopment was piecemeal with a variety of building styles and materials but many still mourned the narrow old street.

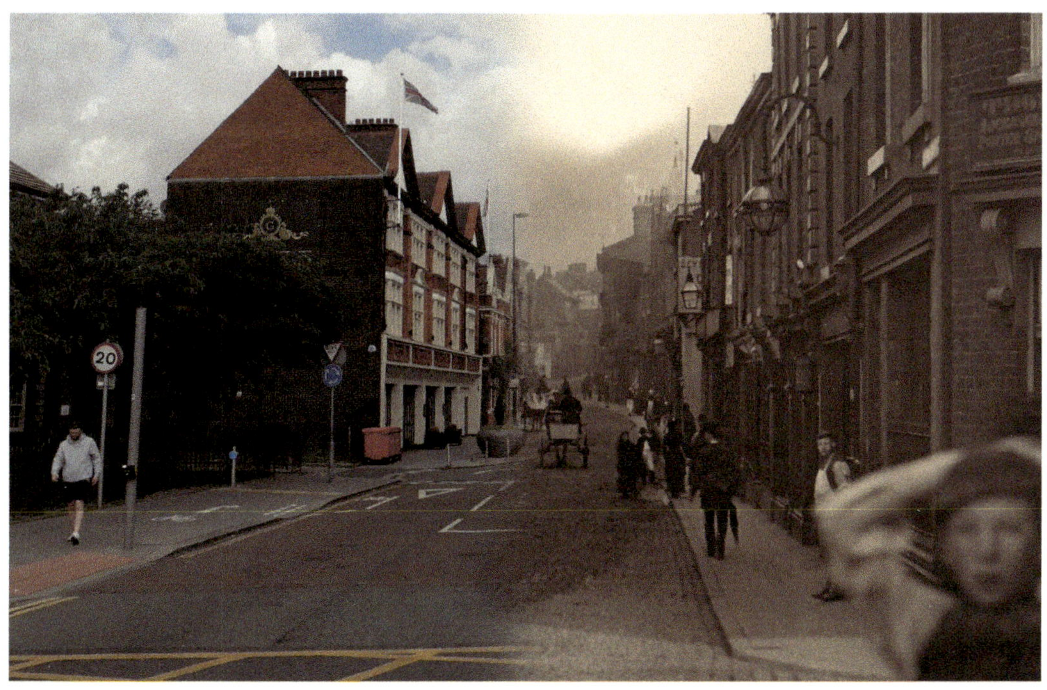

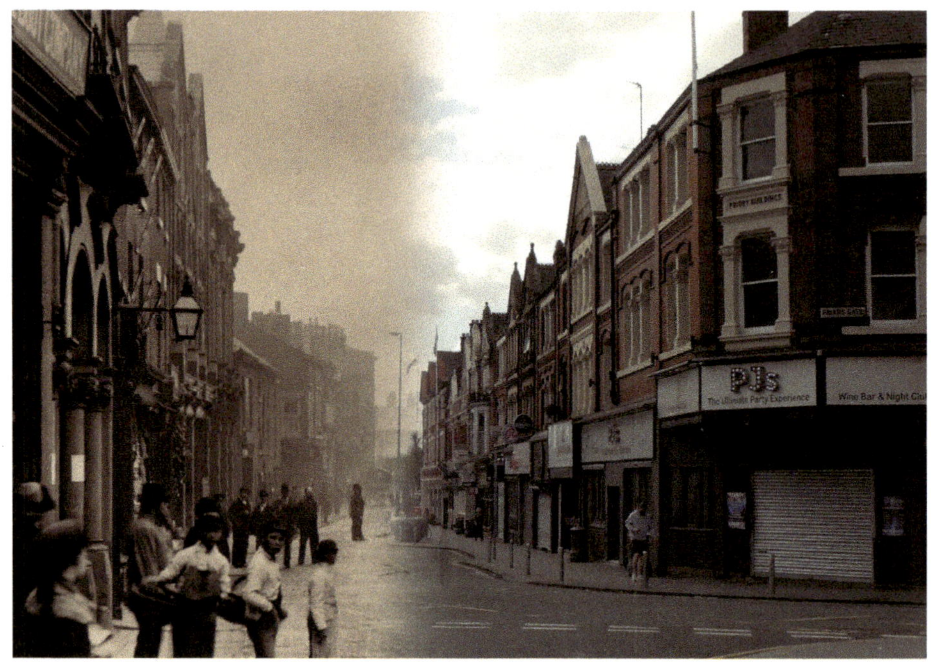

In 1887 curious errand boys came out to watch photographer Thomas Birtles capture the last days of the properties on the right of the street between Friars Gate and distant Bridge Foot. Today the scene shows a wider street which is interrupted by Academy Way, which cut through the properties on the left in the 1980s as part of the inner ring from Legh Street via Scotland Road to Wilson Patten Street allowing Bridge Street itself to be pedestrianised.

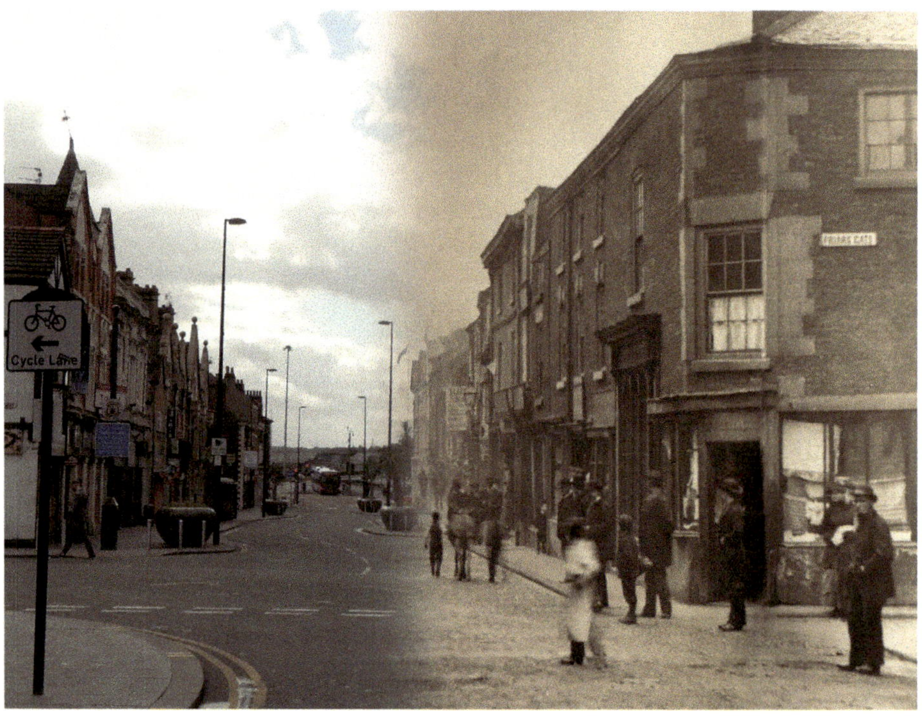

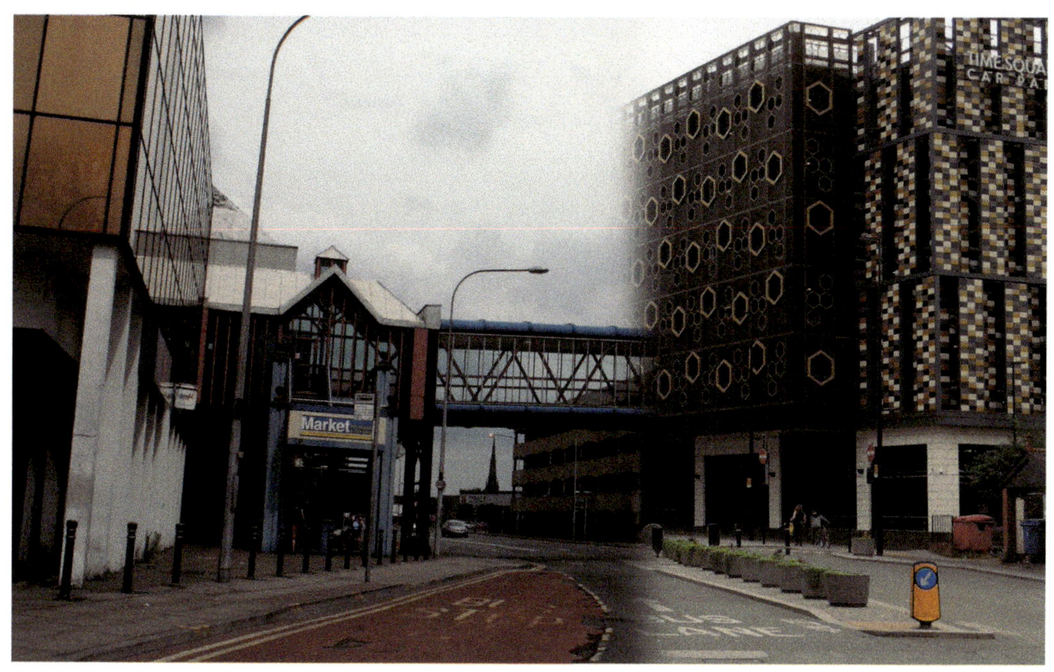

In 2017 the townscape from Bridge Street along Academy Way began its second major transformation in forty years. The distinctive blue pedestrian bridge, the Market Hall with its pyramid-shaped roof and the 1970s Mersey Street car park were swept away. Utilitarian concrete blocks gave way to a distinctive wire-mesh and chequerboard covered the new addition to the town's skyline, which also provides an ideal viewpoint to watch the rise of Warrington's new centre.

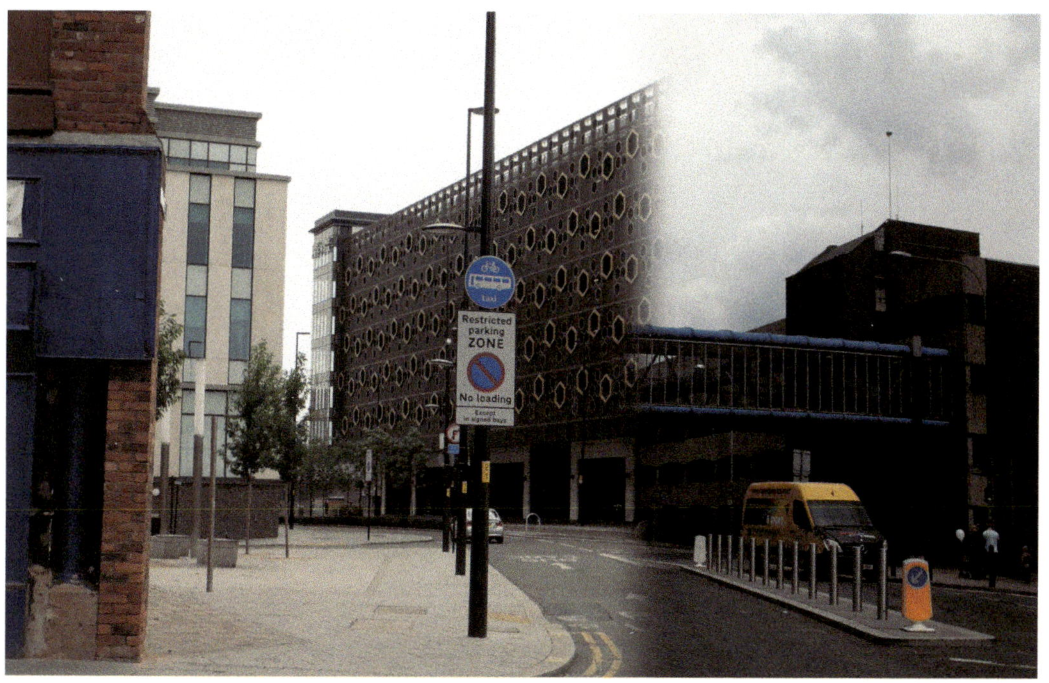

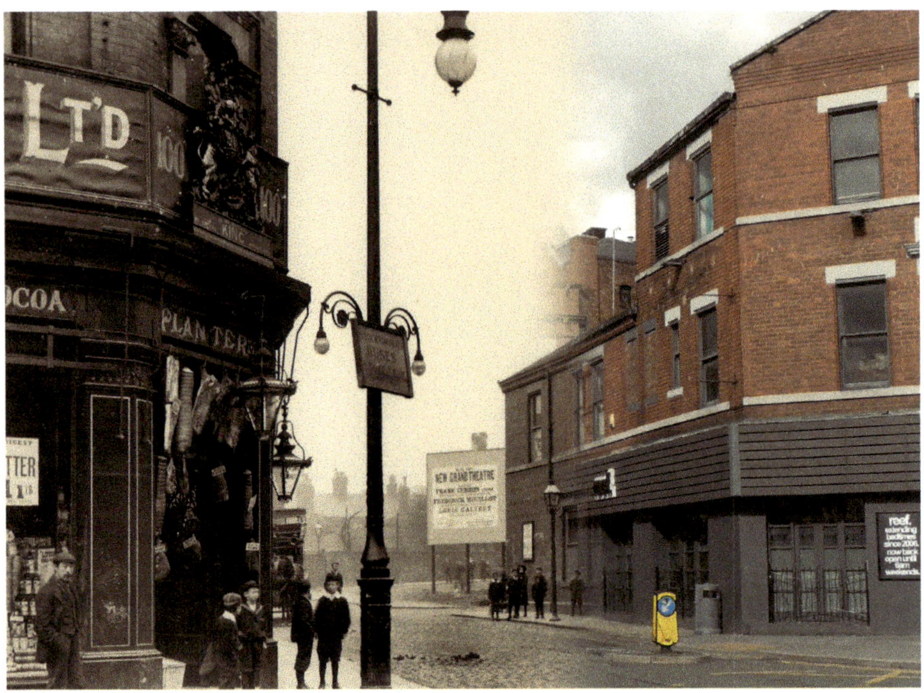

Friars Gate once led to an Augustinian friary which was a large church housing a community of preachers from the thirteenth to the early sixteenth centuries. It was sponsored by many of the town's richer families and similar in style to Norton Priory. A large placard on the right of the older picture shows the site of the new Hippodrome theatre which opened in 1907. This music hall later became the Palace Theatre, a bingo hall and finally a nightclub.

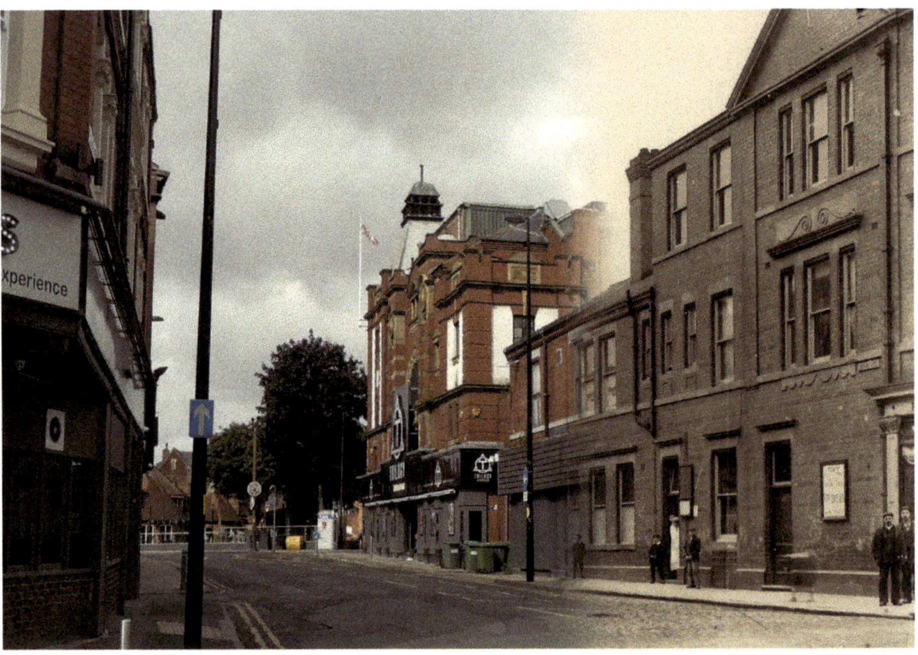

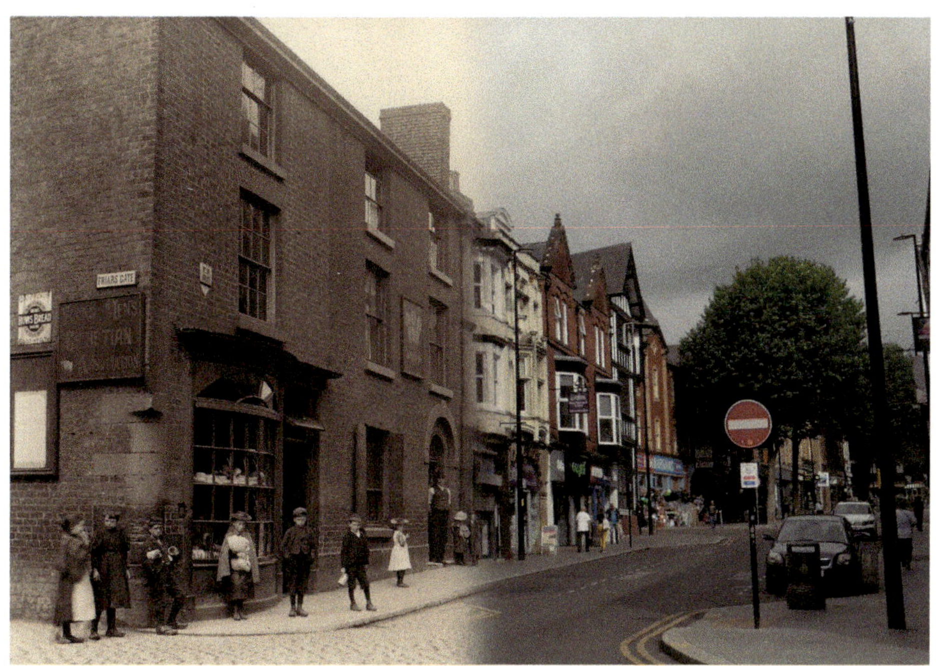

Birtles studio also recorded the last days of the properties between Friars Gate and Rylands Street. The older photograph shows the plain-fronted old Feathers Inn to the right of the bow-fronted shop. This was one of the many hostelries lining the town centre streets to serve the travellers and traders coming to Warrington market. Local architects William & Segar Owen designed its more ornate successor with a distinctive brick frontage contrasting with cream stonework (seen to the right of Reef).

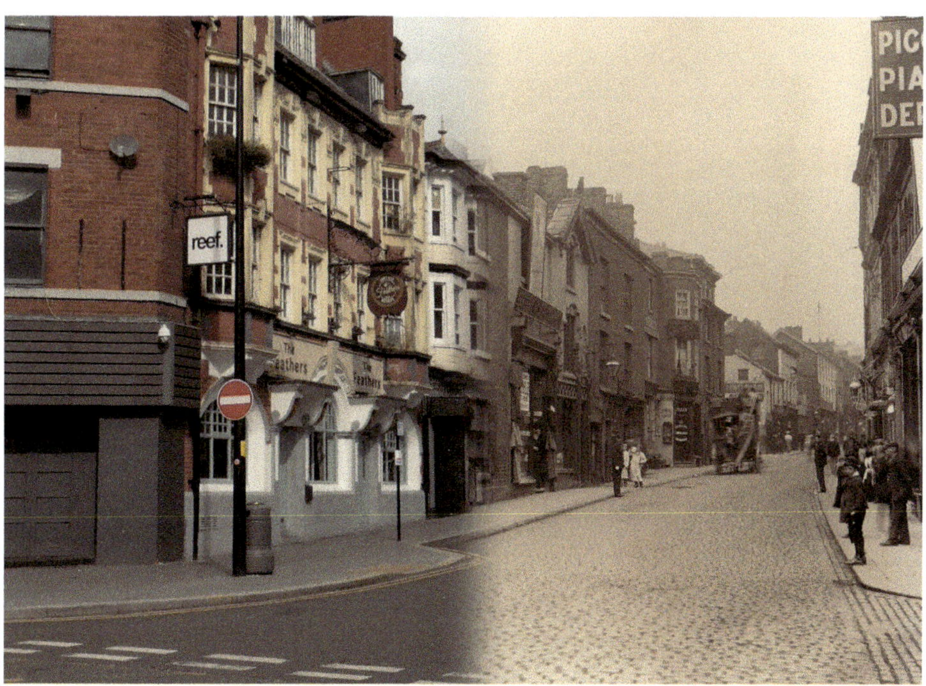

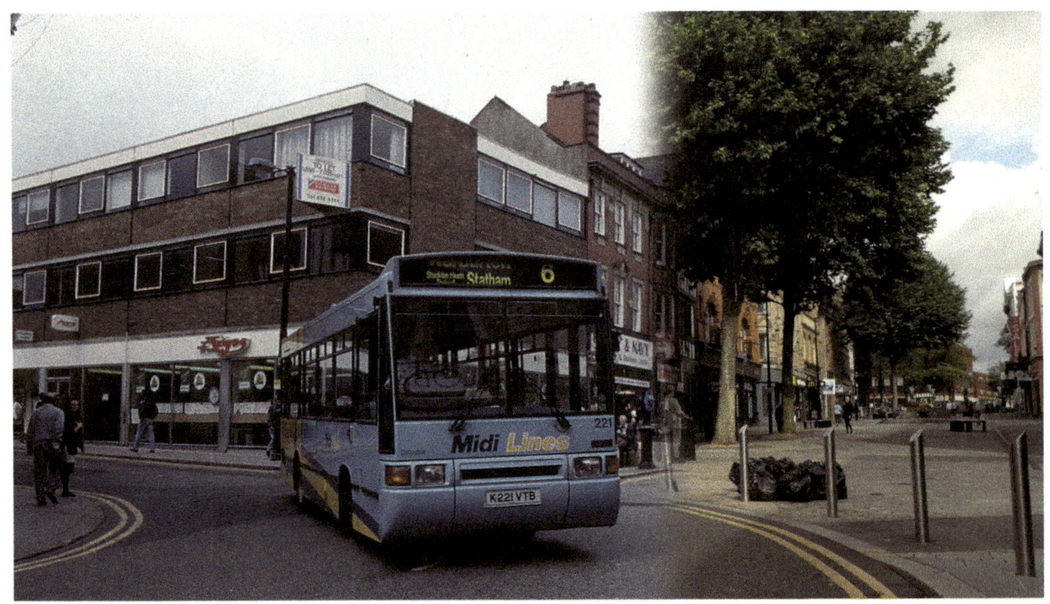

In the 1990s Bridge Street was still free of the trees which line the present-day street hiding many of the facades of the fine buildings. However, many conservationists felt that the 1960s-style Argos showroom on the corner of Rylands Street, which had replaced the Royal Court hotel, needed to be hidden, as it was out of keeping with the rest of the street's Grade II listed architecture. Its recent replacement mimics the brick and stone of neighbouring buildings.

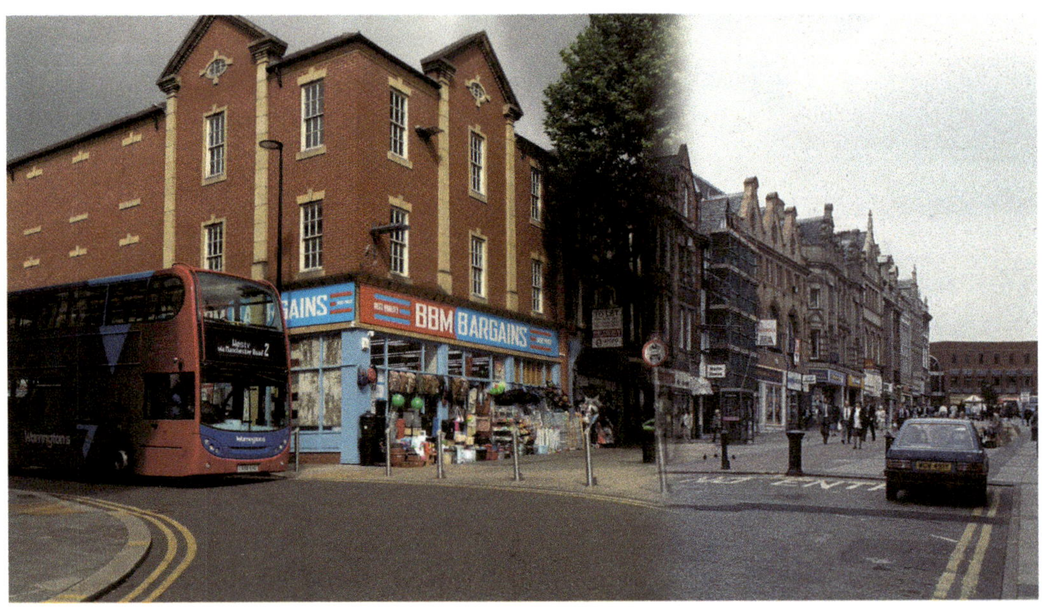

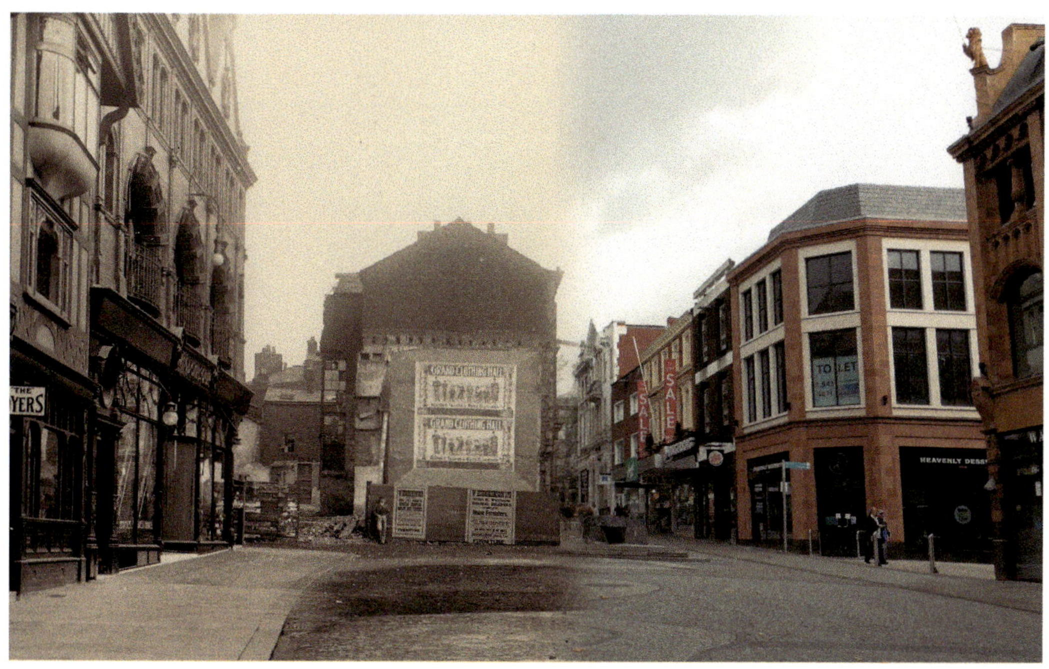

Upper Bridge Street has changed considerably since the 1900s. The older view towards Market Gate shows the emergence of today's familiar shopfronts built behind the line of the old narrow street on the left whilst the shops opposite await redevelopment. More recently they have been transformed as the Bridge Street entrance to the new Time Square. The shop second from the left on the modern photograph was once W. G. Hodgkinson's, one of the town's premier department stores.

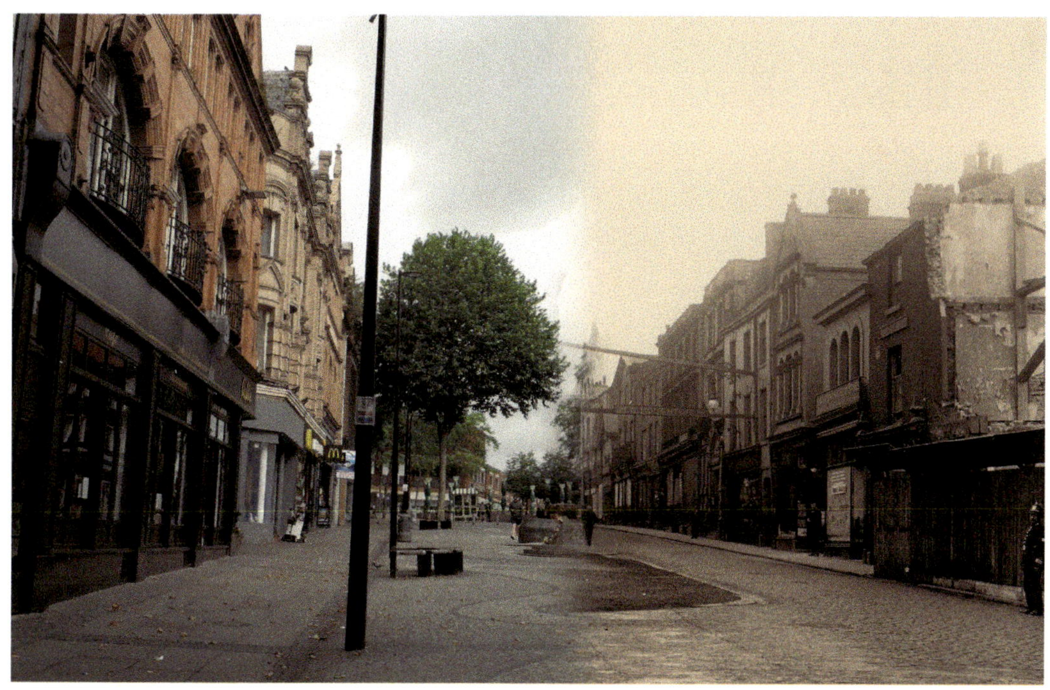

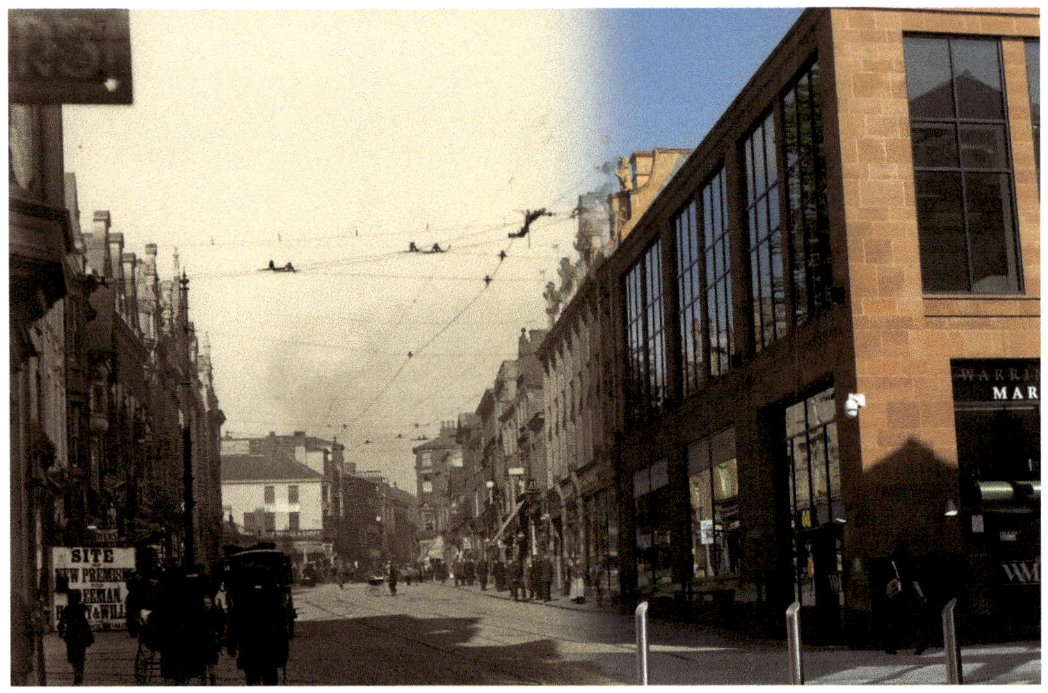

Today upper Bridge Street is a tree-lined pedestrianised area but in the 1900s it was a major tram route. The buildings to the centre right were replaced by the new market linking with Time Square but to their left lions still stand guard on the Howard building. Opened in 1907, it commemorates noted prison reformer John Howard who lodged on the site in the 1770s whilst he was completing his work on *The State of the Prisons in England and Wales.*

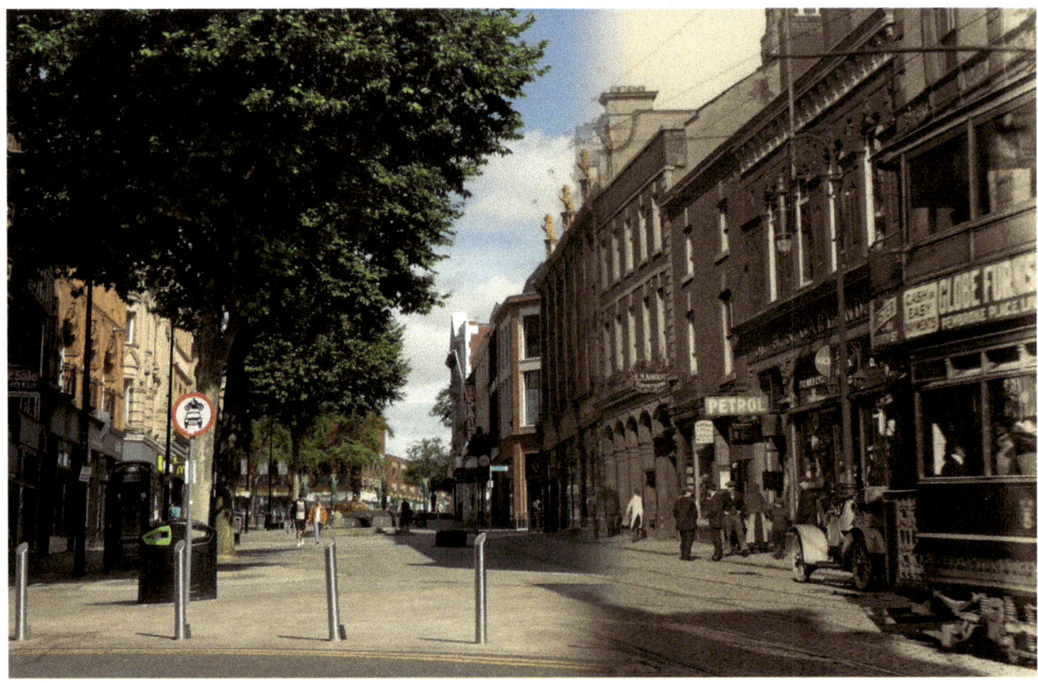

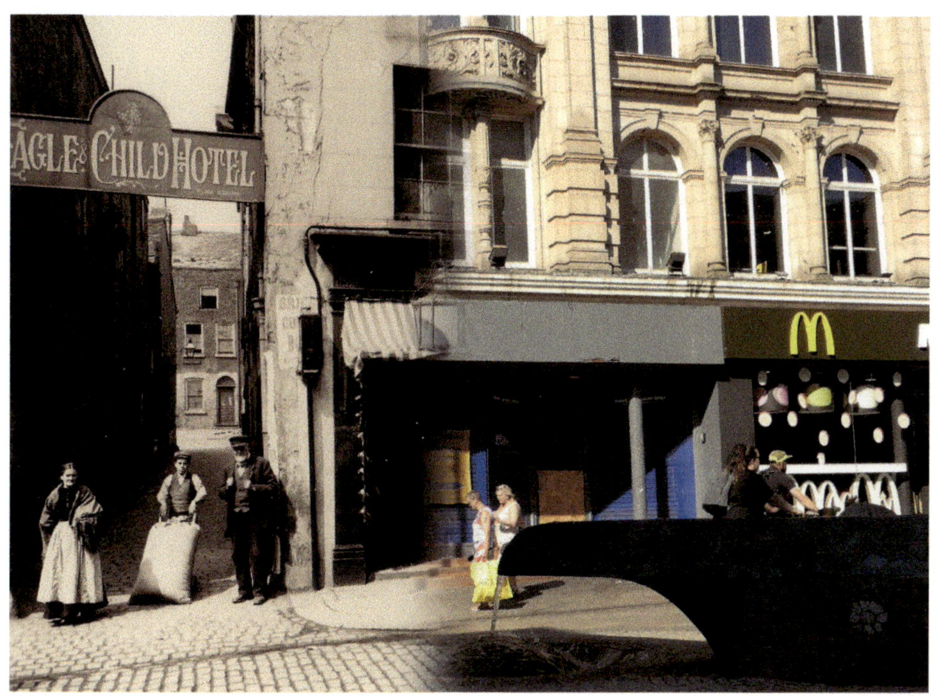

This insignificant little alleyway near McDonald's has a proud history as Patten Lane. In the eighteenth century it was home to Thomas Patten, the wealthy businessman who built Bank Hall, now Warrington's Town Hall. As the older image shows it was also the entrance to the Eagle & Child Hotel, which had been one of the town's major coaching inns. When Bridge Street was widened in the 1900s the entryway survived with Hodgkinson's former shop to the left.

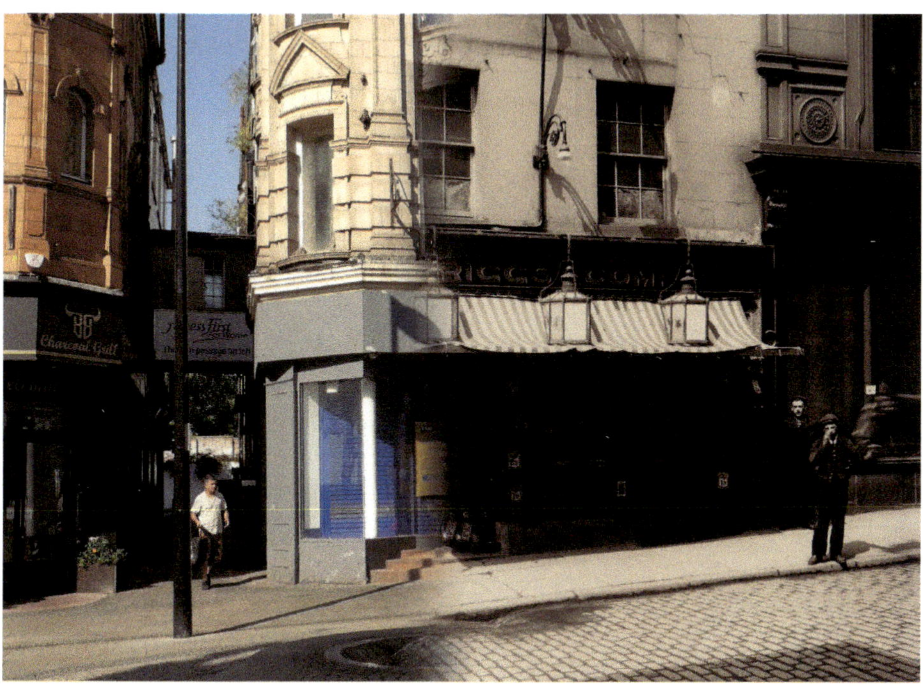

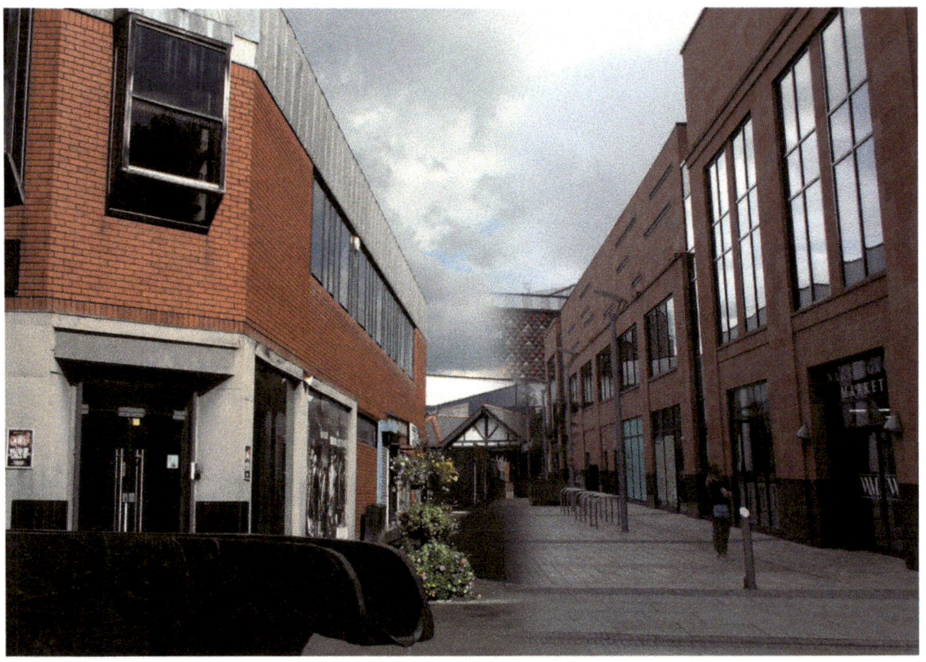

Opposite Patten Lane is another forgotten alley called Dolman's Lane which connects Bridge Street with Time Square. In medieval times this was home to the dole man who gave aid to the poor for burials. By the nineteenth century it was a dark insanitary street crowded with some of Warrington's poorest inhabitants. In August 2017 the alley still led to the old market but by 2022 the buildings on both sides had been transformed by the new Time Square development.

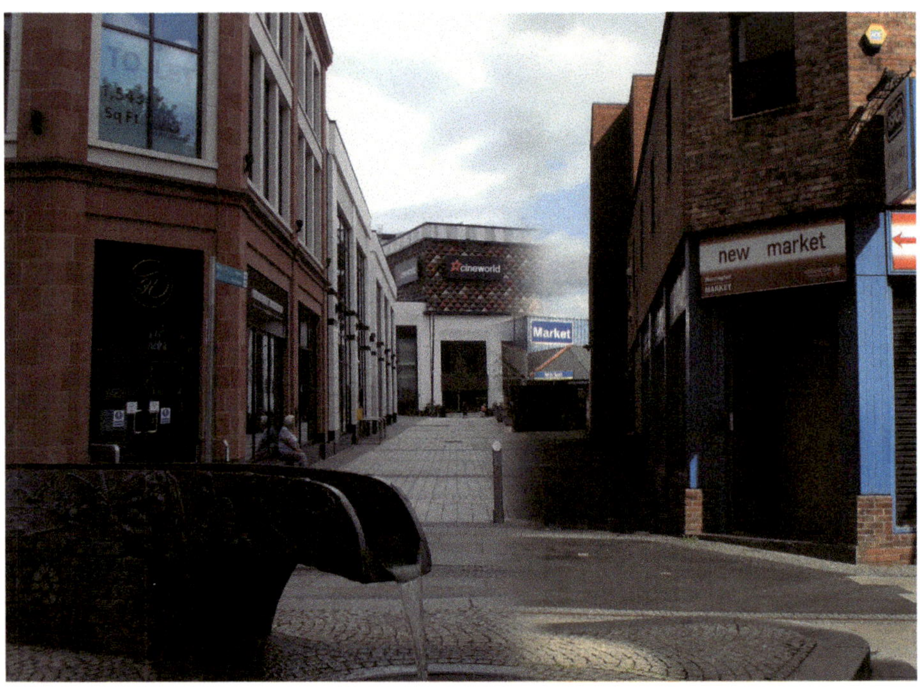

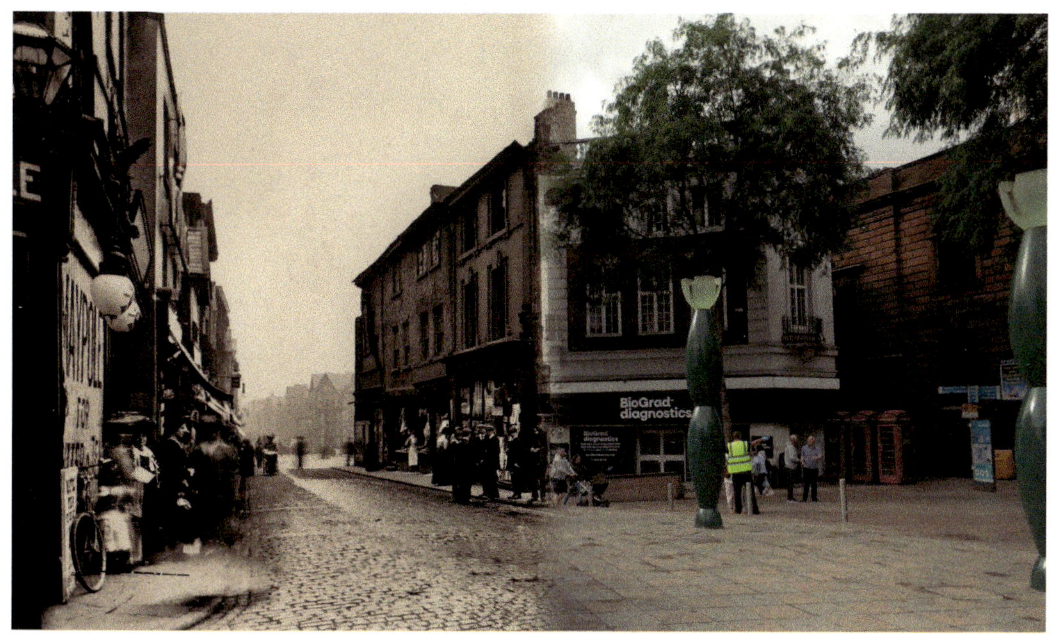

By 1907 the battle to redevelop old Bridge Street was nearing completion. The old postcard view shows that just a few shops on the corner of Sankey Street were resisting the tide of progress. T. J. Lee's prominent advert shows they were clearly anxious not to lose trade as one of the town's key drapers. Changing shopping habits and competition from Golden Square led to the closure of yet another long-established local business in the late twentieth century.

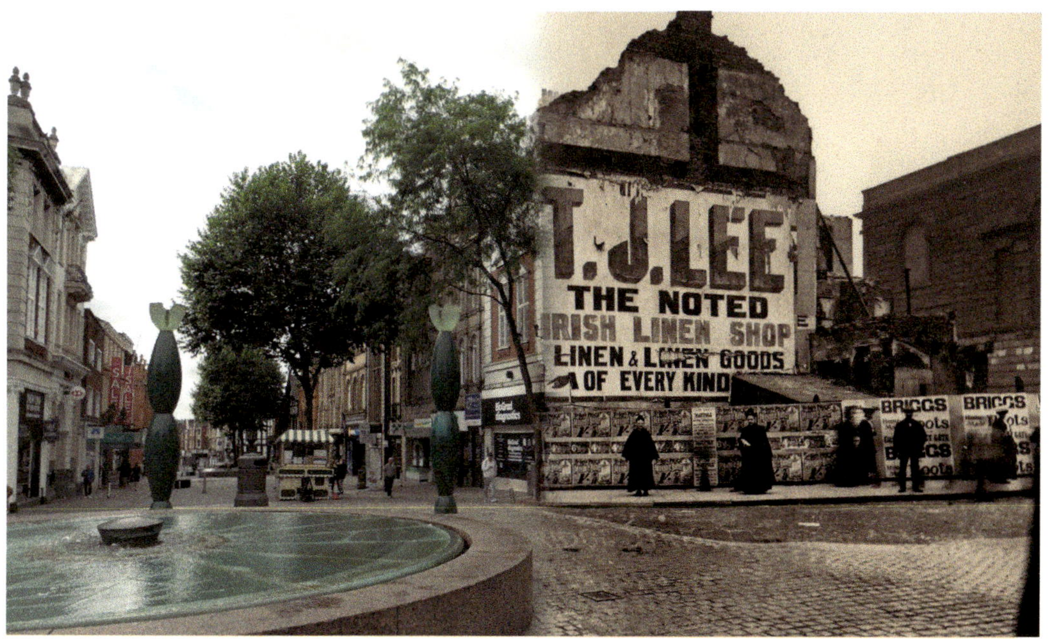

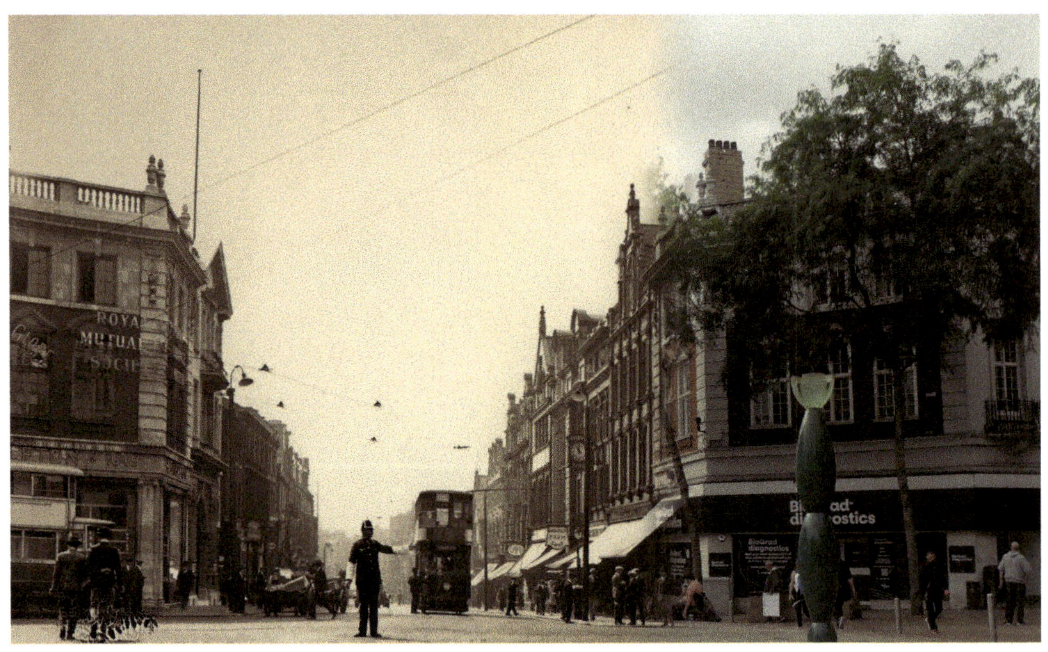

Once Bridge Street had been successfully widened the council chose plans by local architects Wright, Garnett & Wright to create a unified design for each of the corners of the main streets at Market Gate with buildings in brick and Portland stone. Only the corner of Bridge Street and Sankey Street followed the original pattern and a century separates these two views with the tram giving way to a tree-lined pedestrianised street and a central sculpture feature.

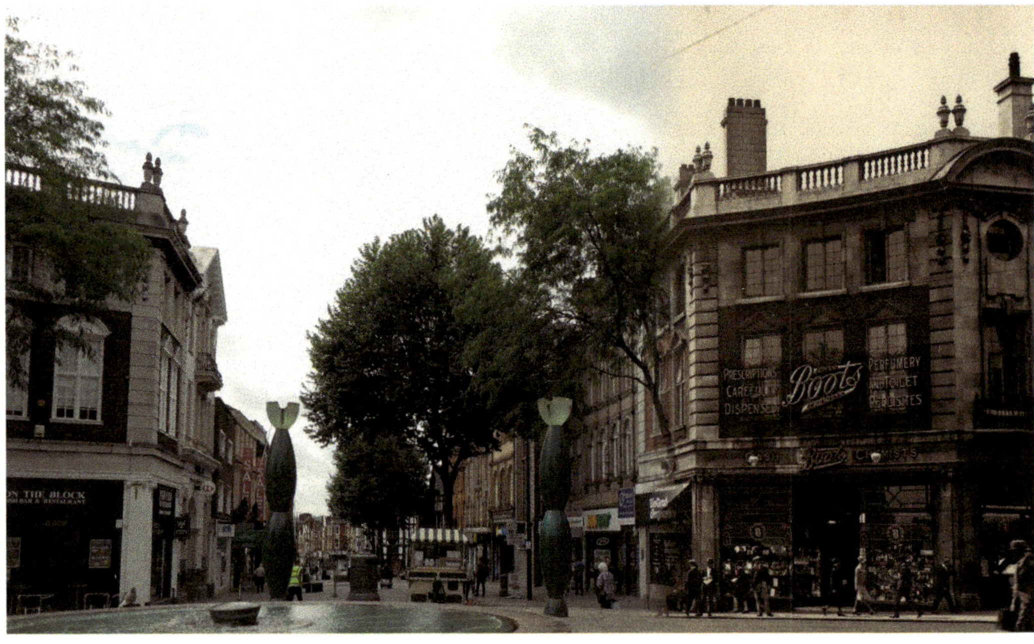

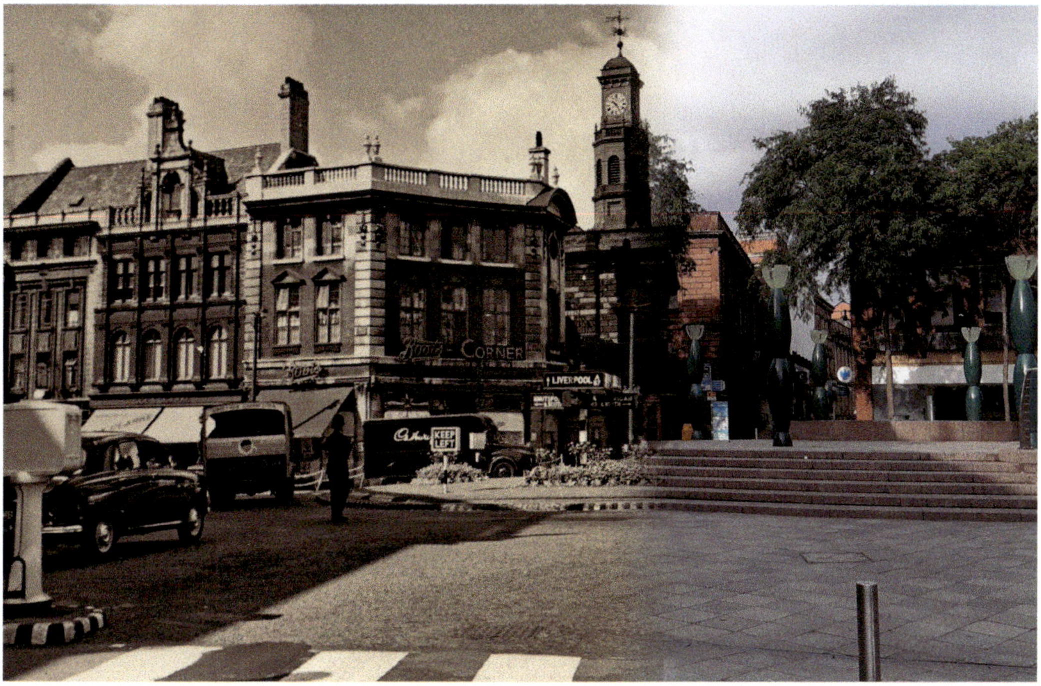

The original vision for Market Gate included a central circular space or circus but this took almost a century to achieve. In 1938 a circular traffic island was added to improve traffic flow but by the 1980s the space was again featureless until the *Guardians* sculpture was unveiled in 2002. This view across from Buttermarket Street has changed considerably since the earlier 1970s image, although the clock tower on Holy Trinity Church in Sankey Street is a constant landmark.

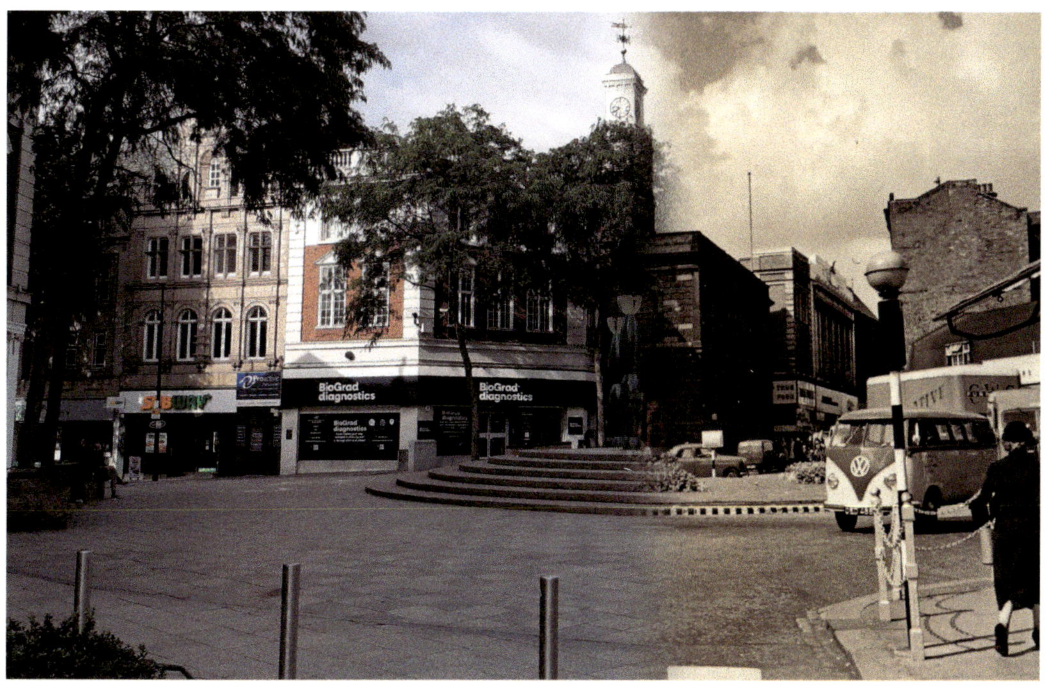

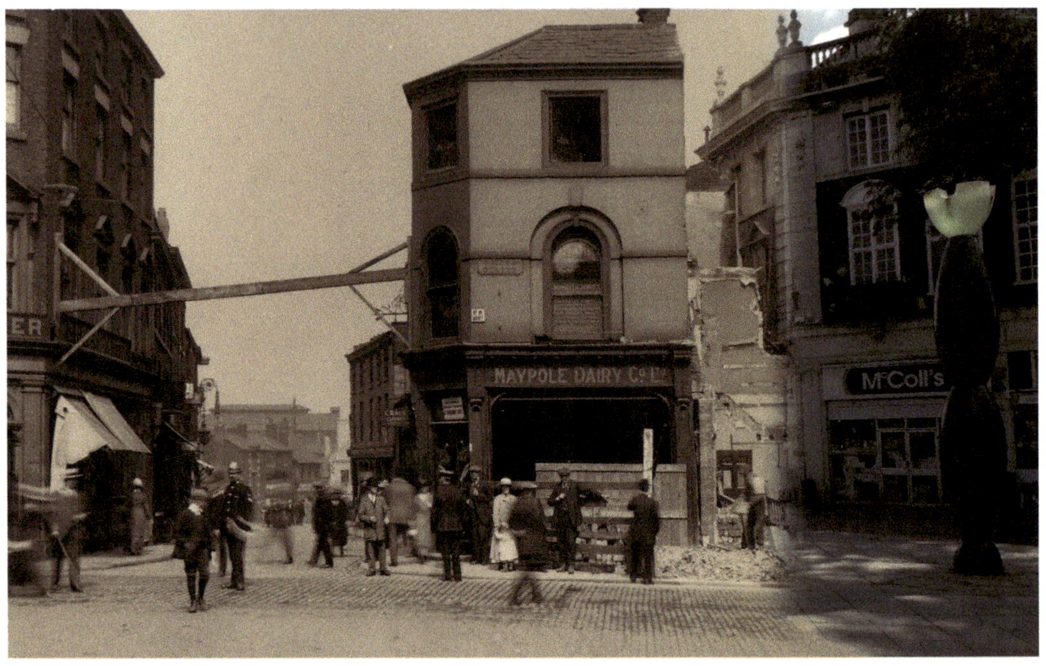

The junction of Buttermarket Street and Bridge Street was the second portion of the Market Gate circus to be constructed in 1913–15. The street corner was considerably widened and built in a similar style to the adjacent corner of Sankey Street. It is unlikely that current health and safety practices would have allowed traffic to pass so close to the partially demolished old Maypole Dairy shop buttressed against the shop on the Horsemarket Street corner!

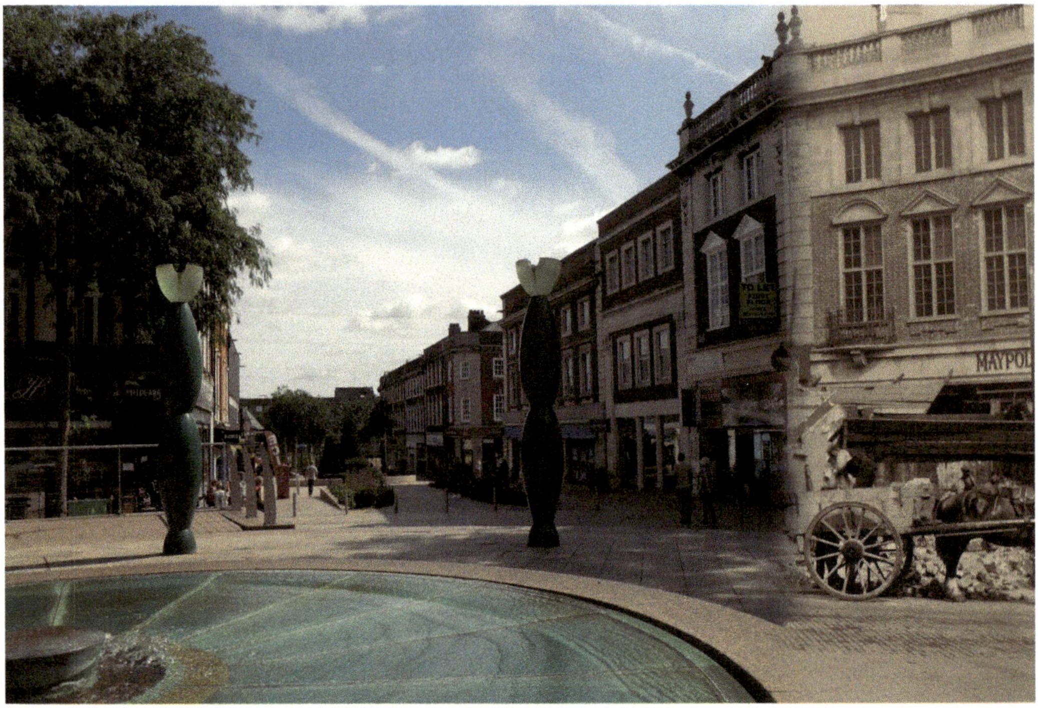

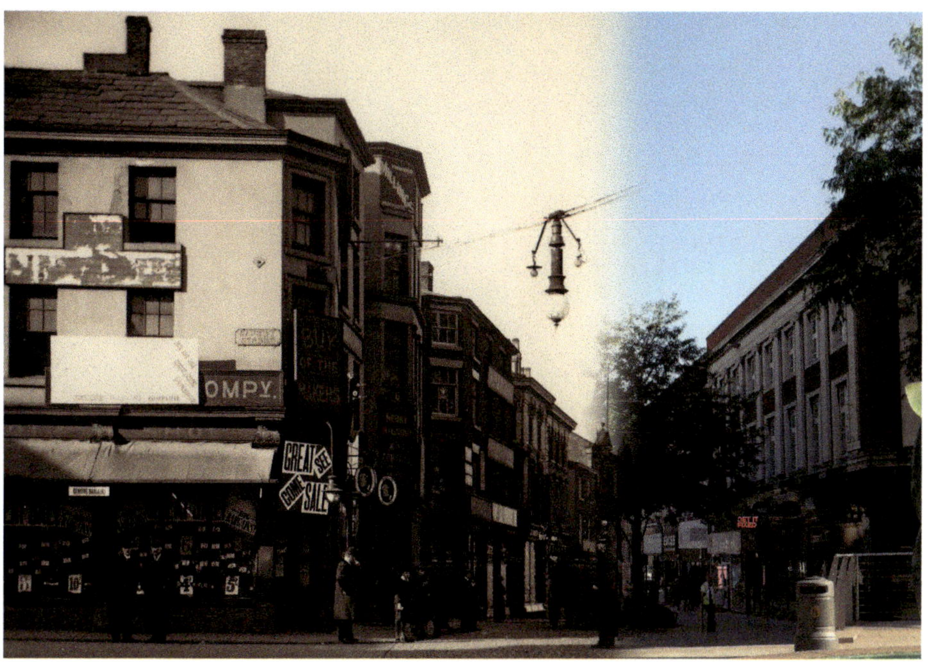

Horsemarket Street was partially widened in the 1930s by the rebuilding of the shops on the right-hand side, adjoining Buttermarket Street. Whilst Brigg and Company's shop on the corner opposite Turner's hosiery business was demolished in 1928, the rest of left-hand side of the street survived into the late twentieth century. Today the *Guardians* look down on a broad vista to Central station.

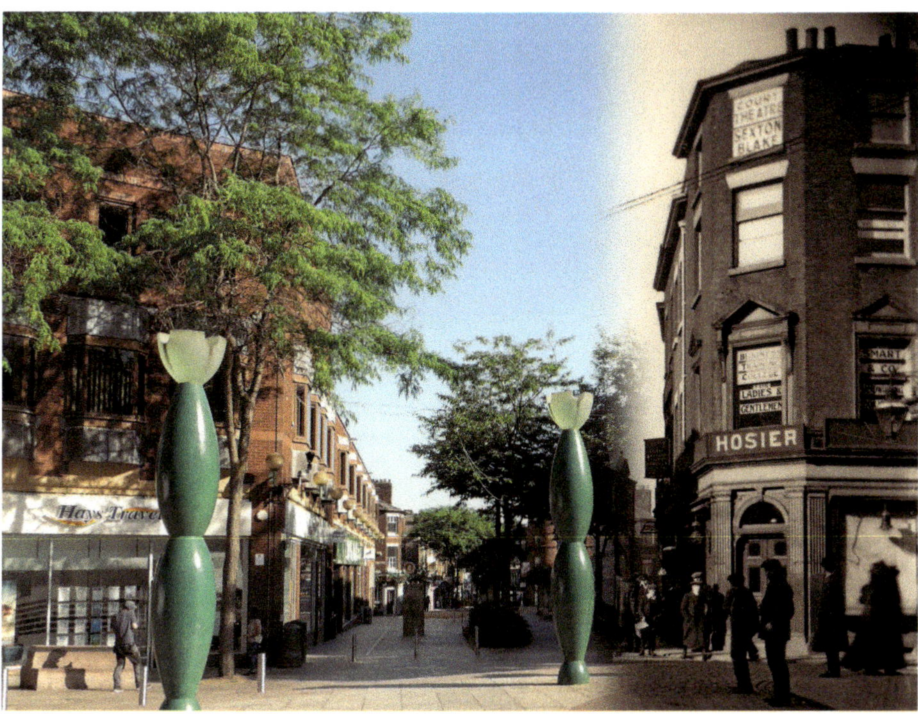

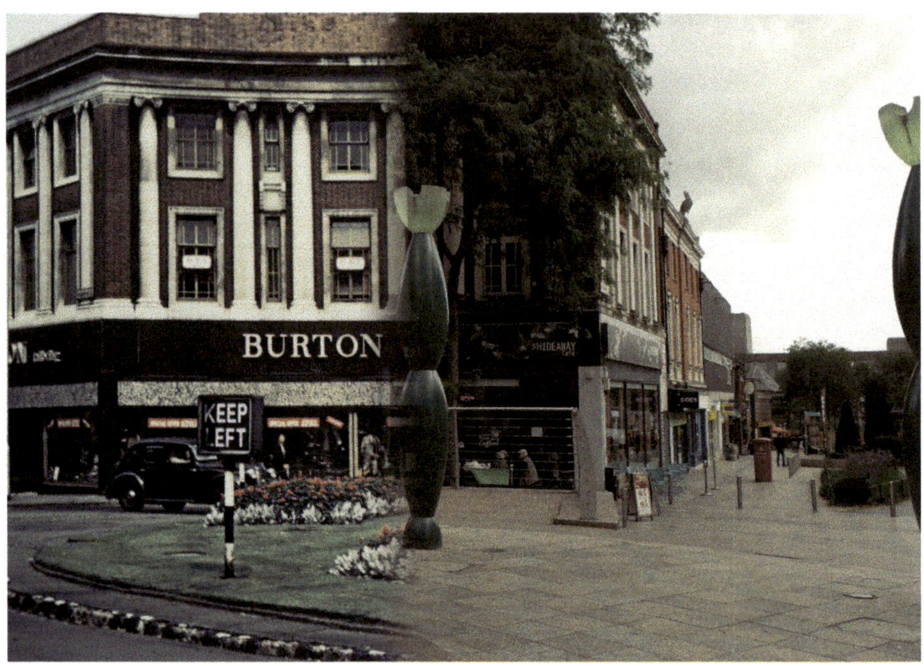

Remodelling the corner of Buttermarket Street and Horsemarket Street was delayed by the First World War and the following economic crisis. This south-east corner of Market Gate was designed for Burton's tailors in the 1930s and reflected the art deco style of the period. The Casino Club above Burton's was a popular entertainment venue and together with the neighbouring Pelican Inn and Empire Cinema in Buttermarket Street created a vibrant nightlife.

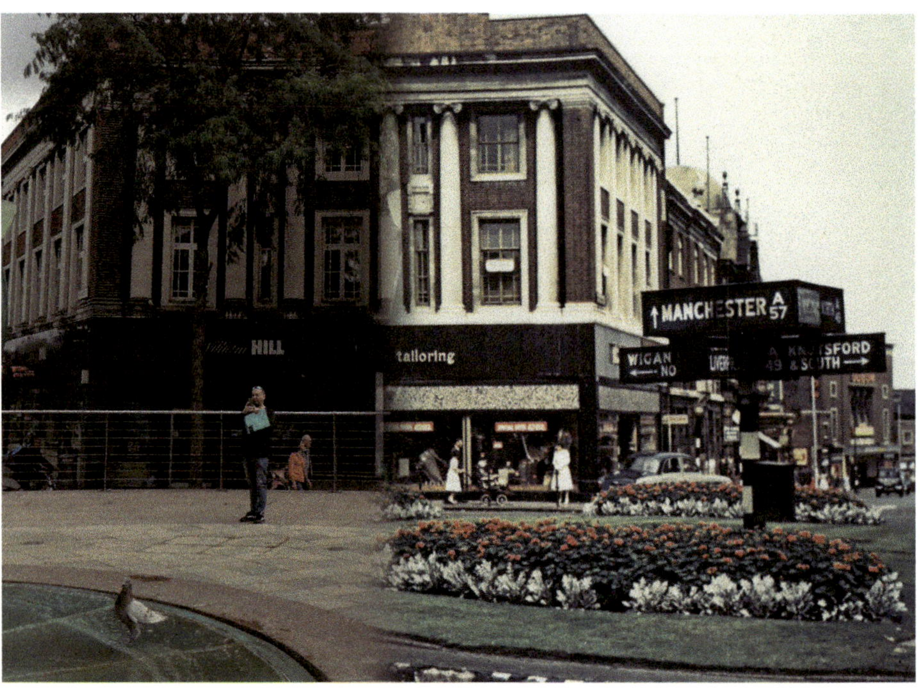

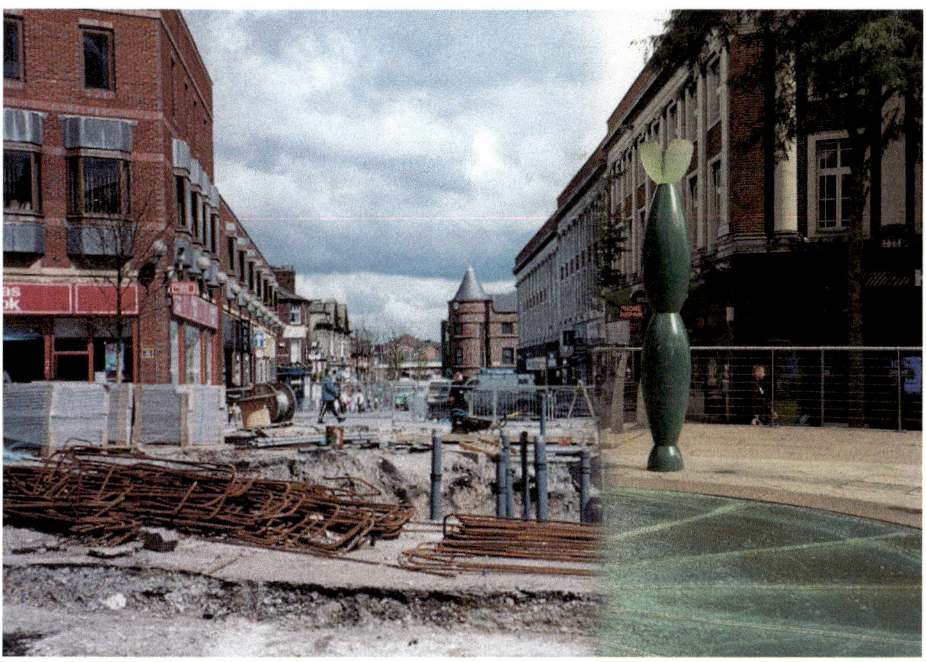

Pedestrianisation of the four main streets by the 1990s had left a variety of unattractive street surfaces which compared unfavourably with the *River of Life* feature in Bridge Street. Leading American artist Howard Ben Tre was chosen from a shortlist of distinguished artists to transform Market Gate, Buttermarket and Horsemarket Streets and link to Golden Square for the new millennium. Central to Ben Tre's scheme is the *Well of Light* at Market Gate surrounded by ten abstract columns or Guardians.

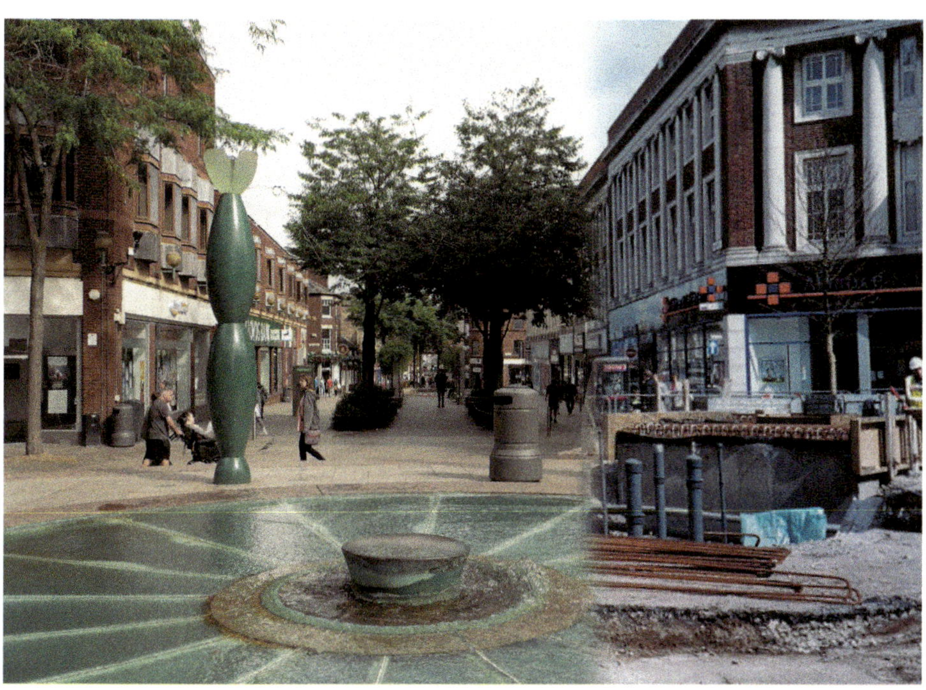

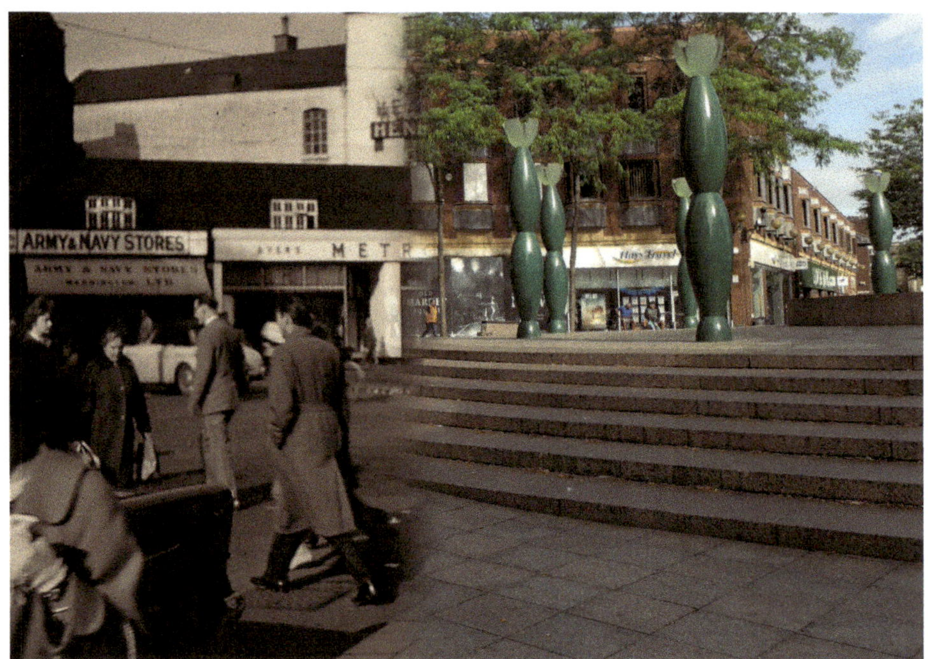

In contrast to today's more tranquil scene these 1960s shoppers clad in overcoats and hats scurry across the busy crossroads where the main north-south and east-west road routes met. Facing them was Horsemarket Street with Sankey Street to the left and Buttermarket Street to the right while the crossroads came to be known as Market Gate (the street leading to the market). Millings and Peter Leigh's high-class grocery stores survived until the building of Golden Square in the 1970s–80s.

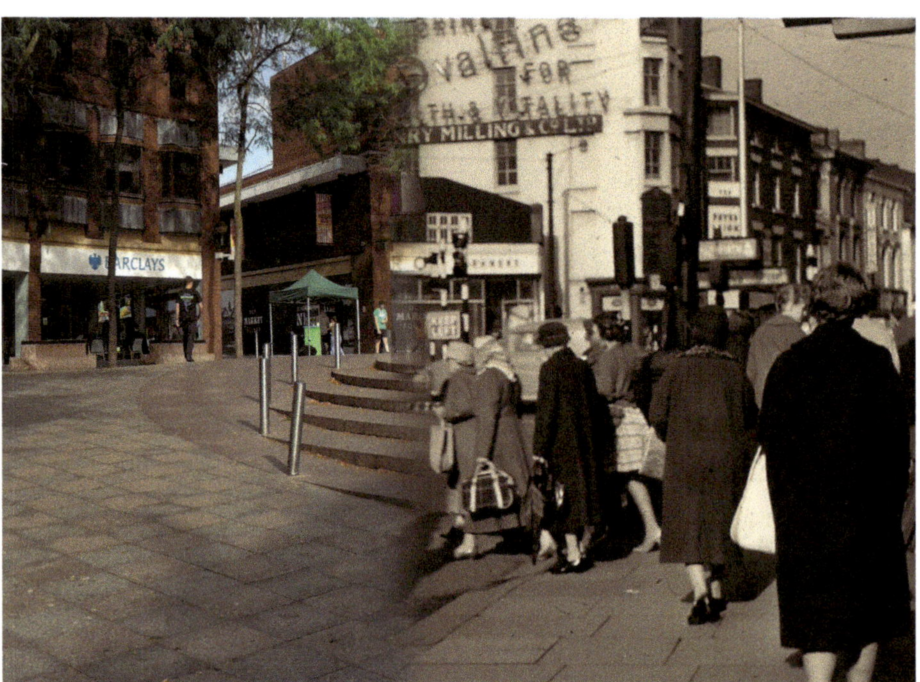

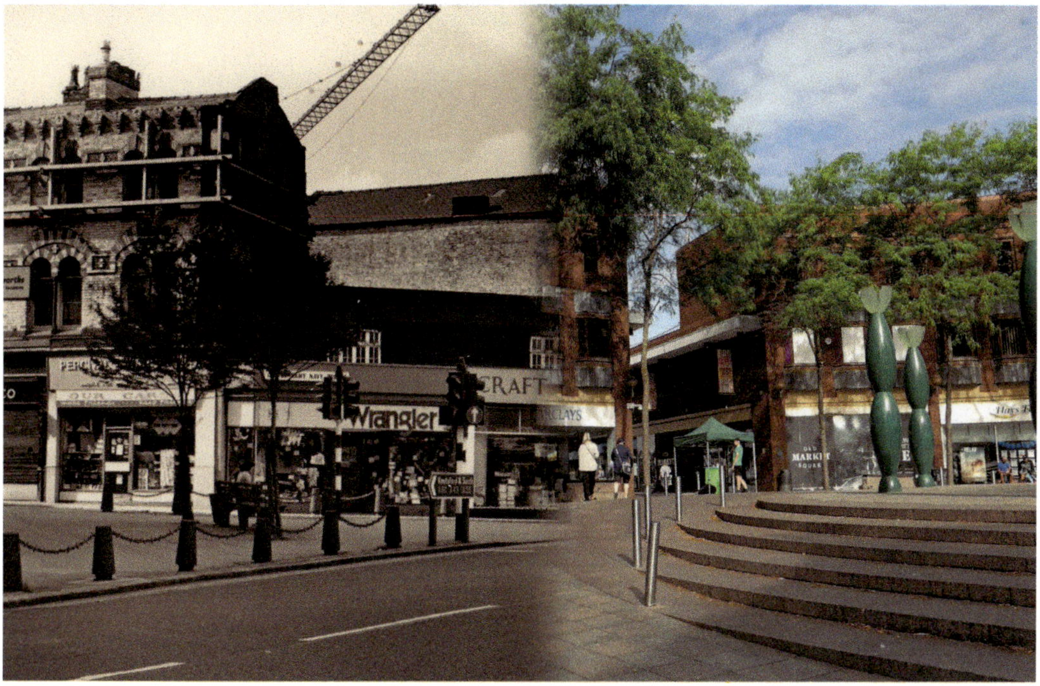

By the later 1970s work was already beginning on the Golden Square development behind
Horsemarket Street and Sankey Street. Many of the old shops were in limbo and the familiar
Ovaltine sign had disappeared with the closure of Milling's grocers shop. To brighten the scene
Greenall's commissioned cartoonist Bill Tidy to bring Moscow to Market Gate in a spoof advert for
their Vladivar Vodka and a few surprised motorists wondered if they had taken a wrong turning!

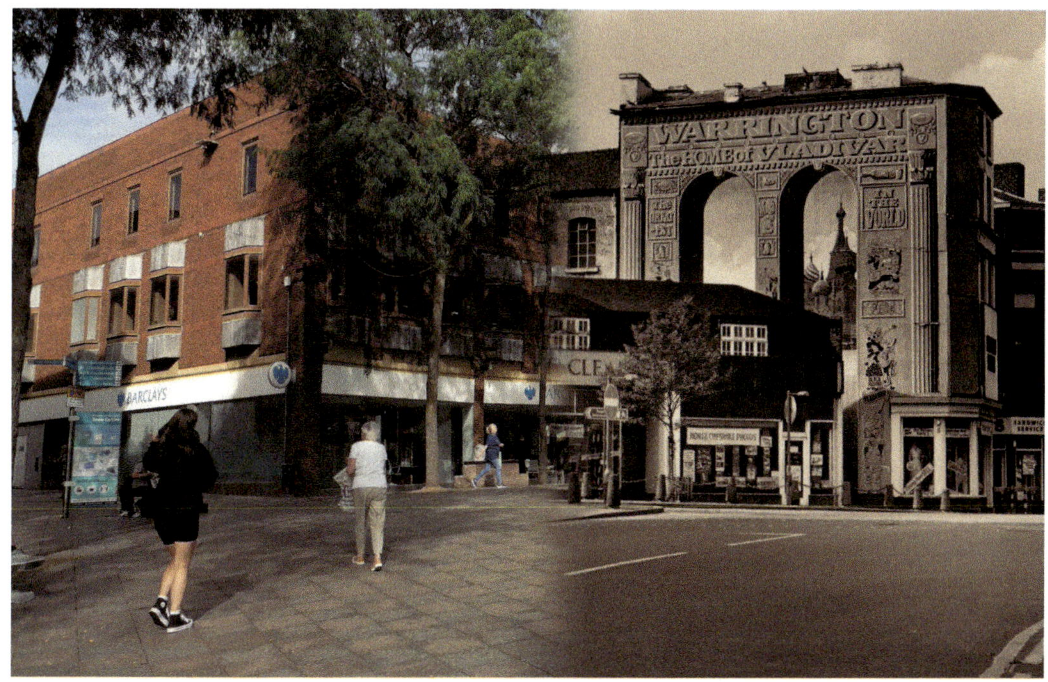

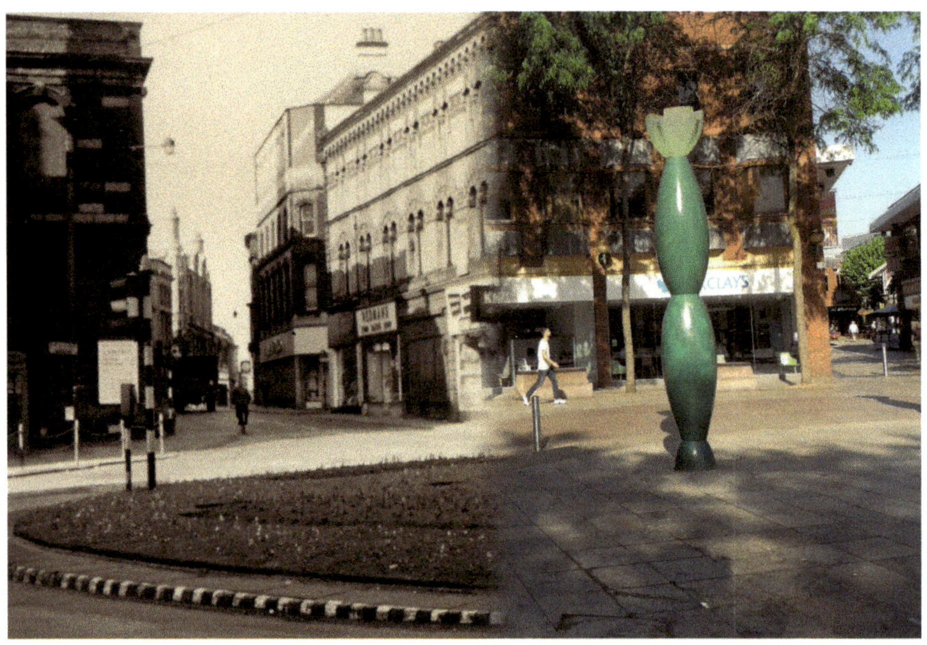

The corner of Horsemarket Street and Sankey Street was the last section of Market Gate to be transformed with the demolition of a number of mid-nineteenth-century shops facing Holy Trinity Church (on the left of Sankey Street). Ben Tre's abstract *Guardian* figures are a prominent feature of the new streetscape, representing those who guard Warrington's heritage in the past, present and future and have a copper-effect surface topped with glass capitals reflecting two of Warrington's past industries.

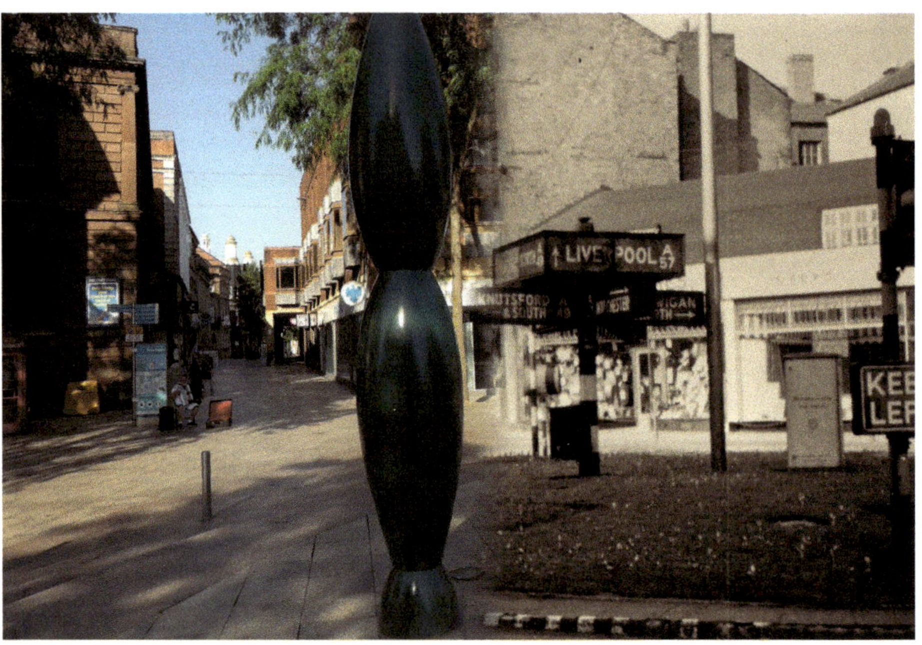

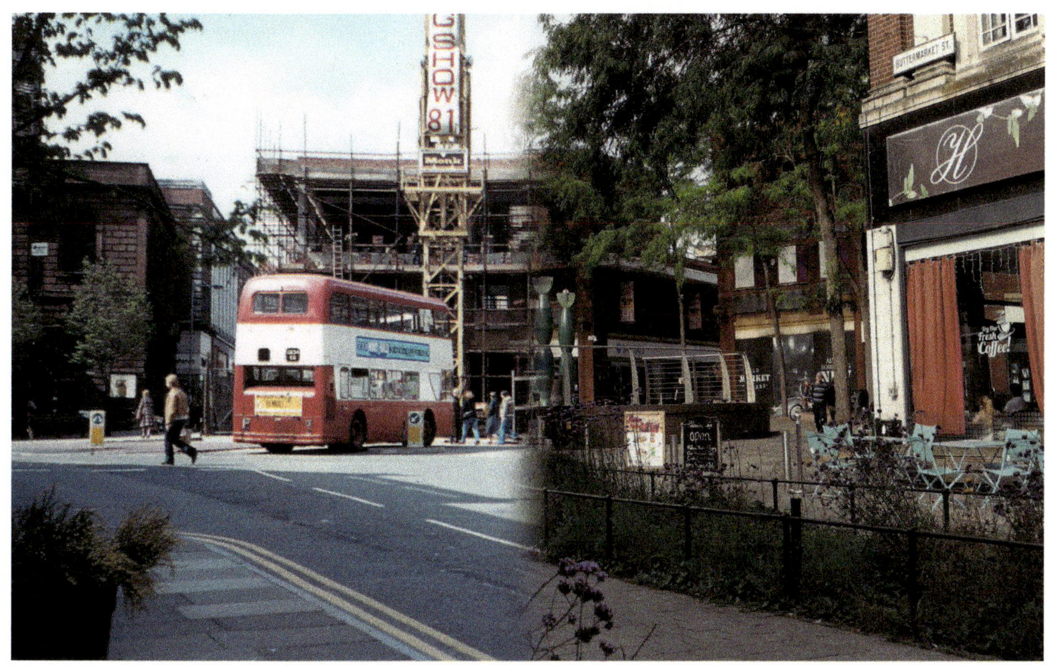

The final corner of Market Gate to be realised was the corner of Horsemarket Street and Sankey Street (seen here from Buttermarket Street), which also marked the third phase of Golden Square completed in 1984. The planners felt they had made a sympathetic addition as 'the beaux arts circus commenced at the turn of the (twentieth) century has been completed by the Golden Square elevations and a 3-storey height has been used to give a uniform relationship with the existing facades'.

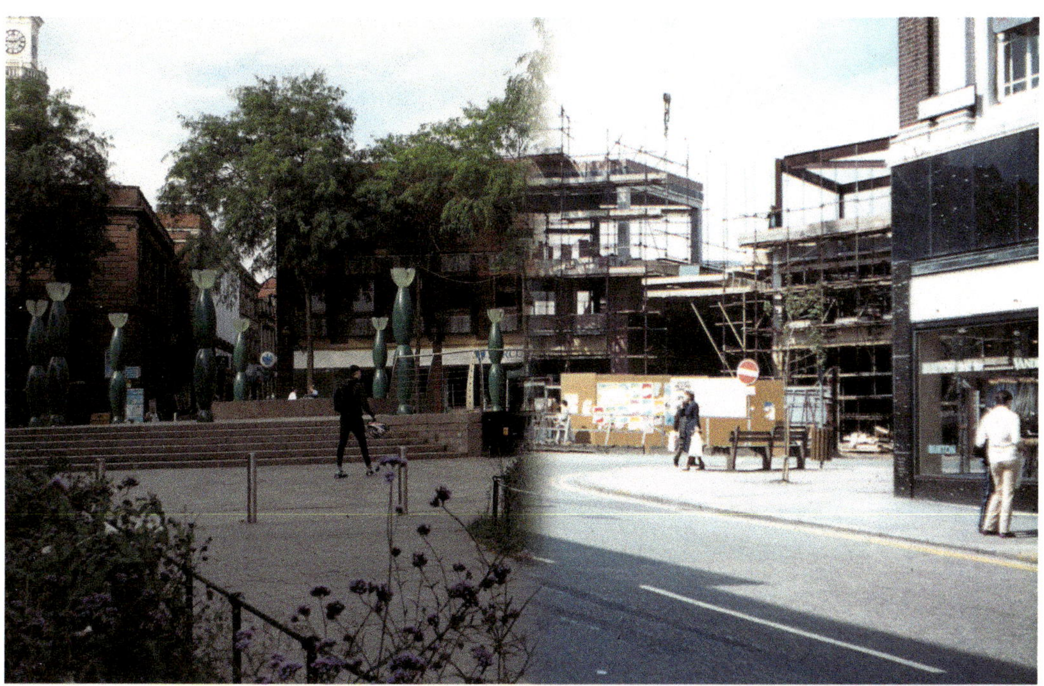

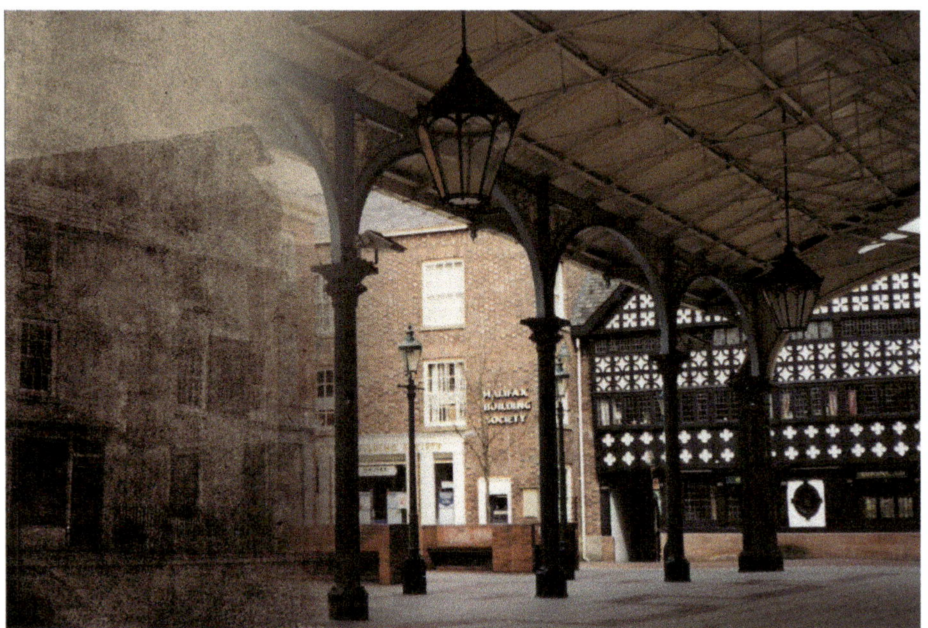

Warrington's market dates back to at least 1277 and by the eighteenth century had moved off the main crossroad into the Old Market Place which was the scene of Warrington's weekly food markets, fortnightly cattle sales and occasional cloth fairs. The early sepia photograph dates from *c.* 1855 just before the old open market was replaced by a covered market hall and open-sided fish market. The half-timbered Barley Mow Inn is just visible to the right of the older Image.

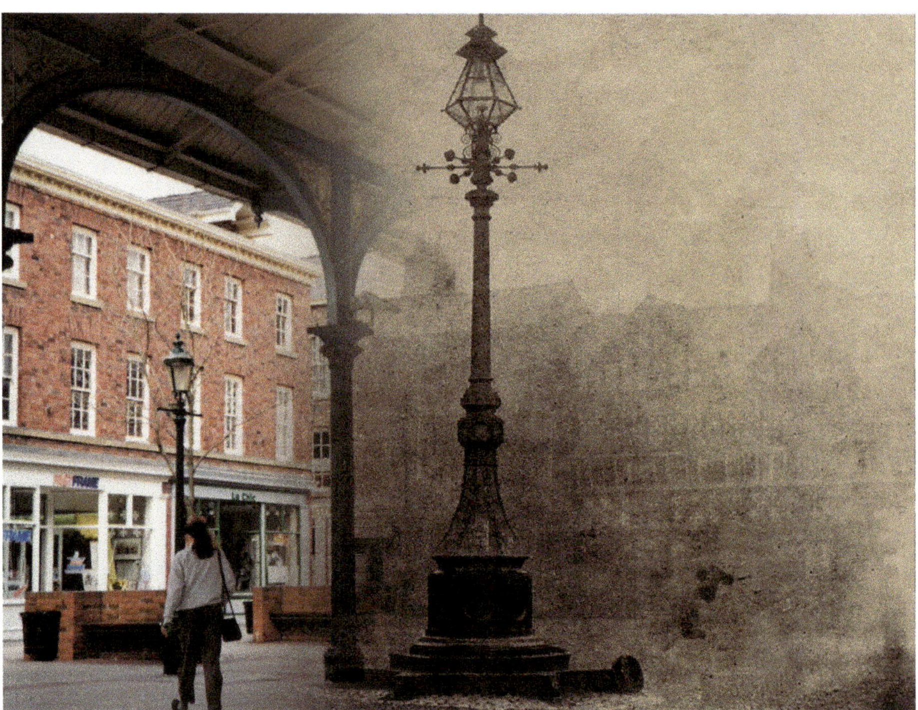

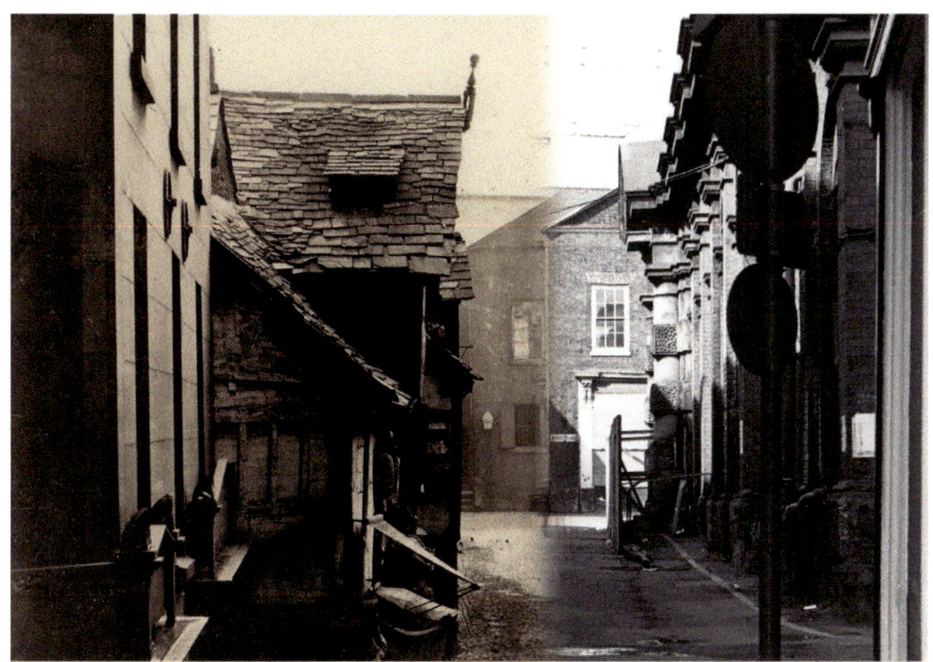

Today's Old Market Place can be reached by an entry from Market Gate which almost follows the line of old Cheapside. The Golden Square redevelopment of the 1980s changed the area almost beyond recognition but comparisons are easier to make between the sepia image of 1855 and the black and white image of the early 1970s. The building with the bell tower survived a 1856 redevelopment which created the covered market hall to the right of the later view.

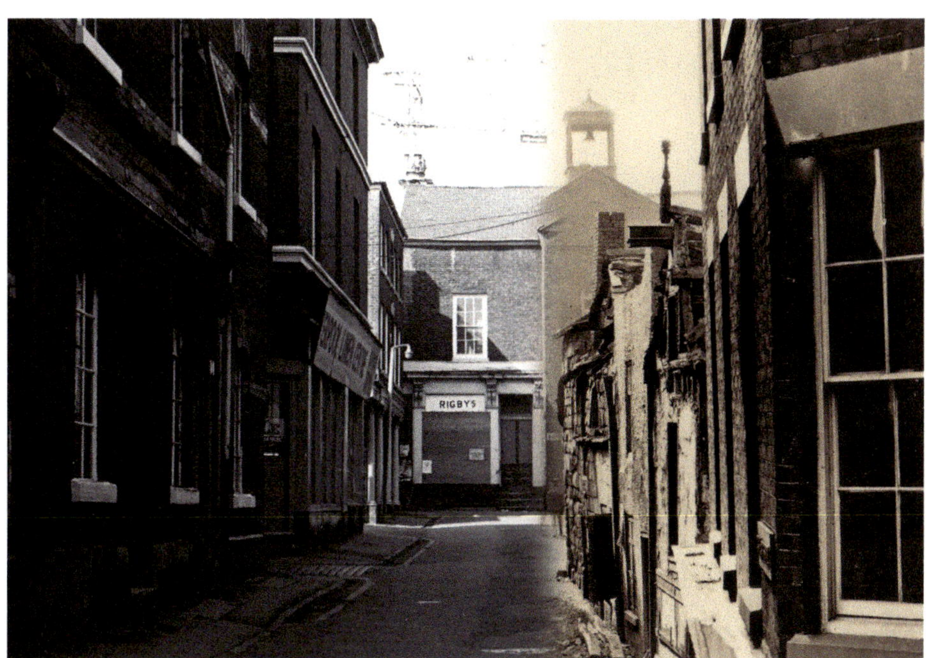

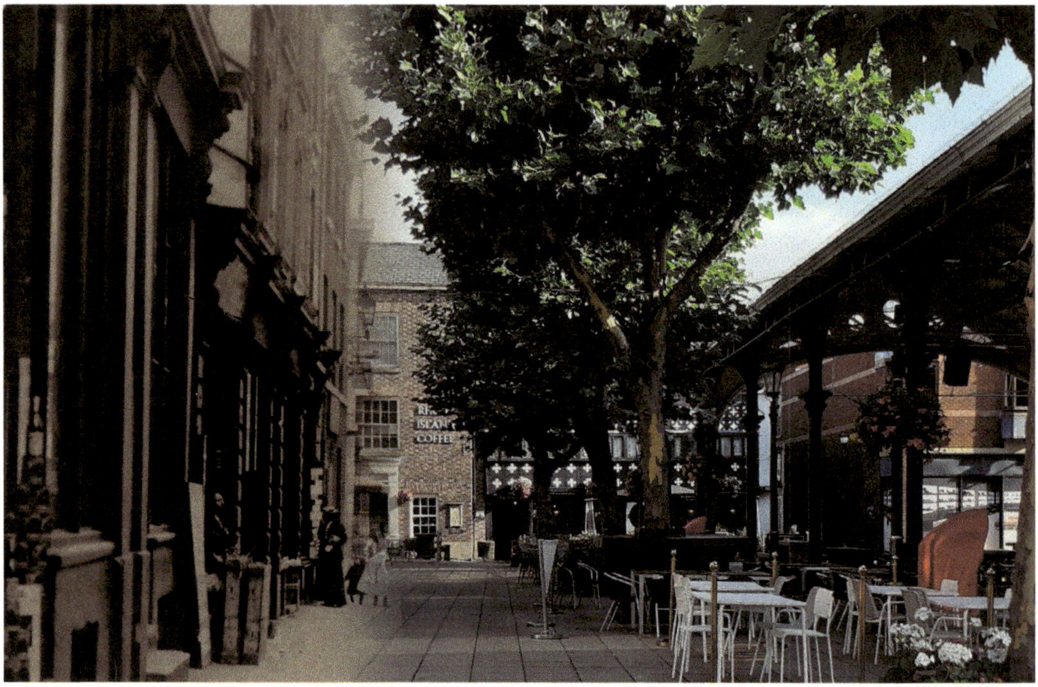

Already known as Golden Square, by 1772 this area was home to Warrington's market until 1974. The decorative cast-iron structure of the Old Fish Market was kept as a centrepiece when the area was redeveloped again in the 1980s. By the early 1900s minor alterations had been made to the Barley Mow's facade and the small oval window appeared at ground level but in the 1980s many of the buildings on the left were demolished and rebuilt in the Georgian style.

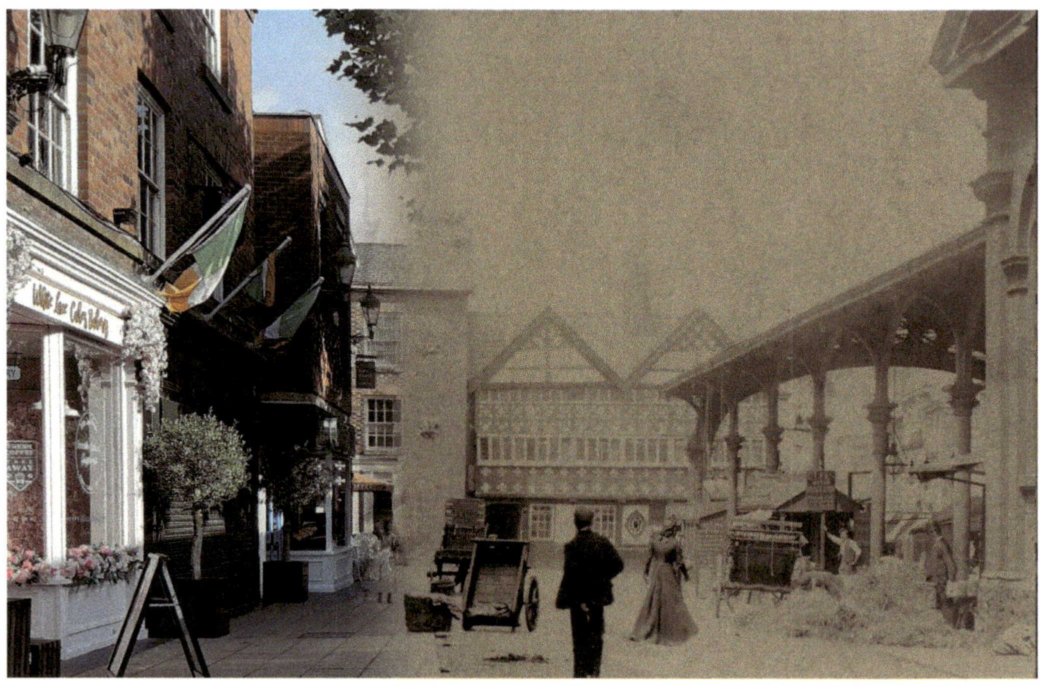

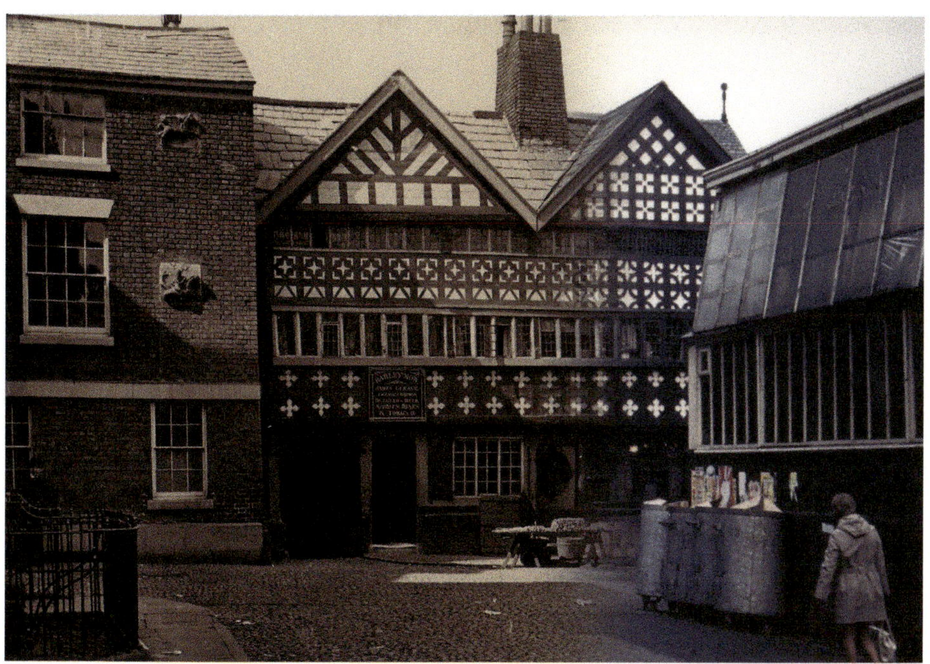

The Barley Mow is the oldest building in the town centre, dating from the later sixteenth century. When the Old Market Place was redeveloped in the early 1980s the Barley Mow was one of the few original buildings to survive as even its neighbour the former offices of William Beamont, Warrington's first mayor, was rebuilt in the Georgian style. The later 1970s photograph shows the Fish Market's ugly side panelling which protected traders and customers from the weather.

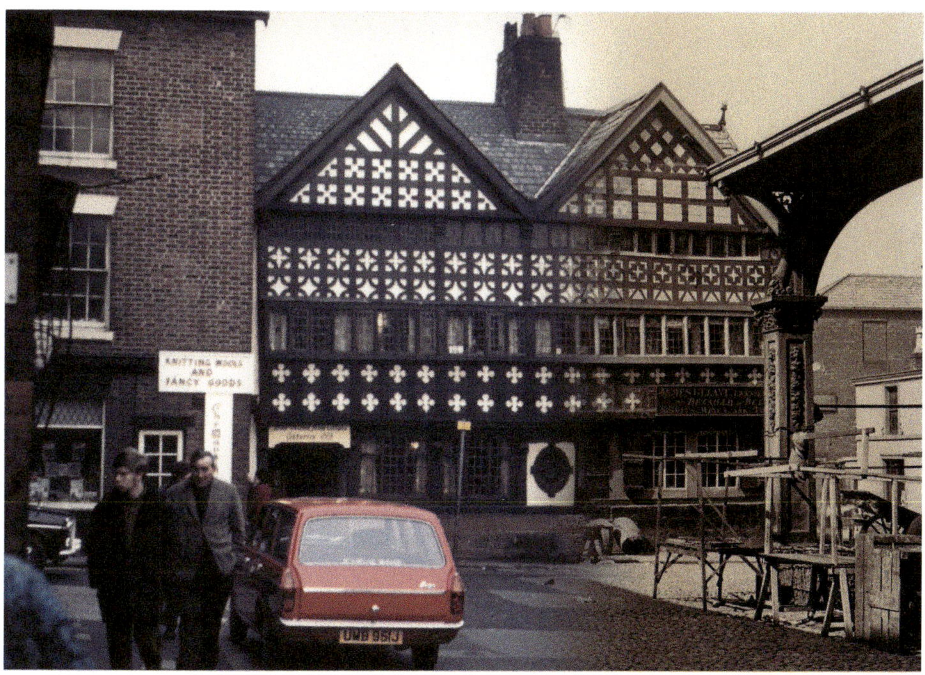

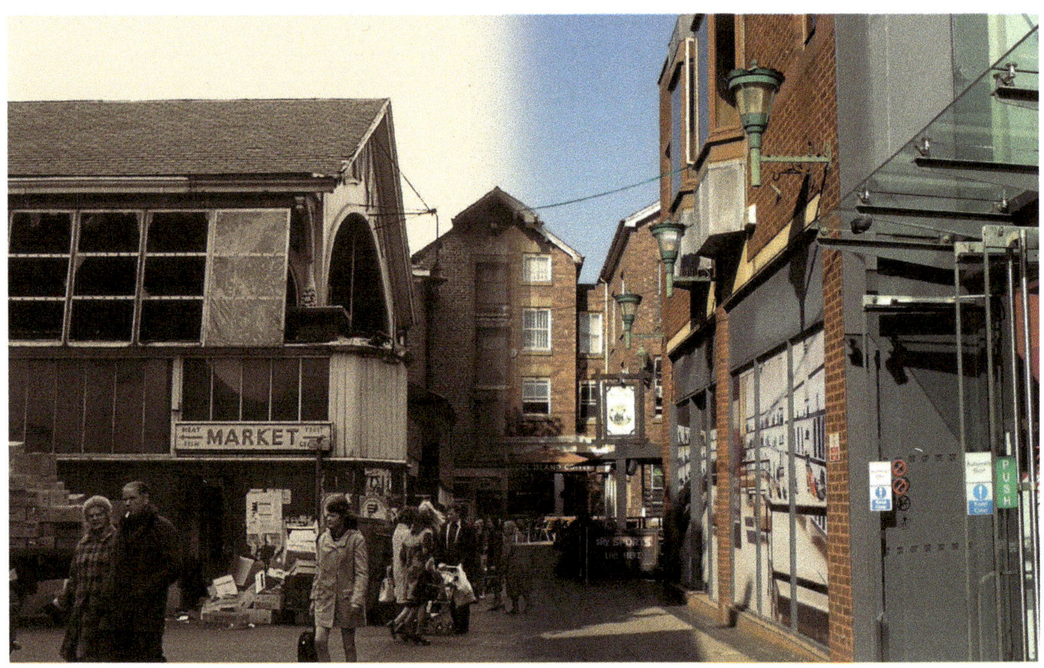

Golden Square shopping malls and the Old Market Place can still be reached from Horsemarket Street by Lyme Street. The 1970s image shows the scale of change. Apart from the Old Fish Market and the Barley Mow the remaining buildings only date from the 1980s when Walker's Vine Tavern (to the right of the old view) was demolished. Beyond that Market Street led off beside the Barley Mow to a general market hall built in the 1880s.

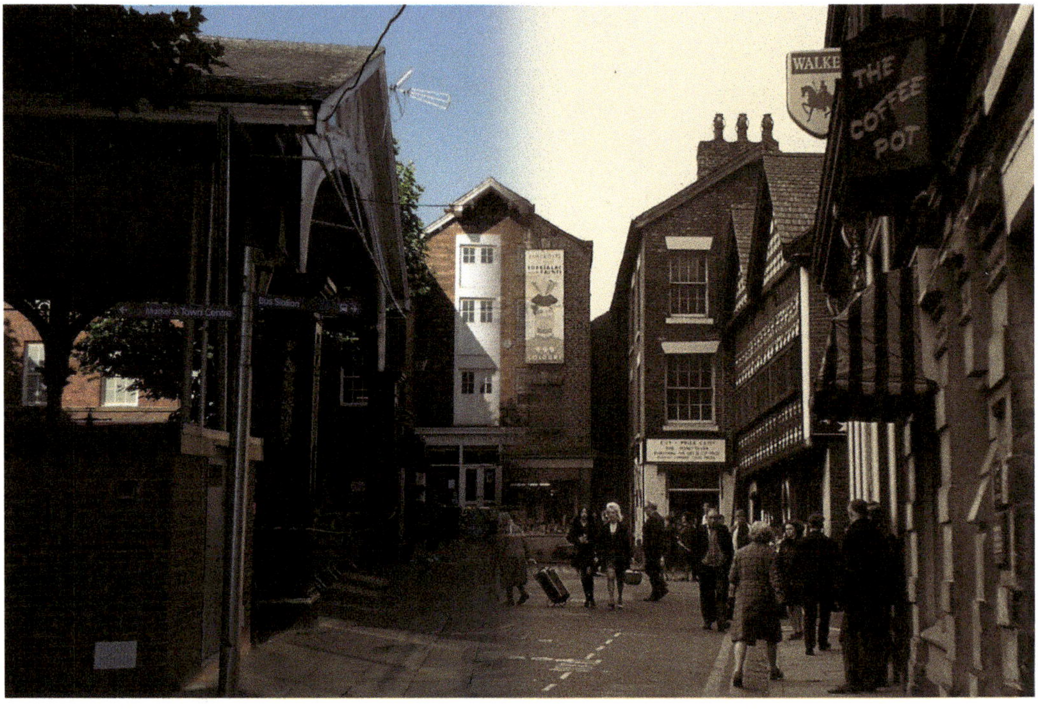

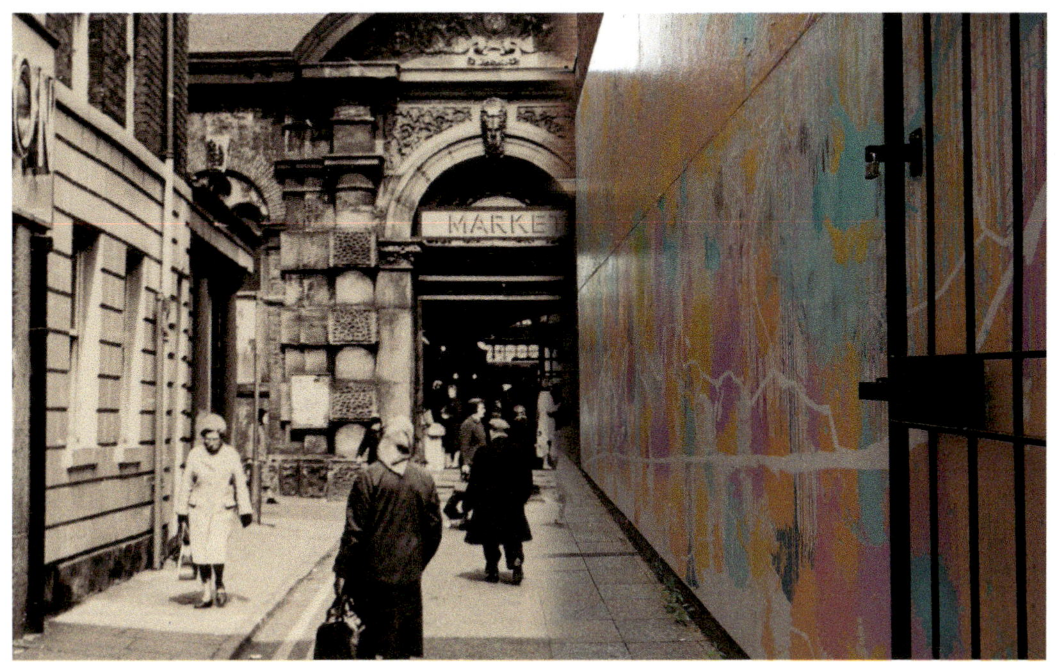

In the 1980s the Old Market Place lost the wide access route from Sankey Street called Corporation Street which led to the ornate covered Market Hall built in 1856. Demolition of this structure was one of the most contested aspects of the 1980s redevelopment with conservationists arguing that it should be retained whilst the planners successfully contended that its demolition was crucial to opening up the area into an attractive square with the retention of the attached Fish Market.

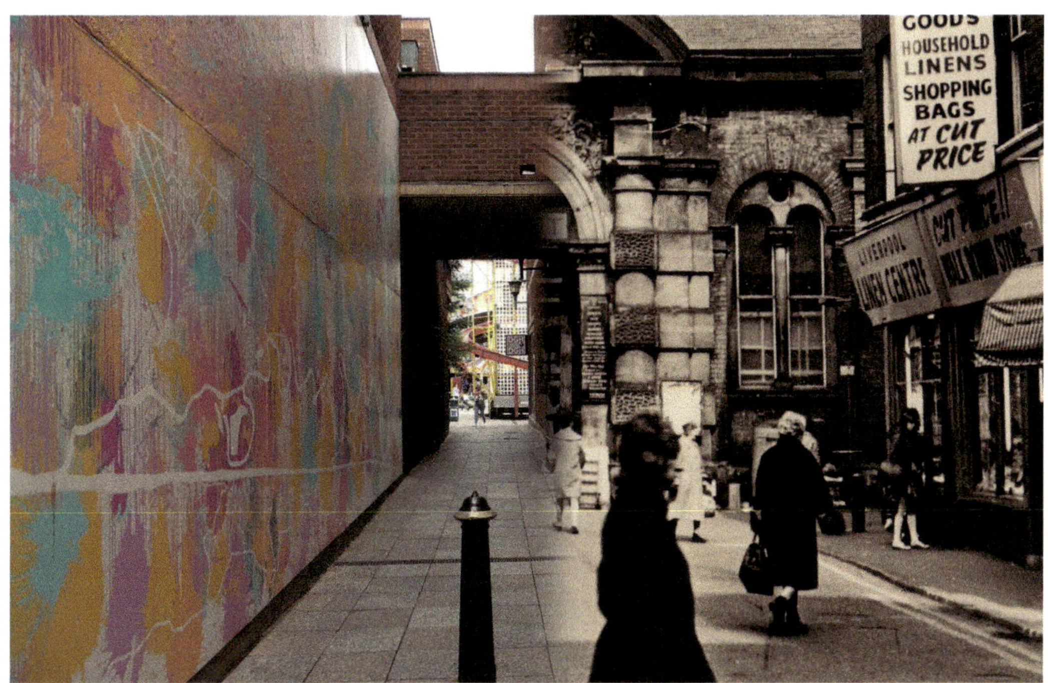

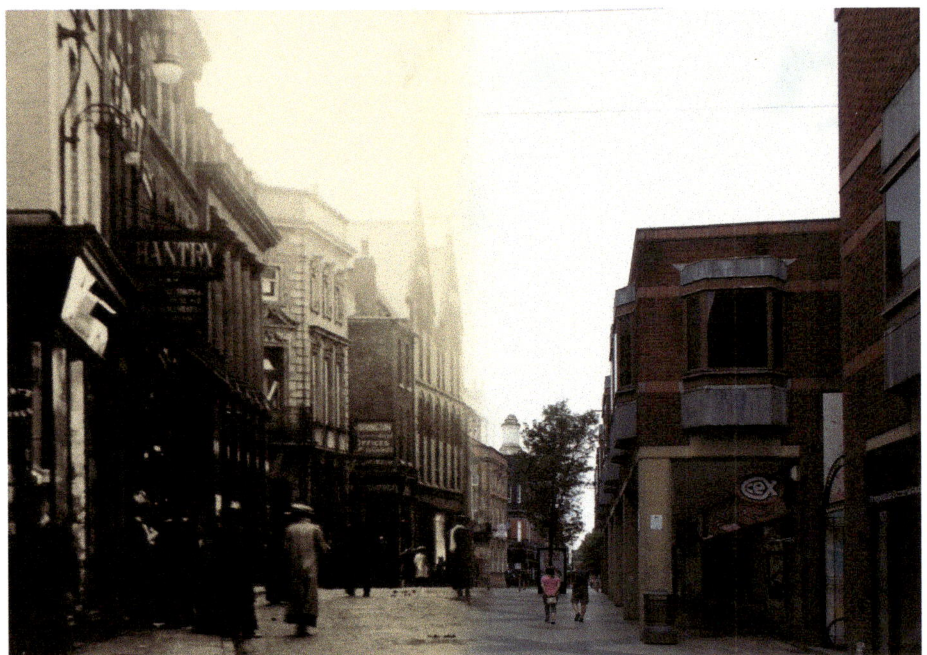

Across from Holy Trinity Church a policeman patrols the entry from Corporation Street into Sankey Street in the sepia postcard view from the early 1900s. Behind him are the imposing premises of J & W Dutton, 'drapers, dressmakers, costumiers, milliners, ladies, gents and children's outfitters, house furnishers', furniture removers etc'. National retail chains had yet to arrive on Warrington's high streets but the town was well served by its own high-class family businesses.

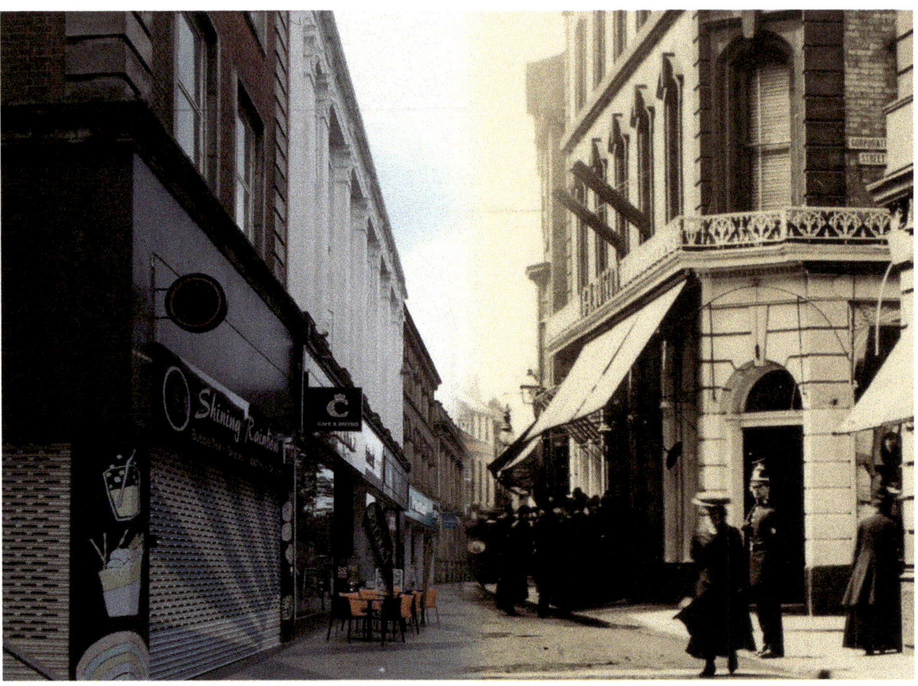

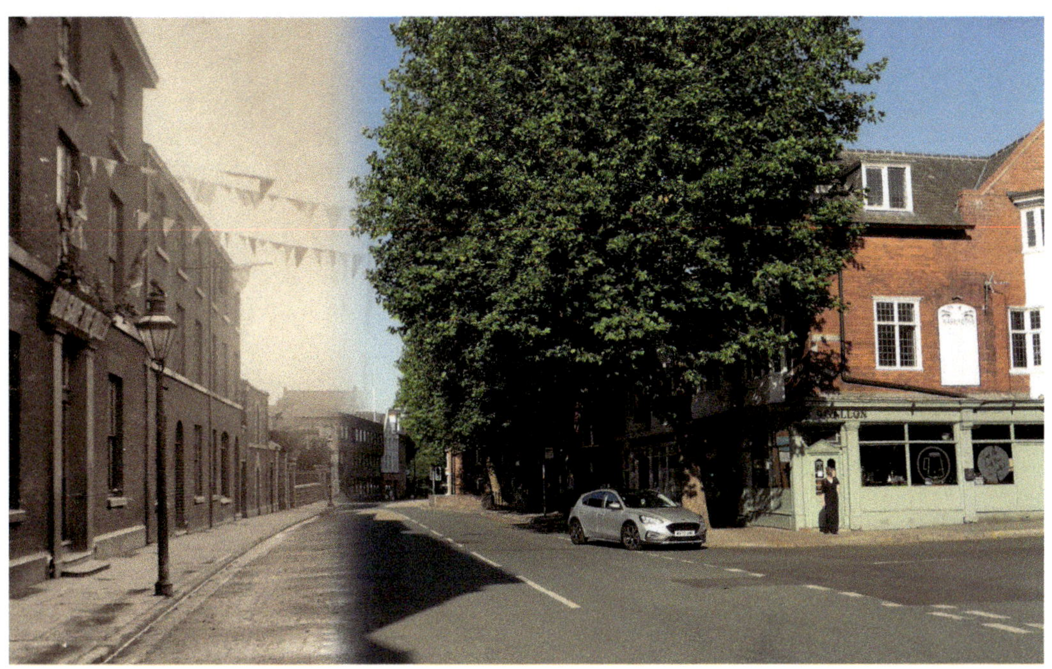

A brisk walk towards Sankey led to a comparatively residential area of the street in the late nineteenth-century photograph from Birtles' Studio whose shop can be seen on the corner of Legh Street to the right. Thomas Birtles was an eminent photographer and local councillor, often commissioned to record the changing face of the town. As his career prospered he followed the pattern of other businessmen who were relocating to the suburbs, leaving their houses to become commercial premises.

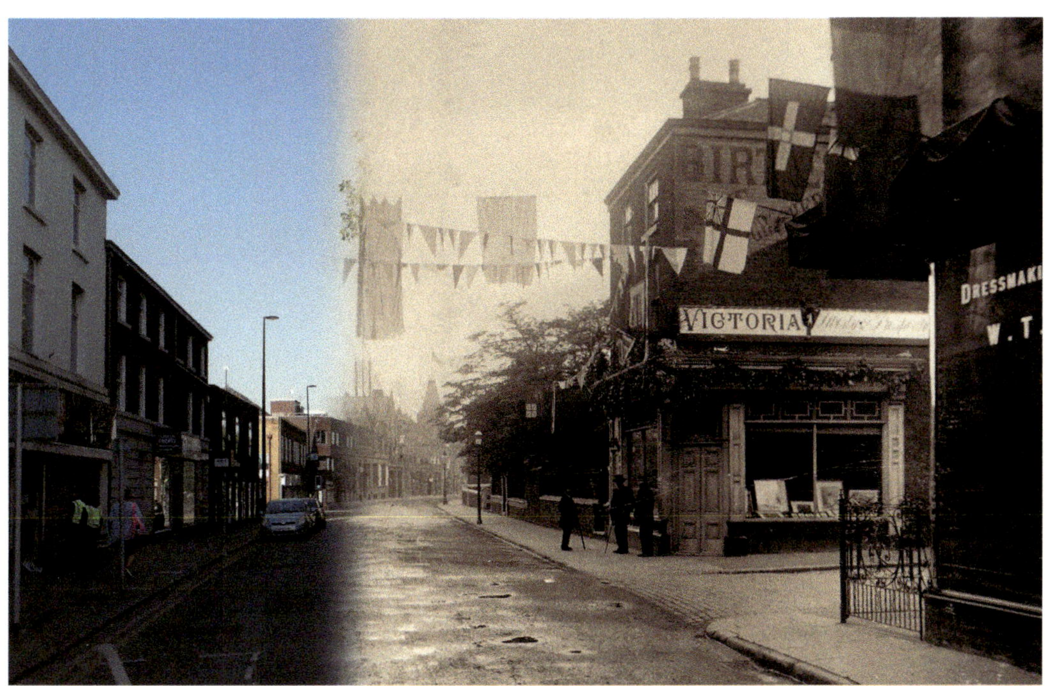

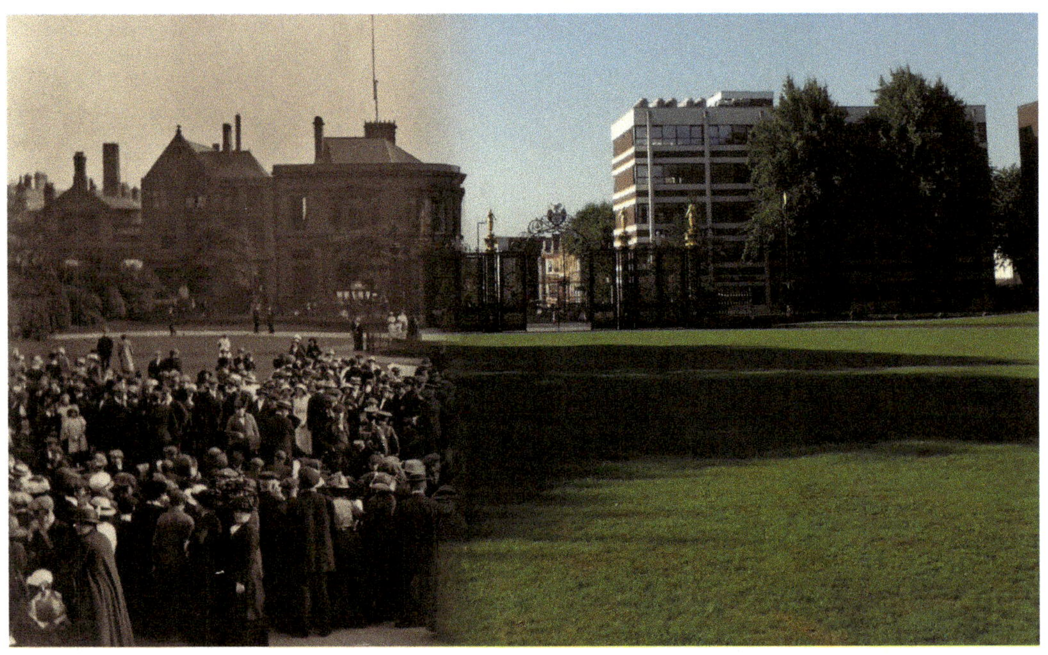

Councillor Birtles would recognise some of the view from the Town Hall steps looking down Winmarleigh Street. However, the white building on the far left is no longer part of Warrington Guardian's headquarters while its neighbour is no longer the main post office. To the right the distinctive towered premises of the Conservative Club, opened in 1884, were replaced in the 1970s by two multi-storey office blocks. Most noticeably an ornate fountain is missing from the Town Hall lawn!

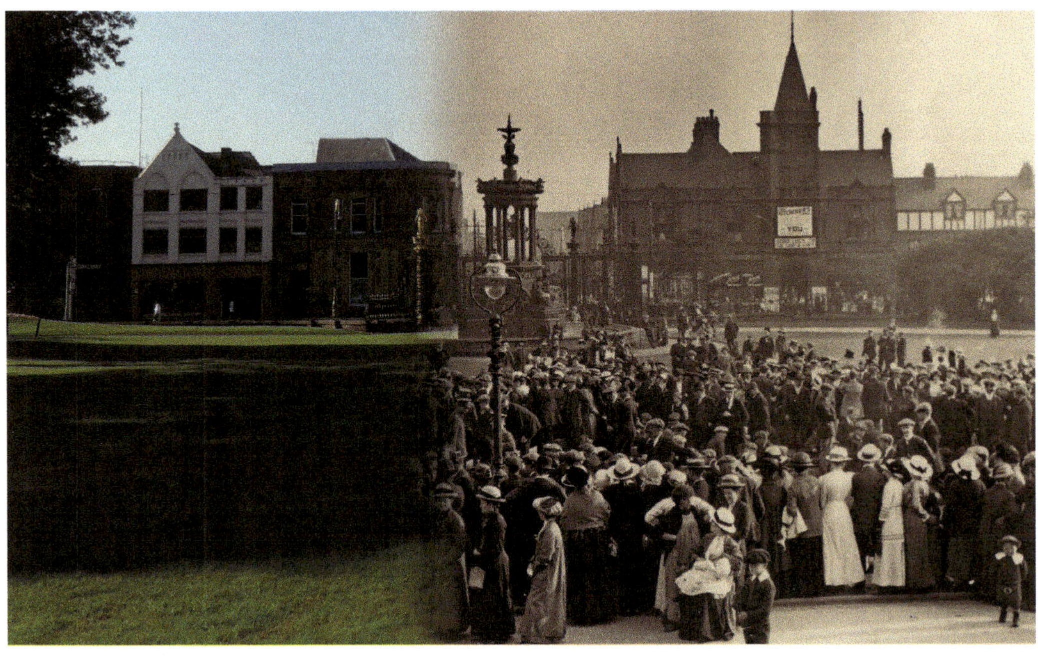

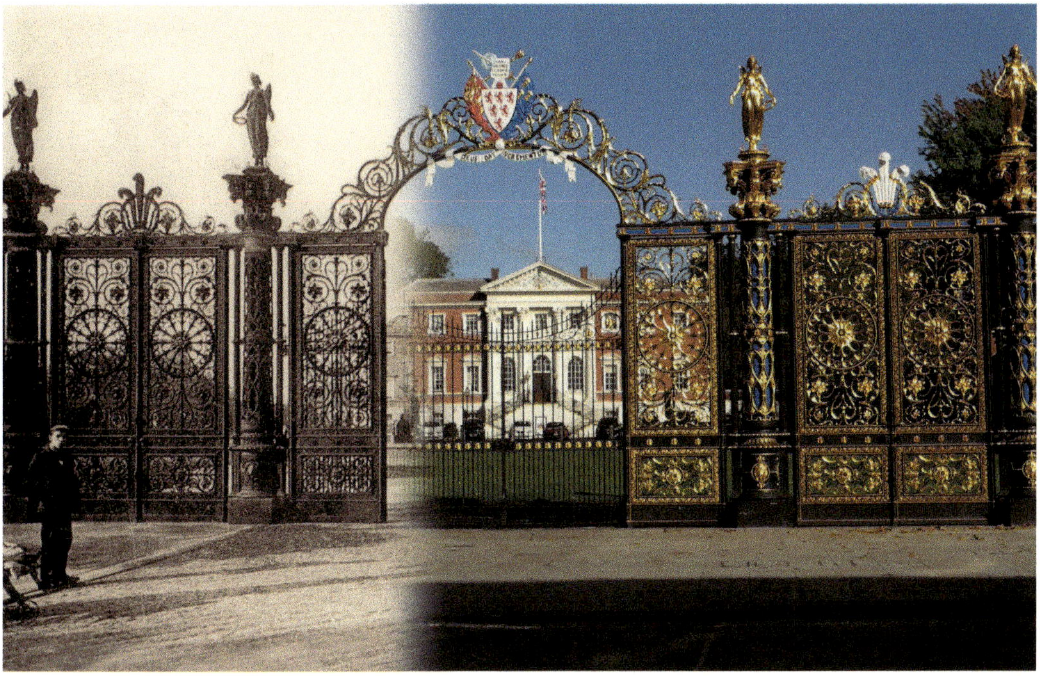

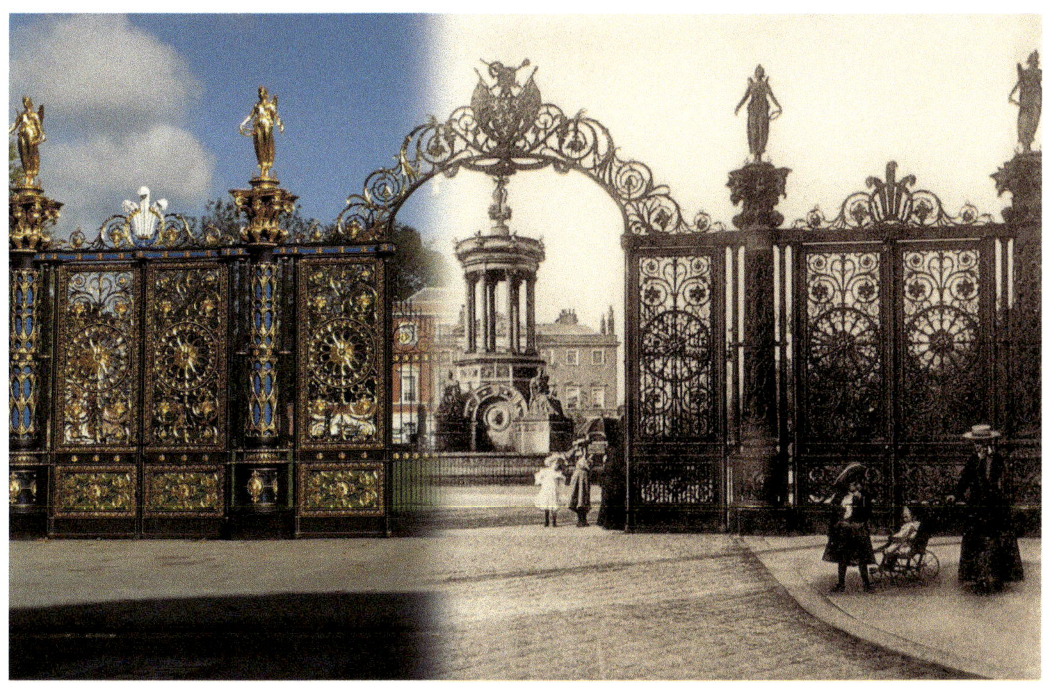

Today Sankey Street has two historic landmarks: the Town Hall and Golden Gates. Once there was a third: the fountain presented in 1900 in memory of Peter Walker of Walker's brewery. Its demolition in March 1942 left a clear view of the Town Hall, built in 1750 by acclaimed architect James Gibbs for local businessman Thomas Patten. Today it is framed by the ornate gates presented to the town in 1895 by Councillor Frederick Monks, of Monks Hall ironworks.

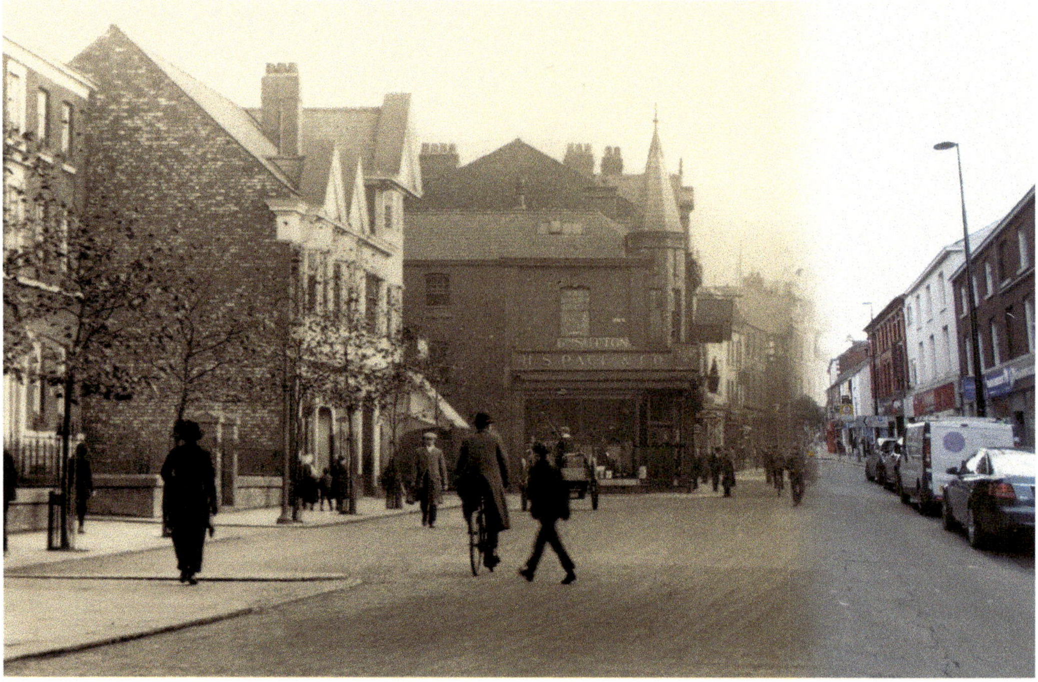

The early twentieth-century view towards Market Gate from the corner of Springfield Street revealed that Sankey Street had yet to become a major traffic route. On the right-hand corner was the ornate façade of the Picturedrome cinema which was remodelled as the Cameo by the 1950s. Nearer to the corner of Legh Street (now hidden by the trees on the left) the street narrowed to a potential traffic bottleneck which has now disappeared.

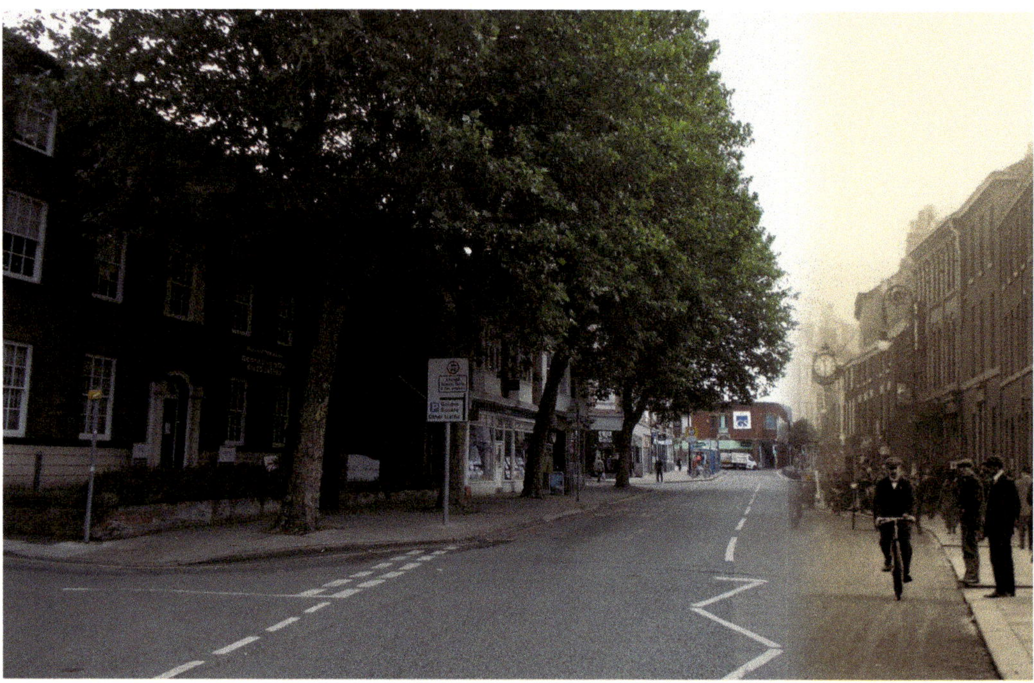

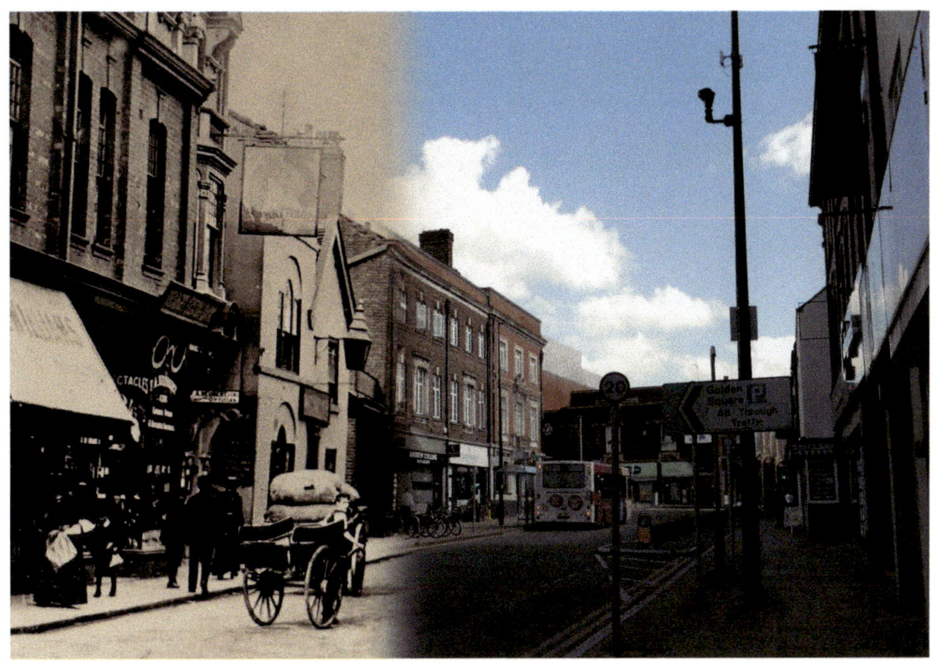

This view of Sankey Street between Legh Street and present-day Golden Square shows the drastic changes which took place from the 1900s to the present. On the near right Dawson's music shop lies shuttered next to the former Ashton's chemist shop. The left-hand side between Legh Street and Golborne Street was completely rebuilt in 1928 as the first stage of widening Sankey Street to Market Gate. The old White Hart (behind the handcart) was demolished and re-sited.

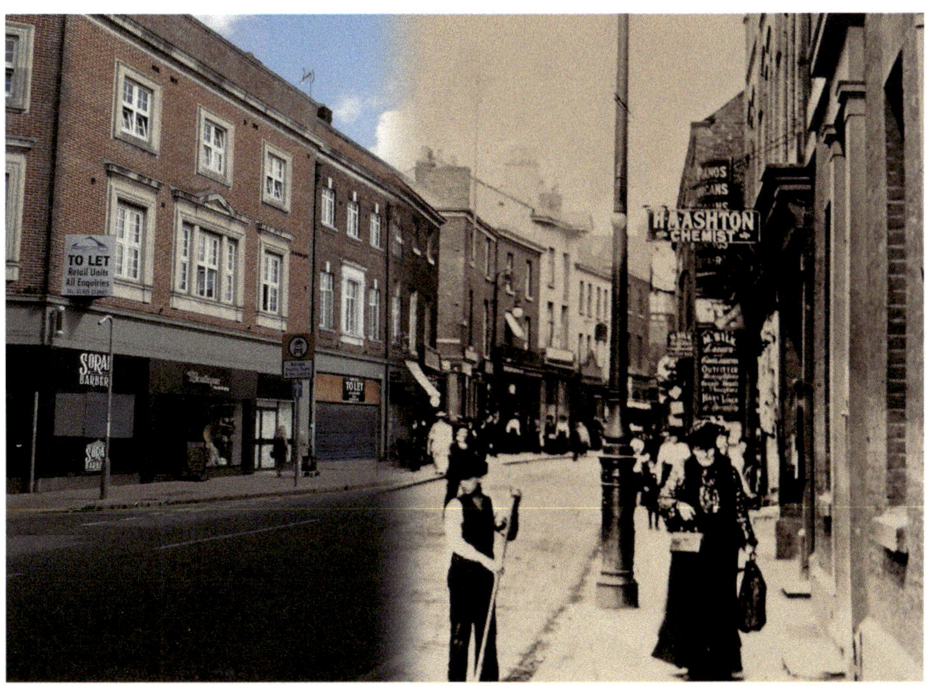

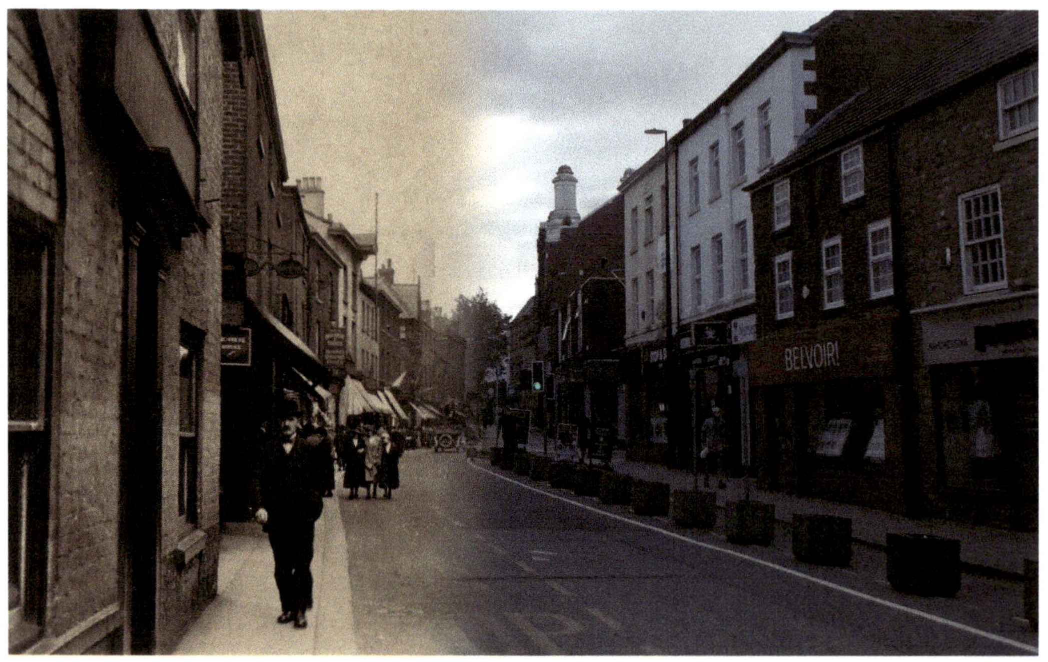

These two views dramatically illustrate the potential impact of turning Sankey Street into a dual carriageway! In 1926 this might have been enough to send the man in the bowler hat scurrying into the old White Hart (near left in the older image) for a reviving drink! On the right-hand side of the street Horobin's newsagents with its stone-flagged floors survived to the early twenty-first century in a block dating back to at least the early 1800s.

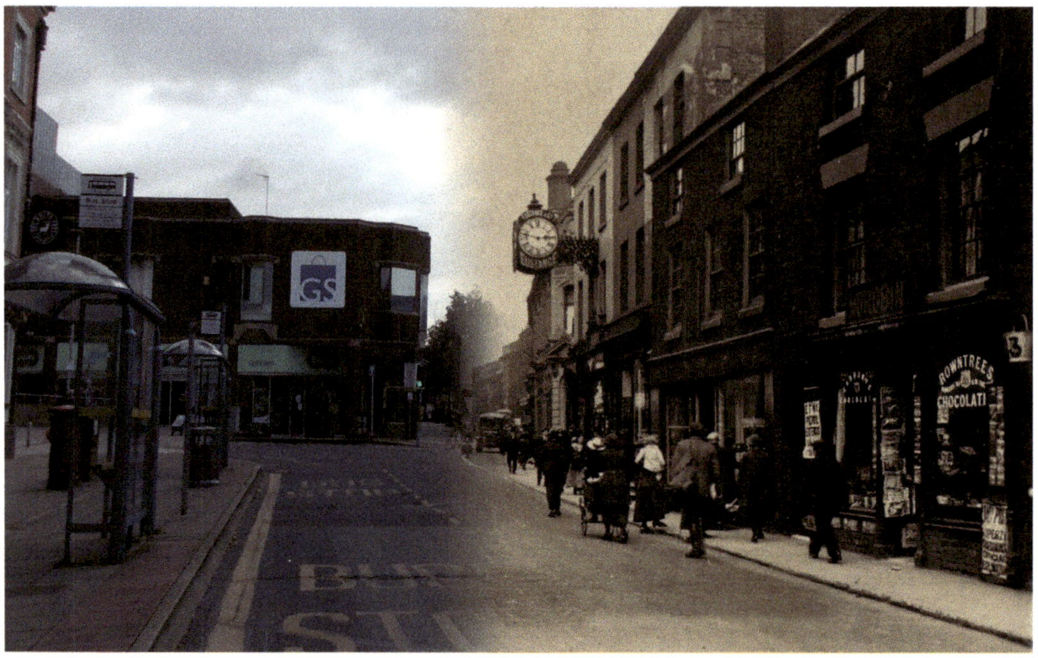

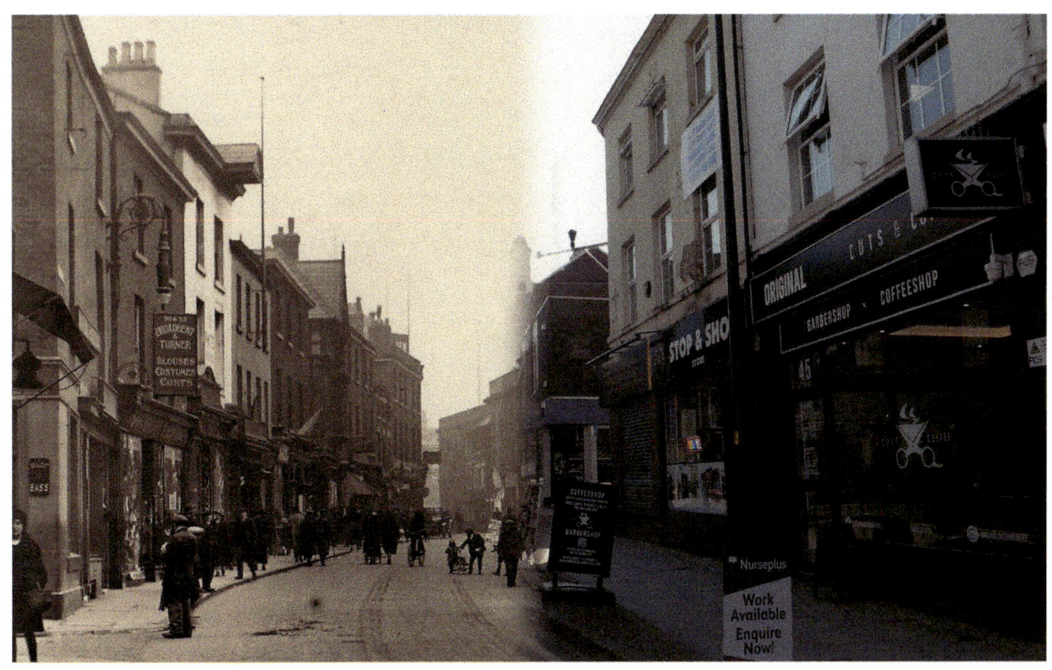

An ornate clock marks the passage of time in these two views of the corner of Bold Street and Sankey Street. Familiar local stores such as Broadbent and Turner and Eustance the jeweller have relocated since the earlier photograph of 1924 whilst the shops themselves were demolished in the 1970s.The elaborate Woolpack Inn on the corner of Bold Street (behind Eustance's clock) gave way to a featureless 1970s block opposite the mellow brickwork of the new Golden Square (left).

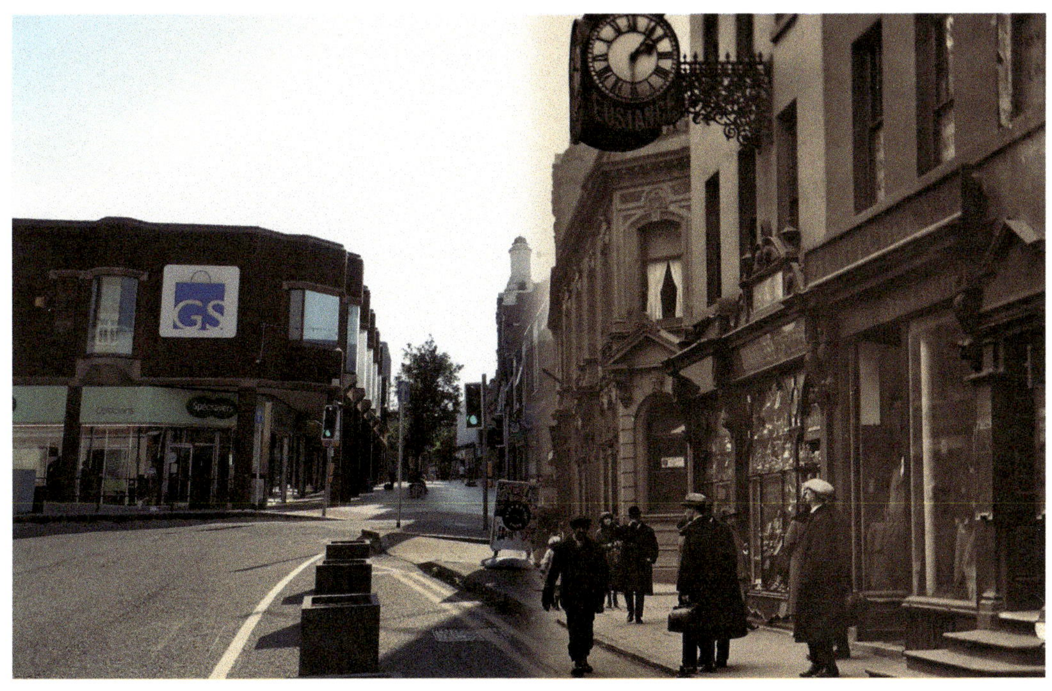

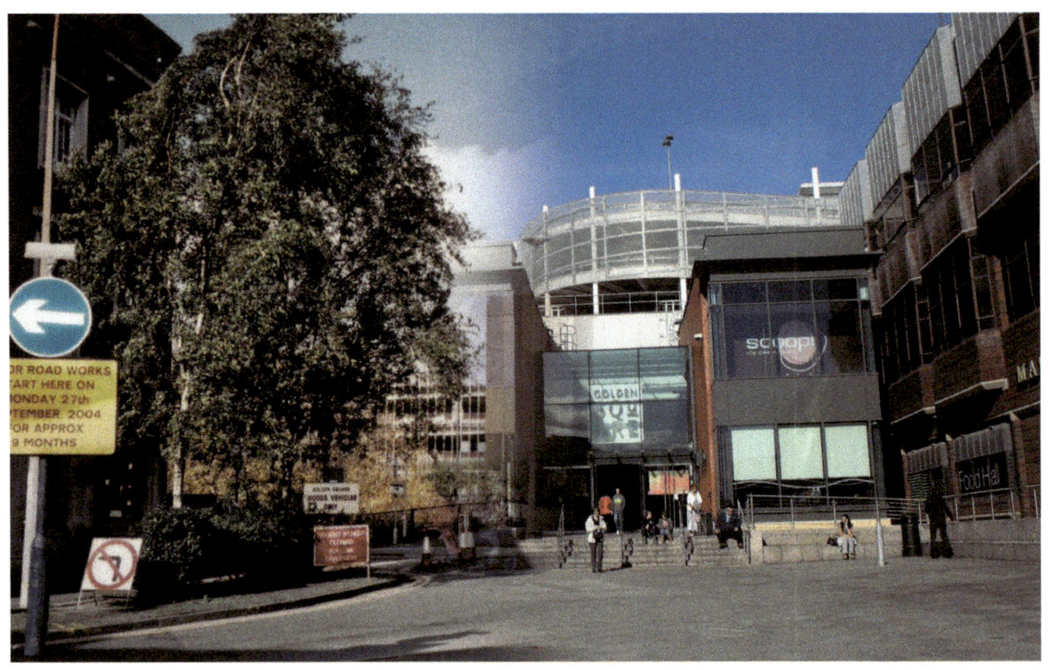

Pedestrianisation of Sankey Street was made possible in the 1970s–80s by the construction of a new inner ring road which diverted traffic via Golborne Street, across Horsemarket Street, Scotland Road and Academy Way to Bridge Foot. A multi-storey car park was created in neighbouring Legh Street and a bus station off Golborne Street. By 2007 the Golden Square extension had replaced the car park and bus station with the new Hilden Platz next to the White Hart Hotel (left).

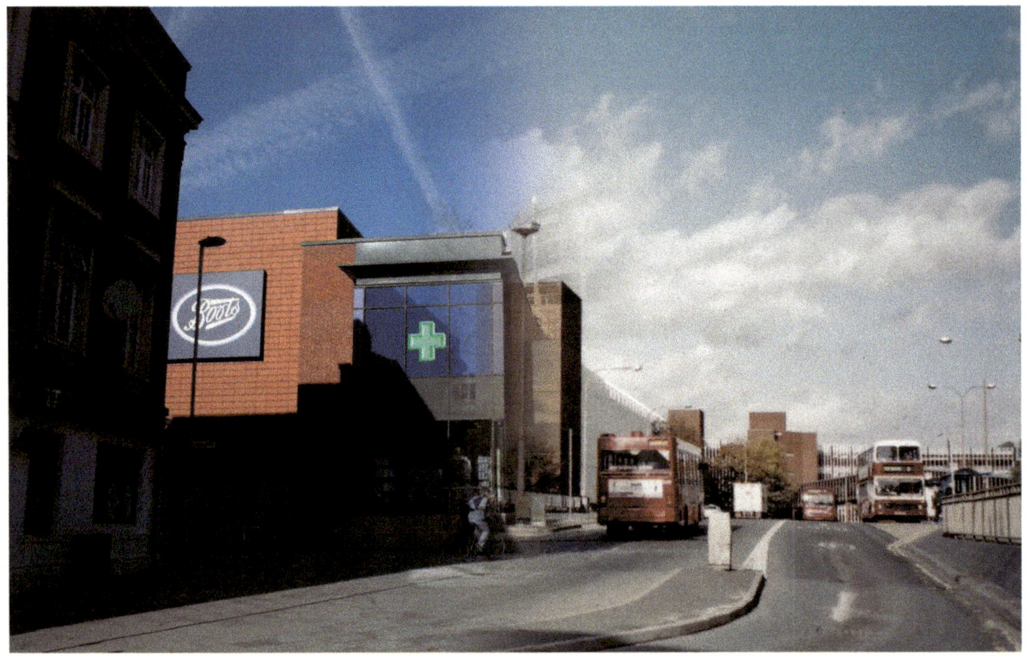

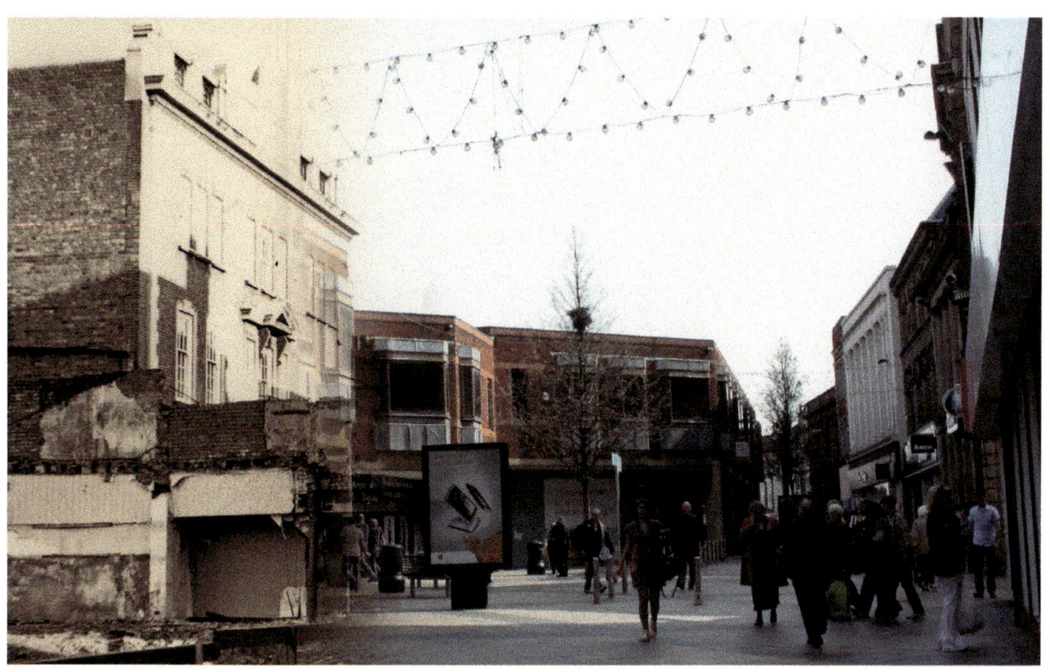

Marks and Spencer's arrived in Sankey Street in the 1930s. In anticipation of imminent plans to widen the street their store was designed with a temporary single-storey frontage which became a permanent feature as the plans were delayed. Pedestrianisation replaced road-widening schemes and a new Marks and Spencer's store opened in 1977 in the first phase of Golden Square. In 1978 the original store and its neighbours were demolished and Marks finally left the town centre in 2017.

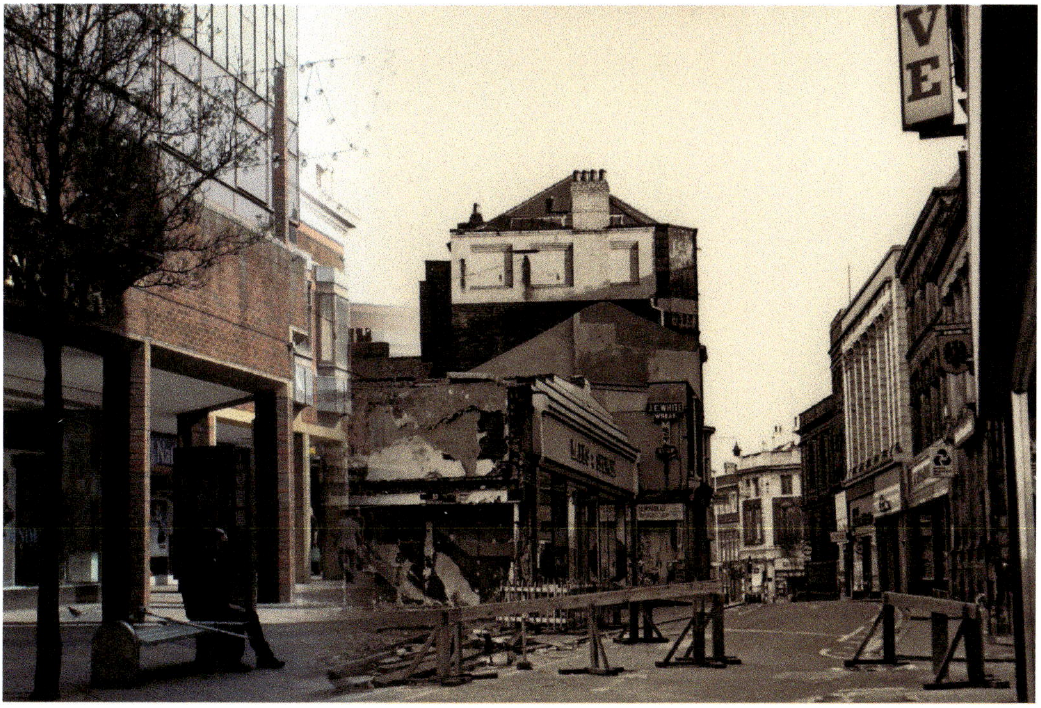

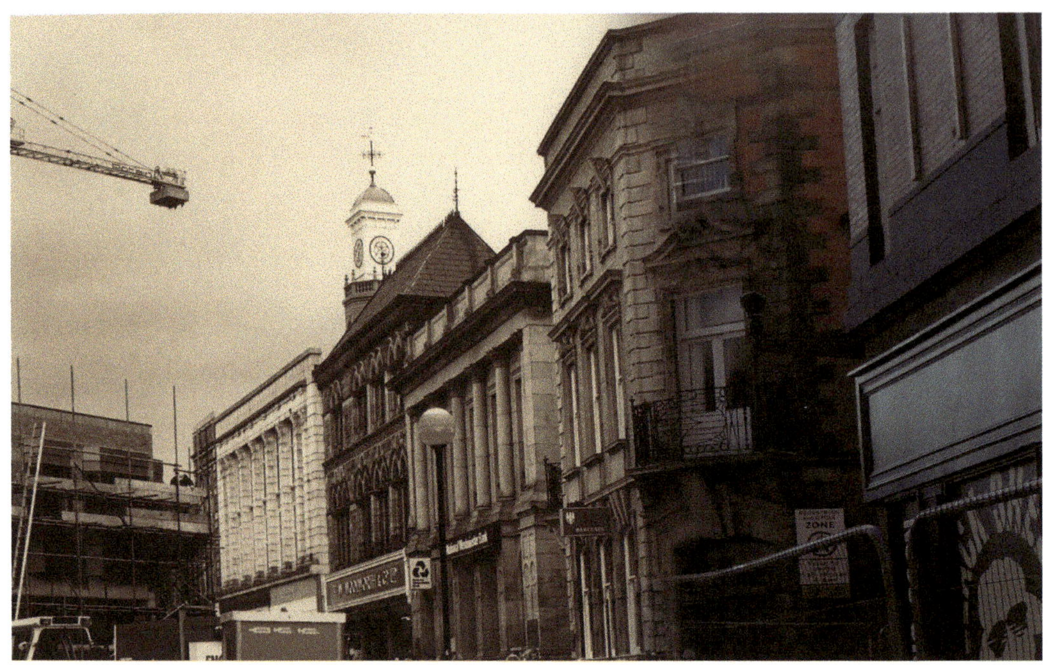

By the early 1980s work was already underway on the extension to Golden Square at its junction with Horsemarket Street. By 2022 the streetscape had seen further changes. The former Co-operative store on the corner of Cairo Street (near right) was undergoing redevelopment. Barclay's was another town centre bank closure in the move to online banking. In 2009 Woolworth's familiar store near to the clock tower closed and eventually reopened as a branch of Poundland.

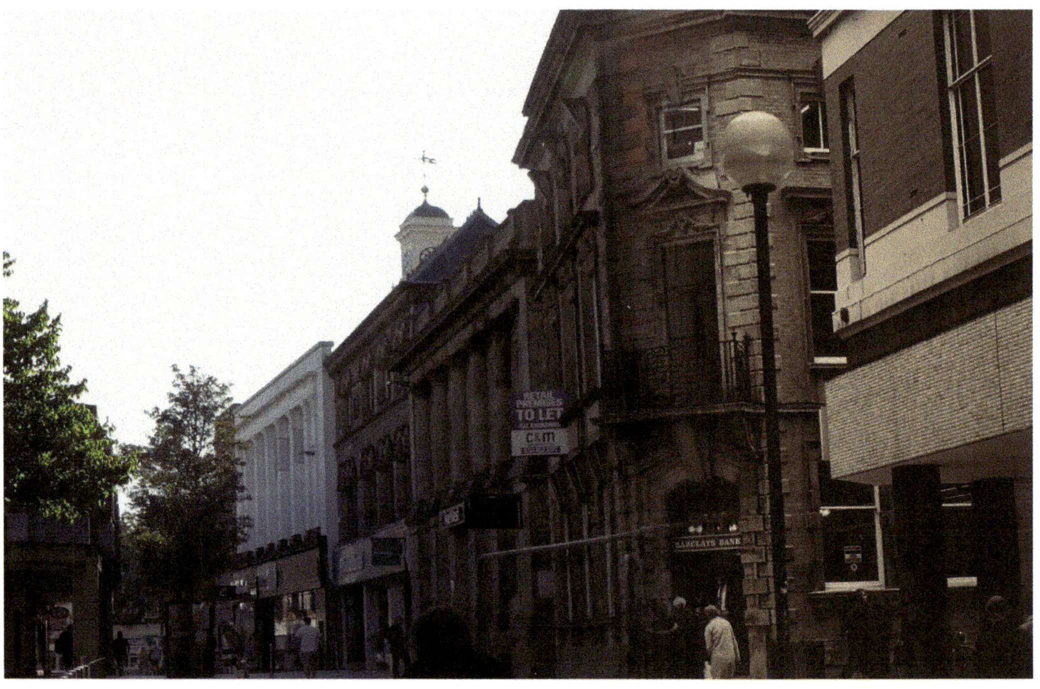

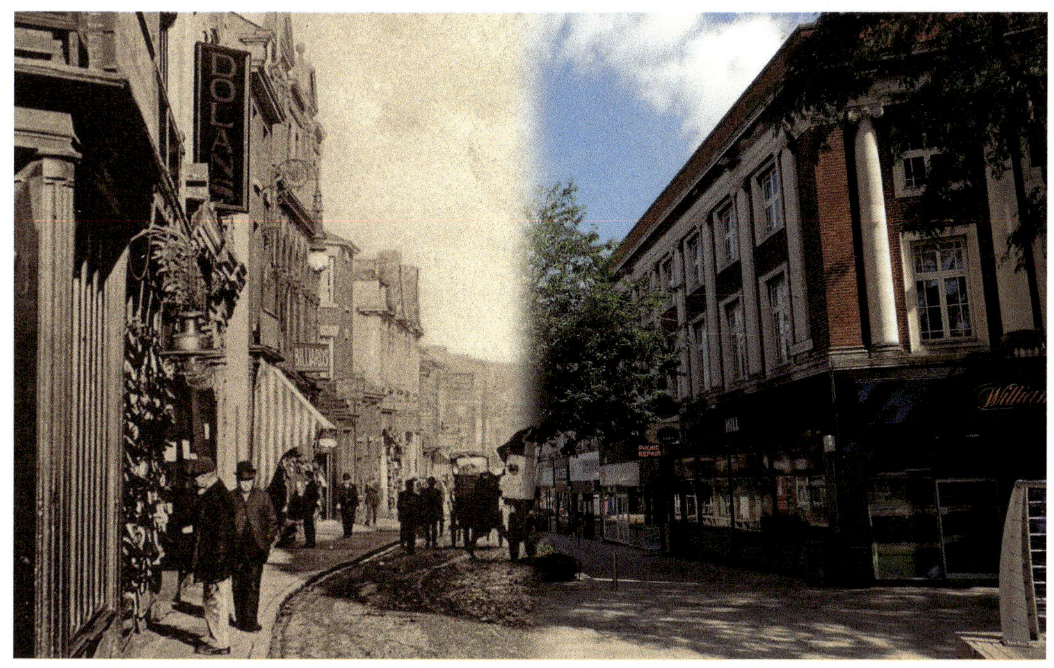

As traffic flow increased on the A49 route through the town centre Horsemarket Street was partially widened in the 1930s removing a bottleneck down to Central Station in the background. The shops on the right-hand side adjoining Buttermarket Street were demolished as far as Town Hill and the street width effectively trebled. The replacement blocks were faced with Portland stone and topped with classical columns as an echo of the original designs for Market Gate.

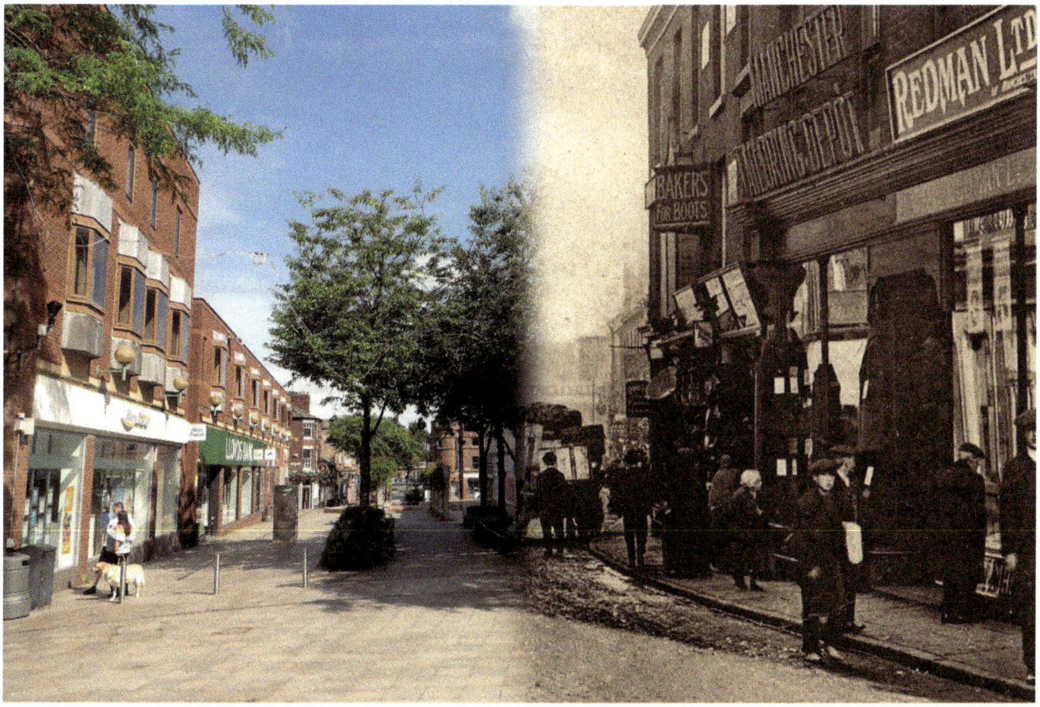

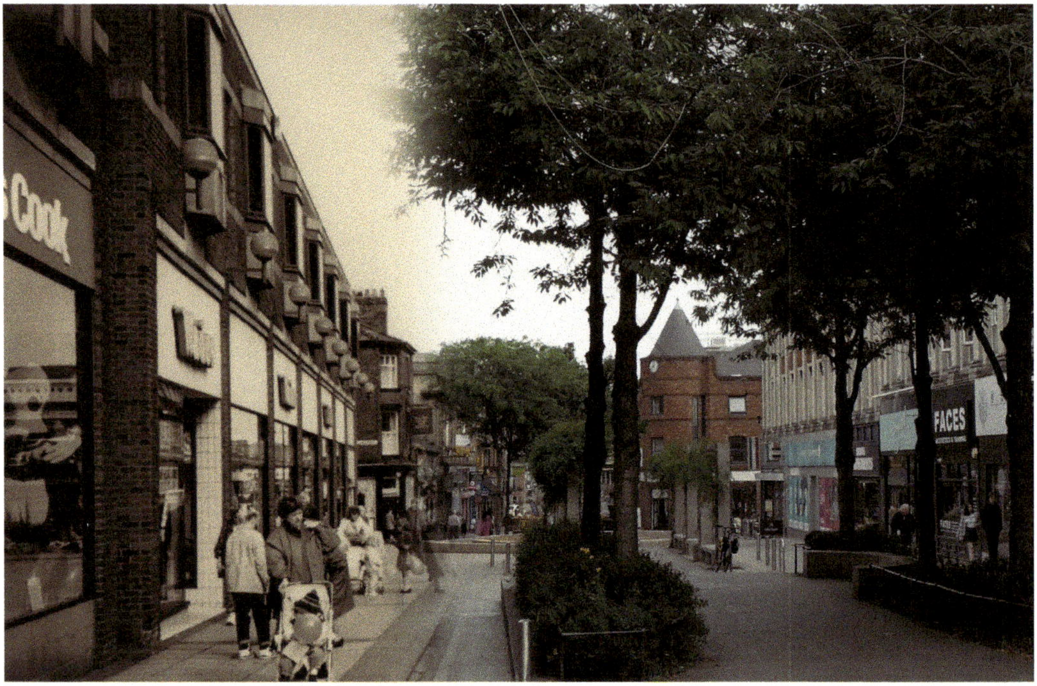

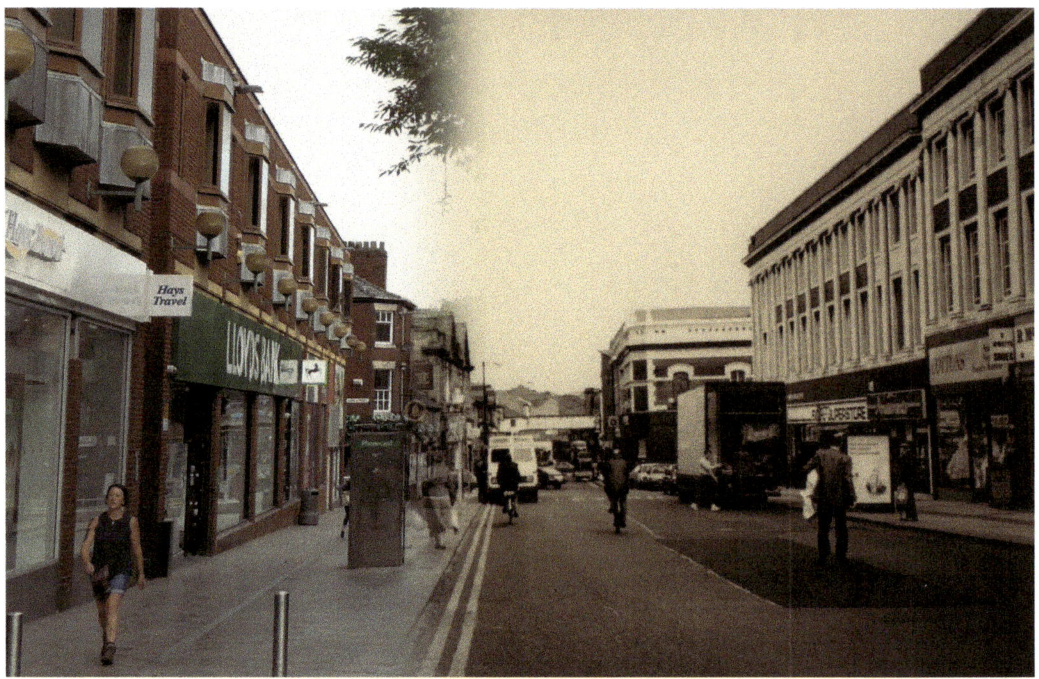

The left-hand side of Horsemarket Street was rebuilt in the 1980s as part of the Golden Square development and a further change took place on the corner of Town Hill. Just behind the delivery lorry on the right of the older photograph is the former late nineteenth-century Griffin Inn. It was later owned by the Royal Bank of Scotland who rebuilt it with a tower in Scottish baronial style in 1992, banishing the griffin figures from its roofline.

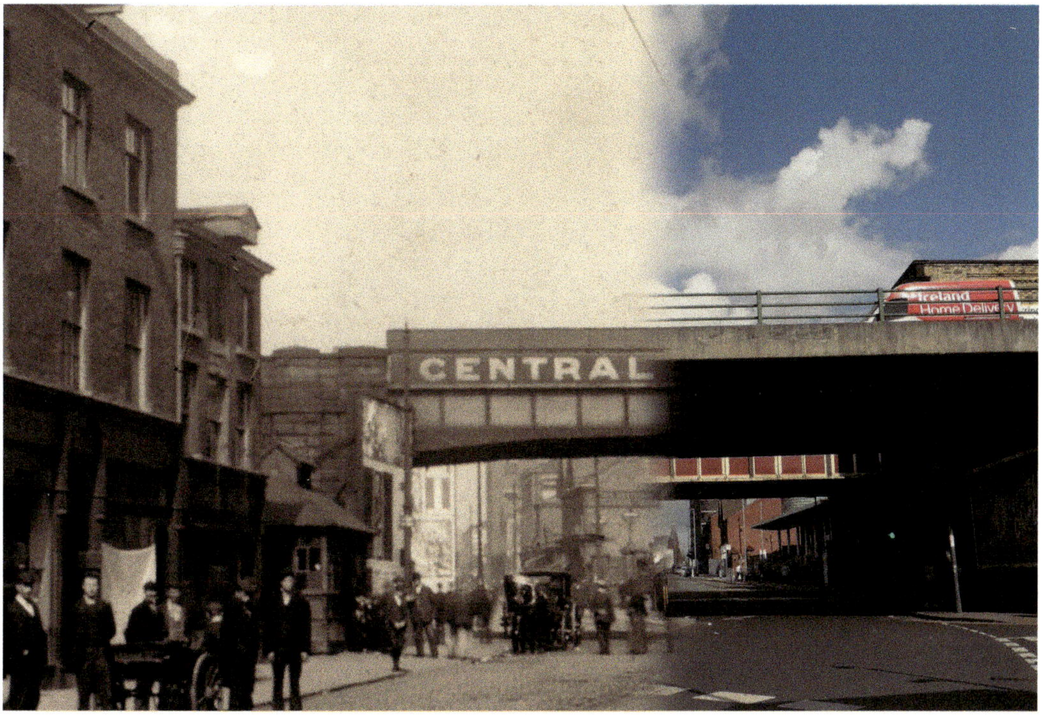

Where Horsemarket Street widens into Winwick Street at Central station was where the actual horse market took place until 1911. The earlier view shows a livelier scene with reductions on prams at Pendlebury & Company's extensive shop on the left. These buildings on the left were demolished to make way for the new bridge carrying road traffic over the road and obscuring the old railway bridge. This once vibrant area of the town has become something of a backwater.

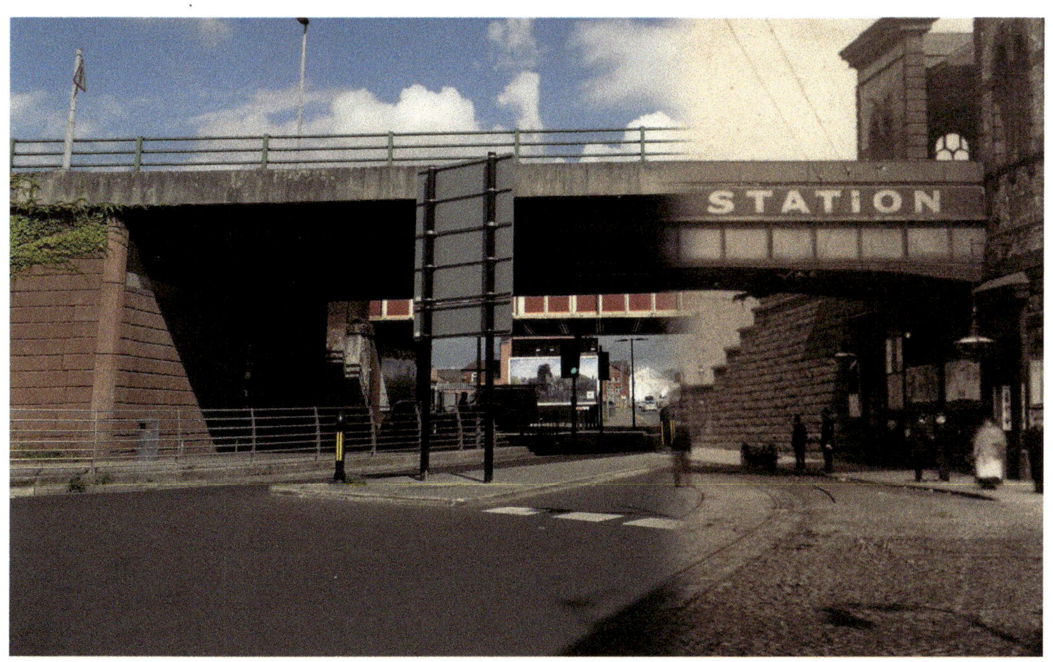

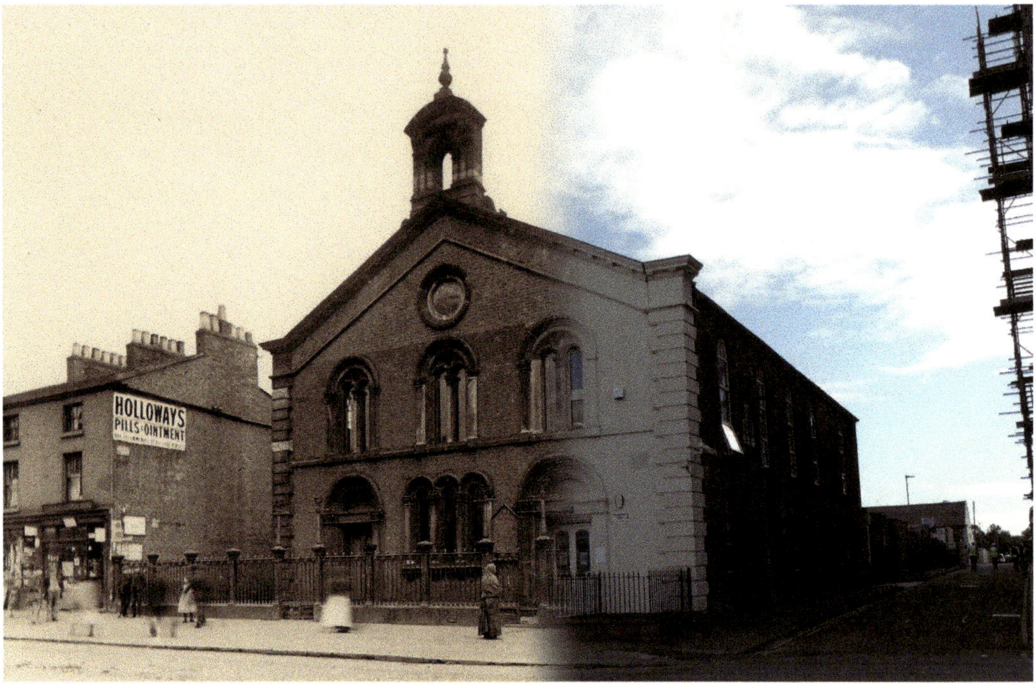

Winwick Street beyond Central Station used to be a thriving working area with enough inhabitants to sustain a large Co-operative store at Tanners Lane. As the terraced houses disappeared other buildings had to find new purposes including the former St John's Chapel, in use from 1808 to 1910 when its congregation moved to Wilderspool Causeway. The building was next occupied by W. A. Boulting's electrical engineers and to its right new apartments are in development on a former tannery site.

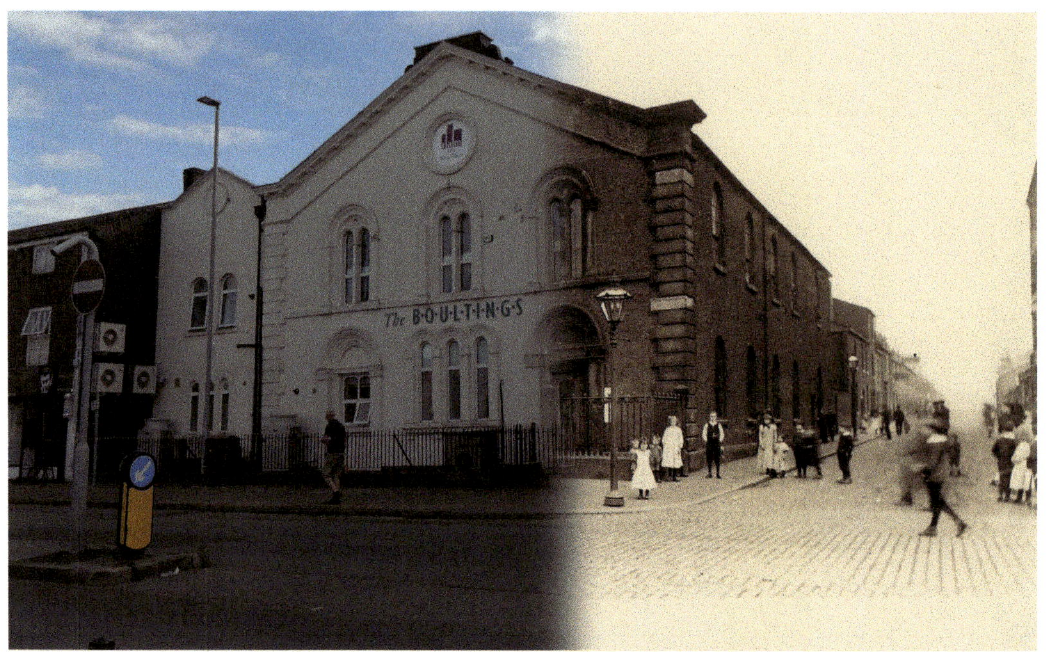

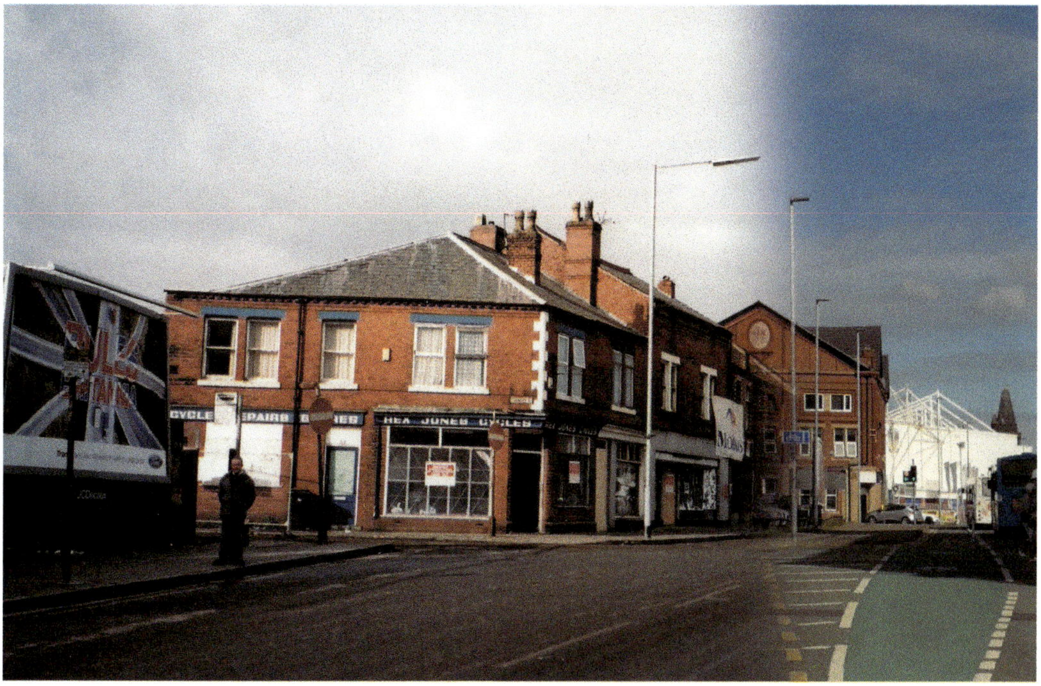

The northern end of Winwick Street used to be known as Townsend as the street left Warrington to become the road to Winwick. By 2022 the area had an air of desolation as development on the housing block to the right had stalled and the left-hand side was a temporary car park. The former Co-operative store on the corner of Tanners Lane is one of the few surviving buildings before Warrington Wolves' gleaming white rugby league stadium.

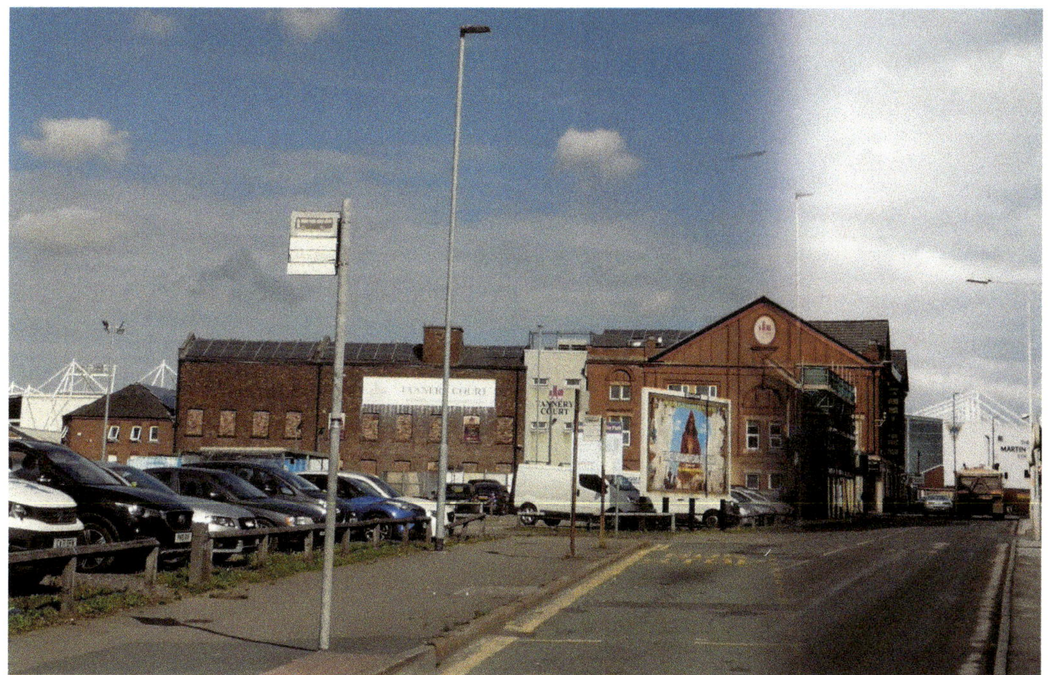

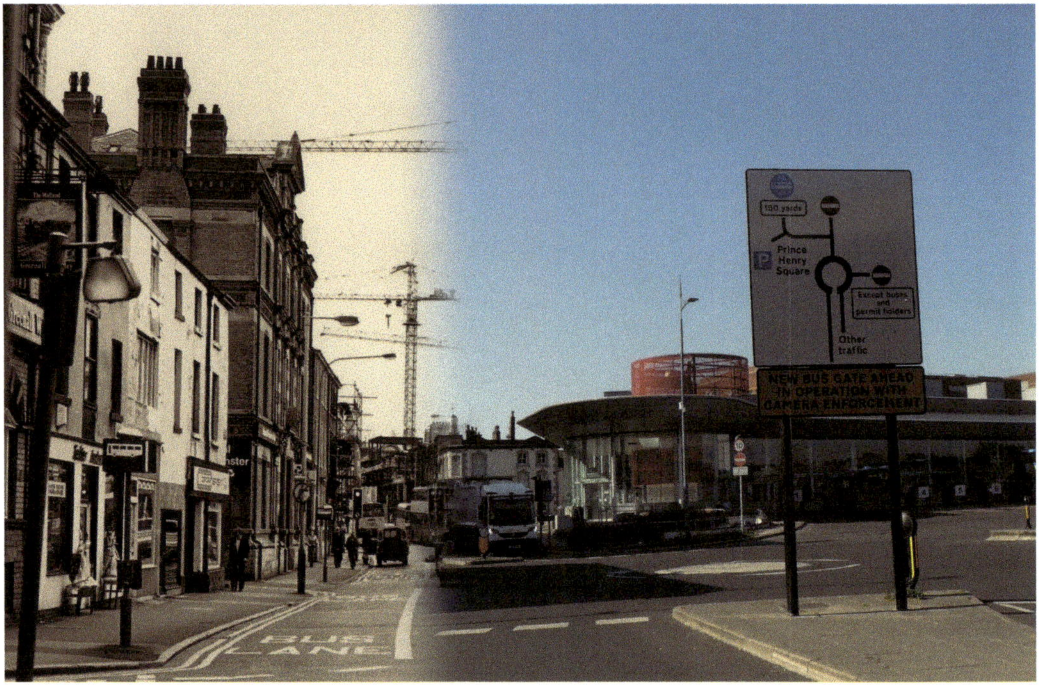

While the cranes in the background point to the redevelopment work at Golden Square many of Horsemarket Street's buildings on the left-hand side of the road towards the junction with Scotland Road survived. The impressive Old Bank towers above its neighbours. Established in 1788 by Joseph Parr and rebuilt in 1877, Parr's Bank had become part of the National Westminster Group by 1968. This branch closed in 2015 before finding a new use as a coffee shop.

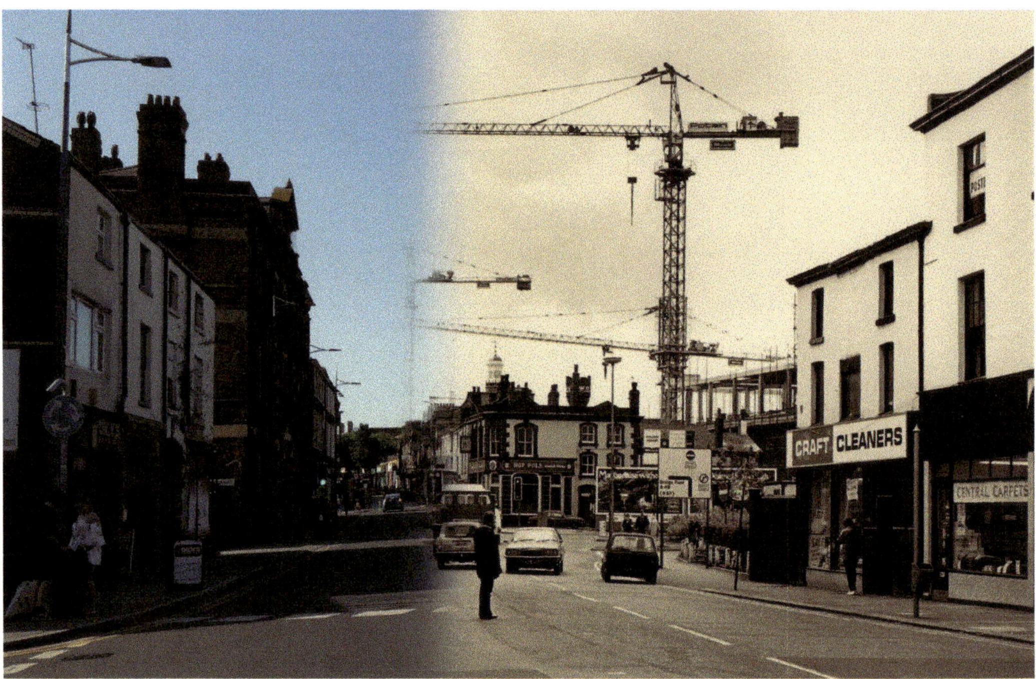

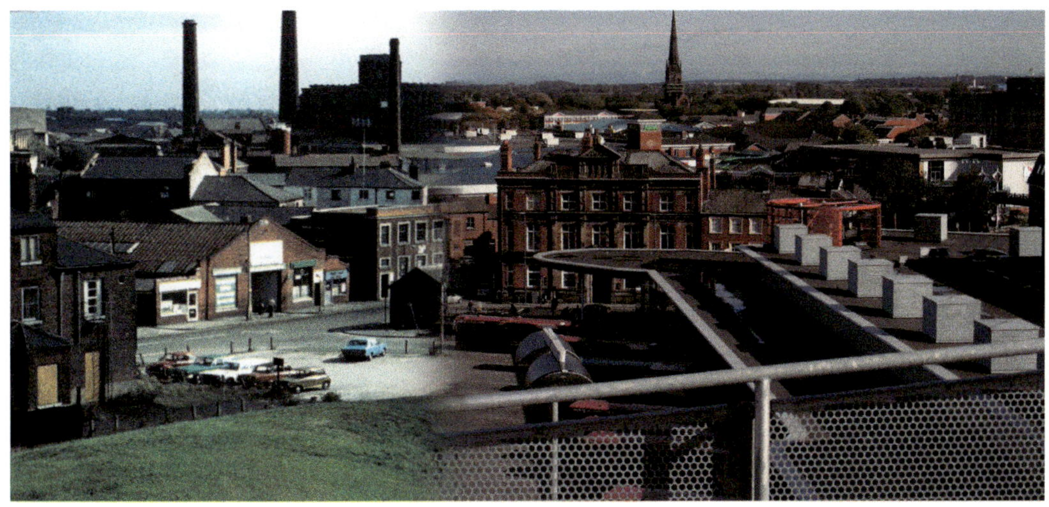

These bird's-eye views over Horsemarket Street record the changes in this area of the town. The early 1980s view shows Cockhedge Mill and its chimneys on the skyline left of the Parish Church spire with the new inner ring road leading to Buttermarket Street to the right. The view over the new bus station reveals that the mill has been replaced by a shopping complex; the spire reigns supreme and the proximity of the transport interchange to Central Station.

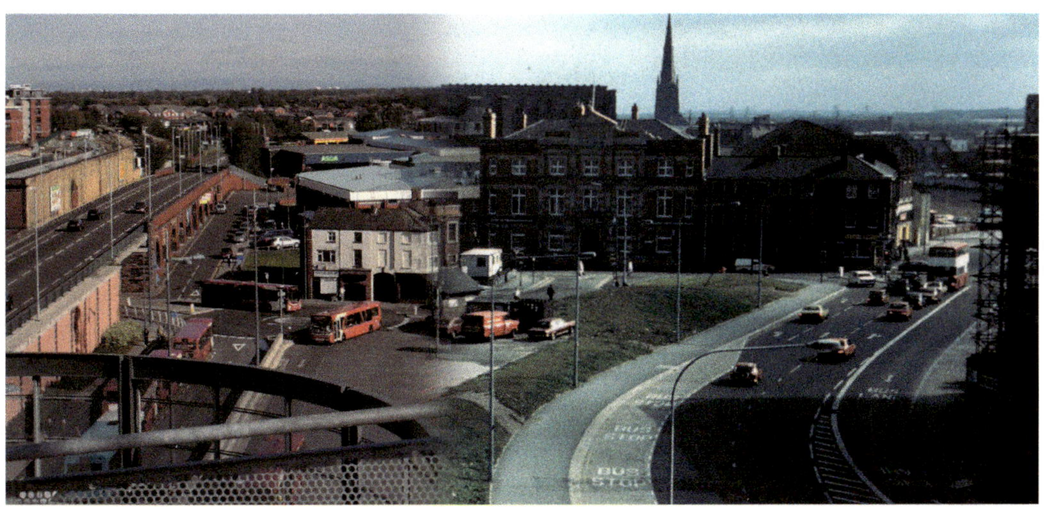

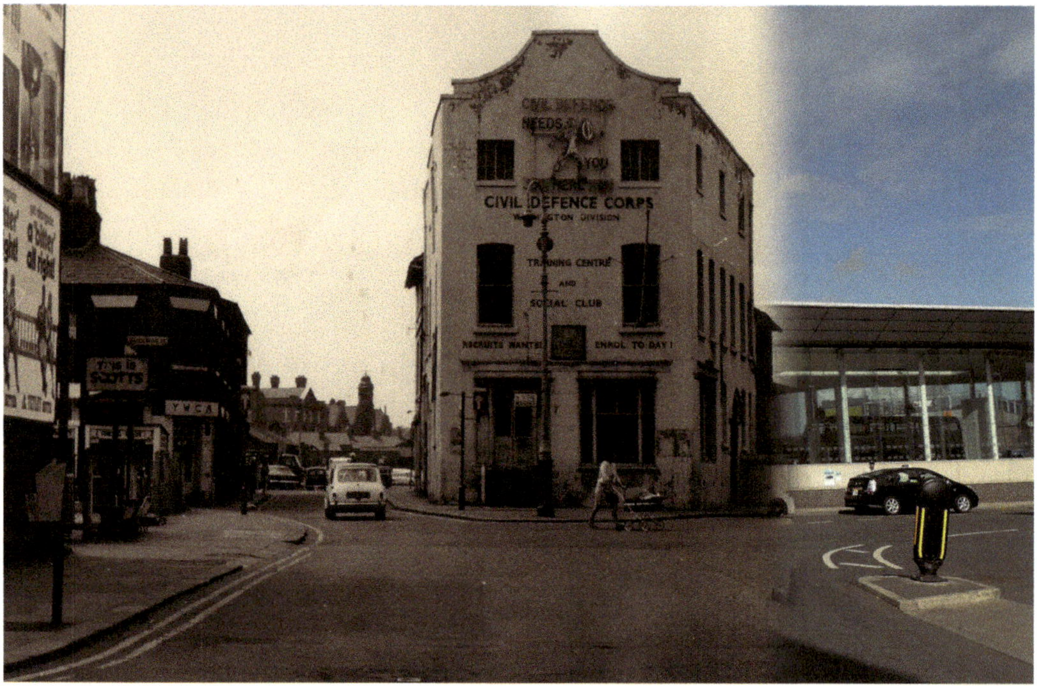

Away from Market Gate there have also been several dramatic changes to the landscape of Horsemarket Street. The 1970s photograph shows the premises at the junction with Queen Street and Bewsey Street which were demolished during the construction of the inner ring road in the 1970s. In the background (left) the roofline of the old Infirmary building can still be seen shortly before its demolition for the Legh Street end of the road.

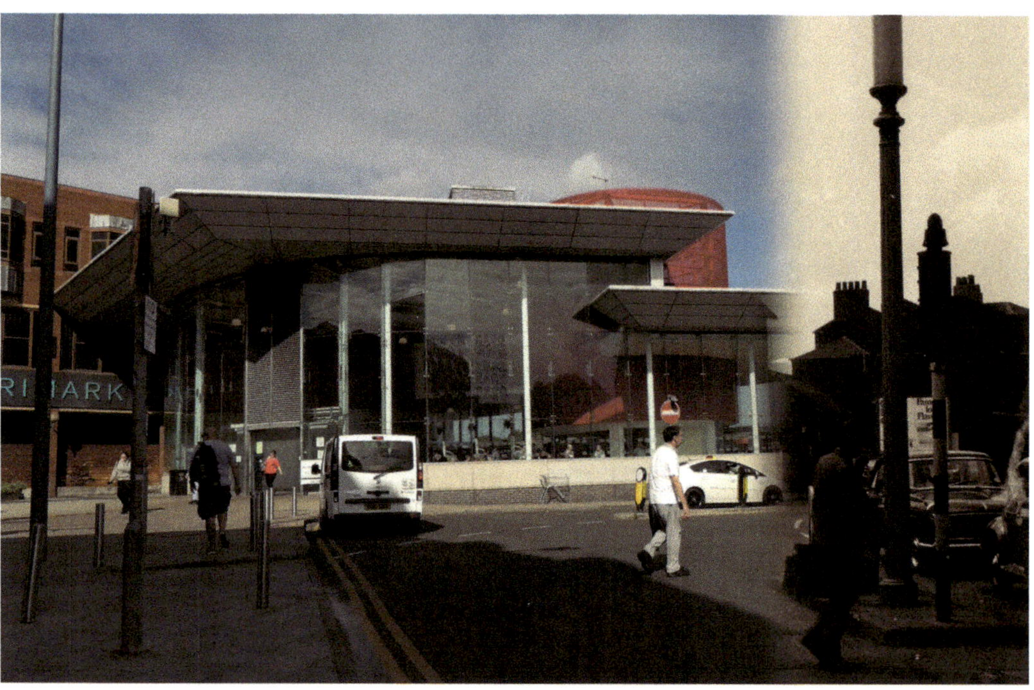

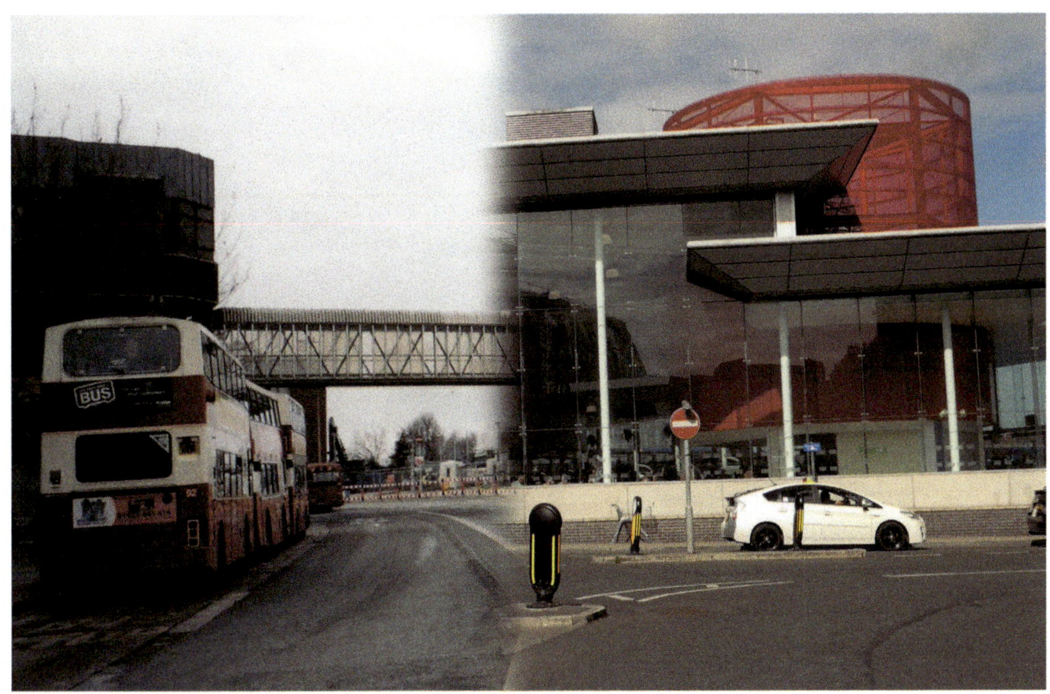

In 2006 a second major upheaval saw the striking new Warrington Interchange materialise there to replace the 1979 bus station. The inner ring road was replaced by Midland Way and the link bridge from Golden Square was removed. The huge Legh Street multi-storey car park was also demolished in this second phase of the development of Golden Square which also attracted Primark to locate there in the former Littlewoods store.

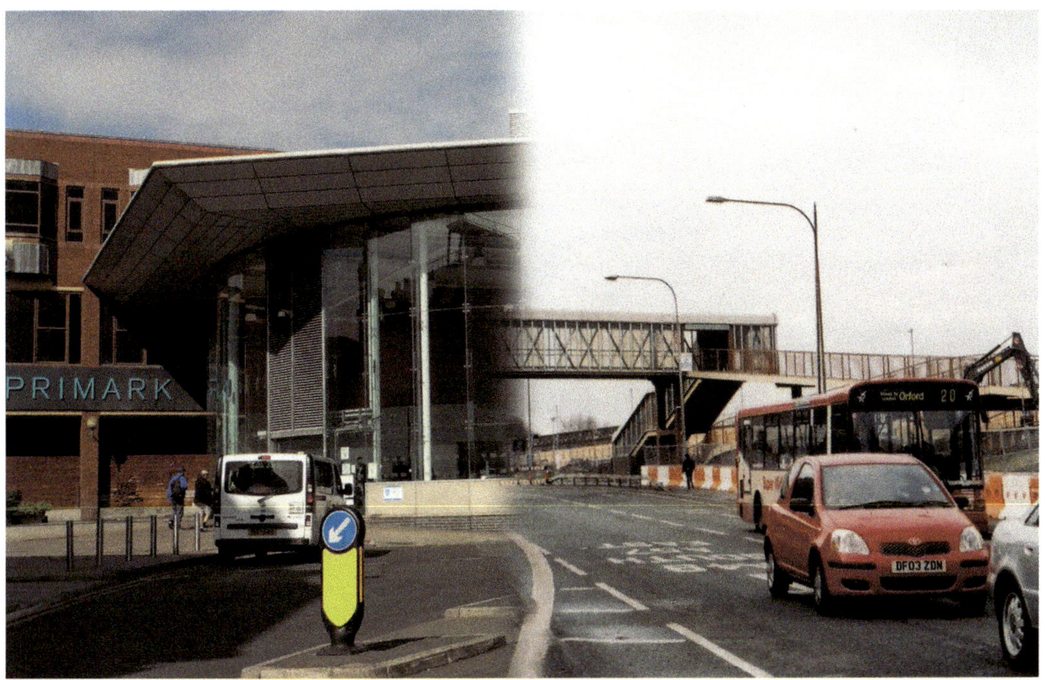

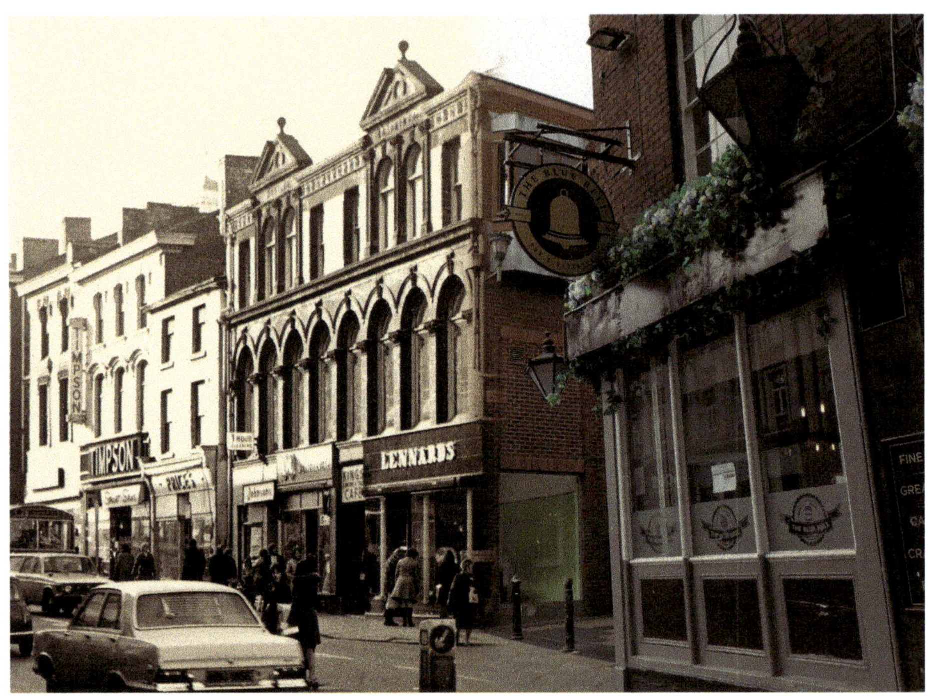

The view back to Market Gate near Town Hill has also changed since the earlier 1970s photograph. The Blue Bell inn still stands on the corner of Lyme Street but all the other shops were swept away. Nearest to Lyme Street was Lennards shoe shop which occupied the impressive Jubilee Buildings, a reminder of one of Queen Victoria's jubilees in 1887 or 1897. The elaborate side window and striking roofline contrasted with the plainer appearance of its older neighbours.

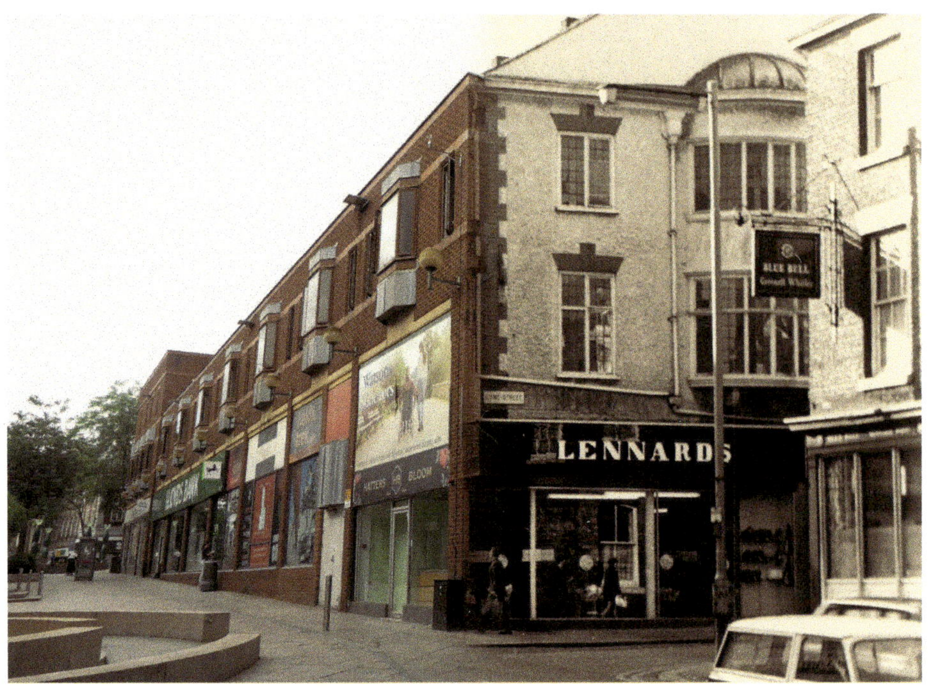

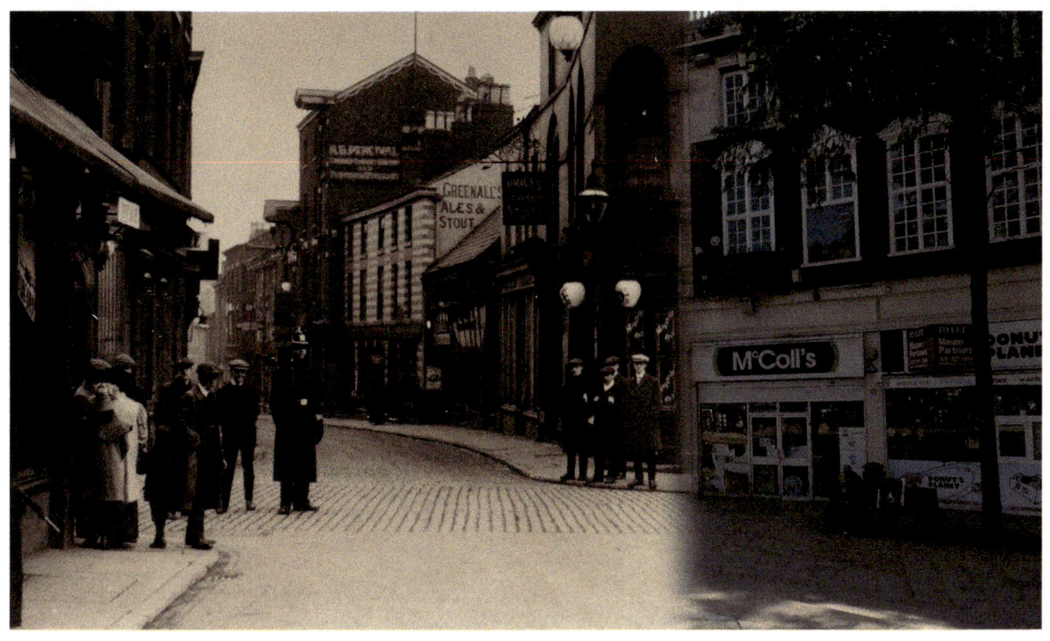

Today the view down Buttermarket Street from Market Gate reveals a pleasantly wide street with many fine buildings dating from the 1930s. In contrast old Buttermarket Street in the 1900s was a narrow road with the quaint Old Fox Inn or Old Curiosity Shop next to the sign for Greenall Whitley's ales on the adjacent Crown and Sceptre Inn.

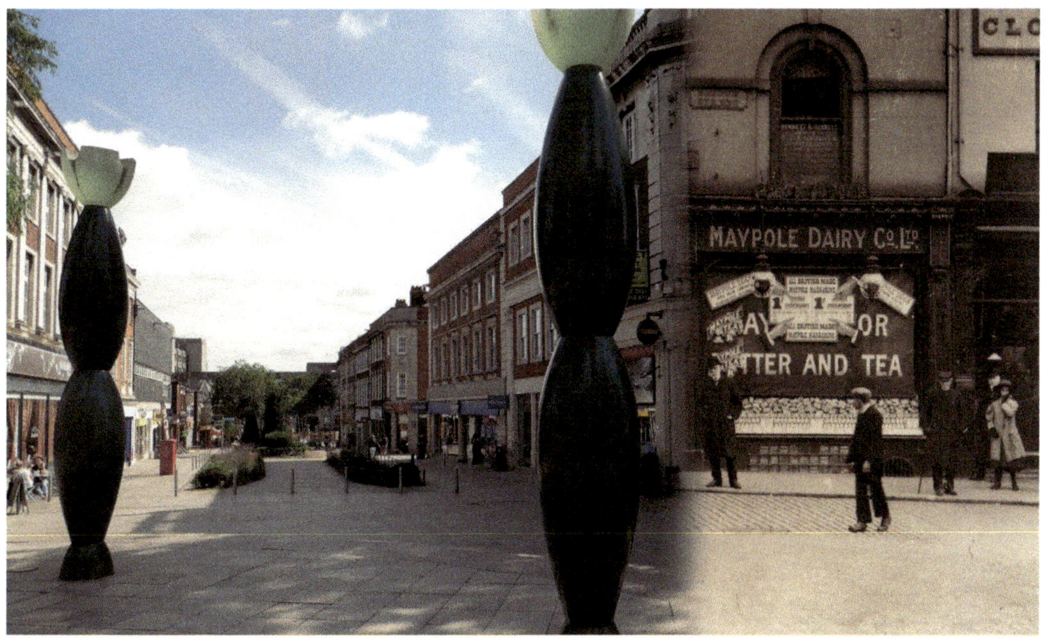

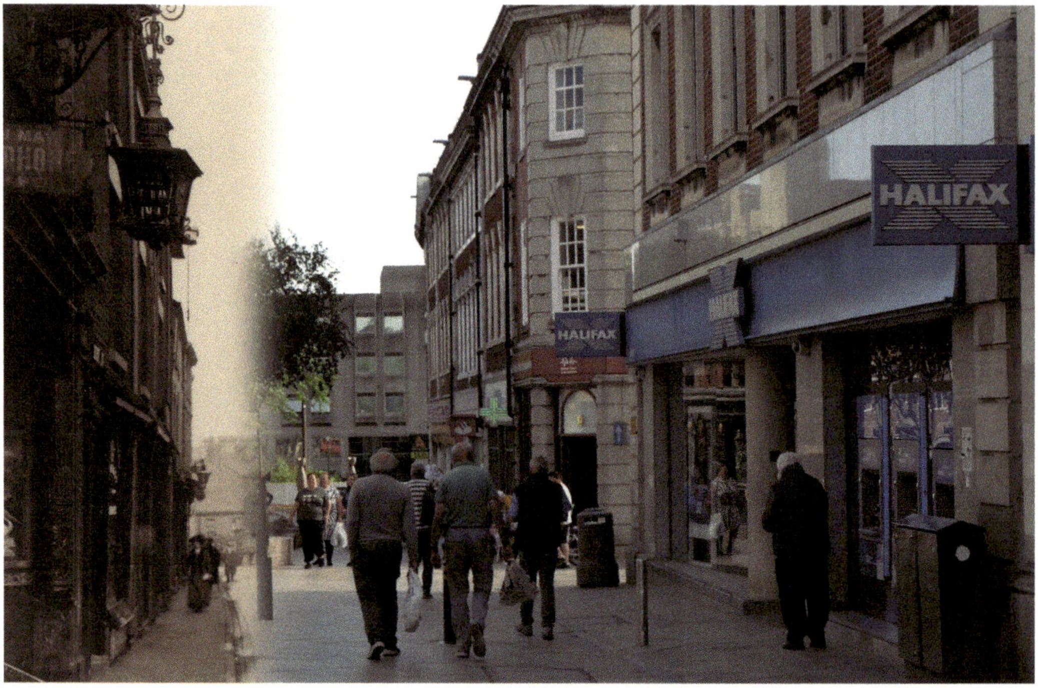

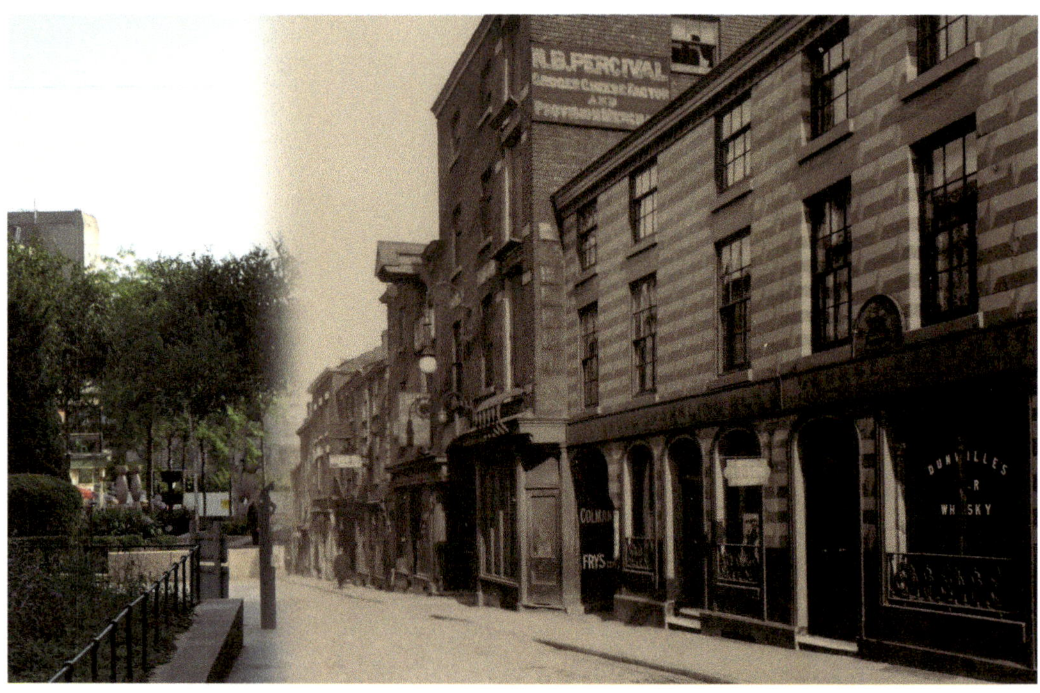

The view from Market Gate towards Scotland Road has seen considerable changes. In the 1900s view an ornate glass lantern hangs outside the old Pelican Inn (left). Facing the Pelican on the right-hand side of the street is the Crown and Sceptre Inn with its striped façade and a sign proclaiming 'You may telephone from here'. Between Percival's grocery store and Edwin Allen's shop is an archway leading into Bank Street and the area now known as Time Square.

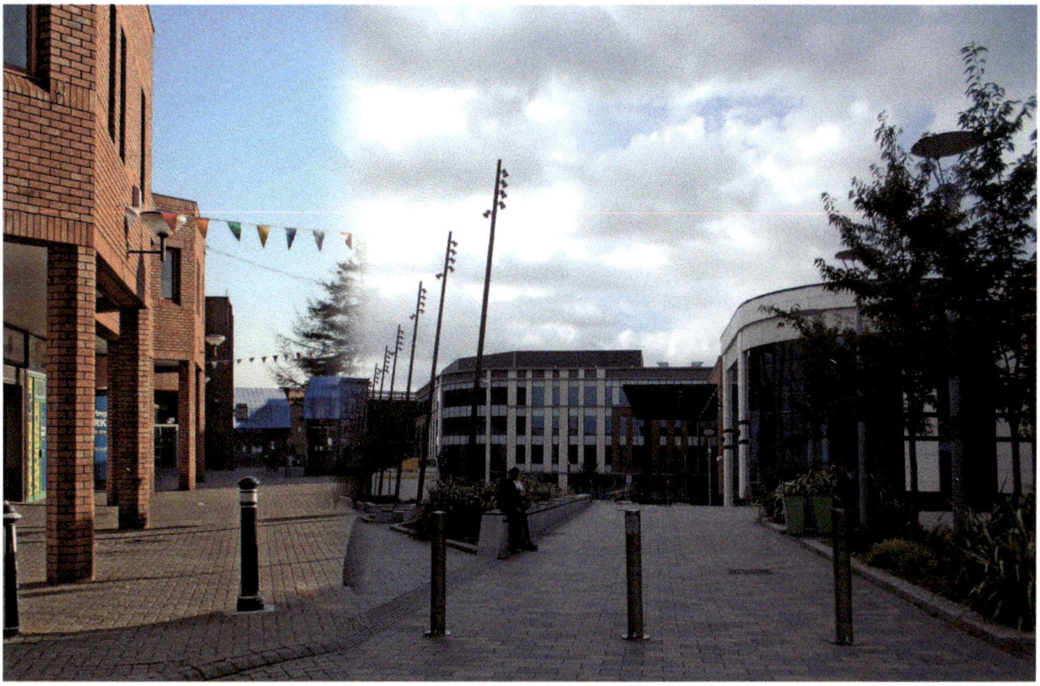

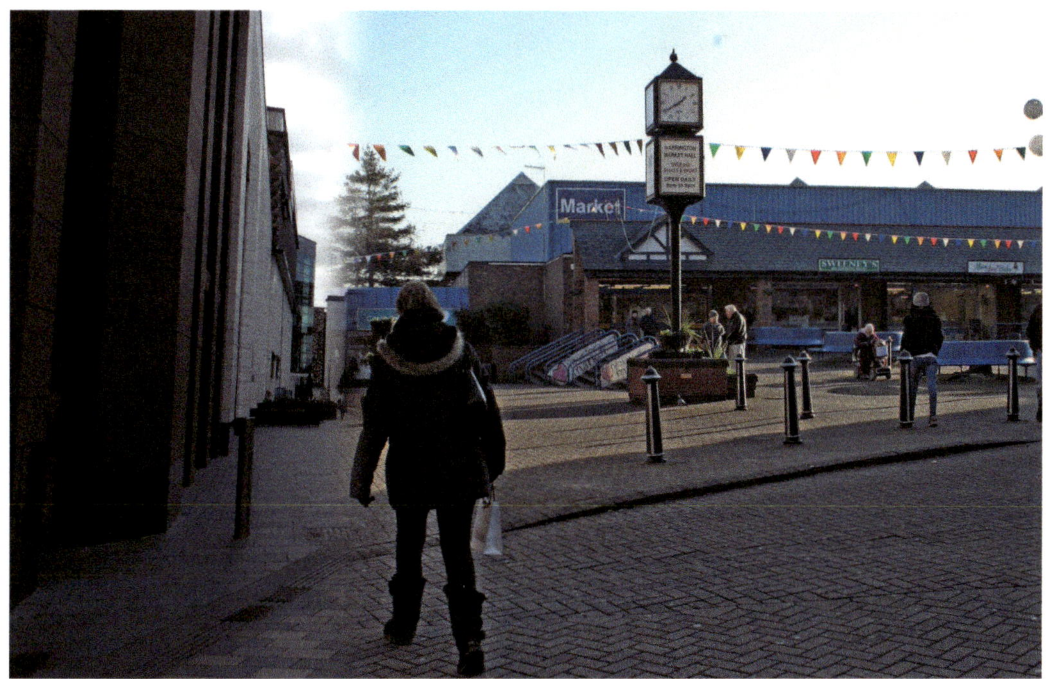

In the early 1900s Bank Street led to an area of densely packed slum housing. From the 1990s the land between Buttermarket, Bridge and Mersey Streets was progressively redeveloped into Time Square. The earlier view shows the retail market built between 1972–74 enabling the redevelopment of the Old Market Area into Golden Square. By 2022 the area was transformed with a new market, and variety of commercial operations served by a new car park off Mersey Street.

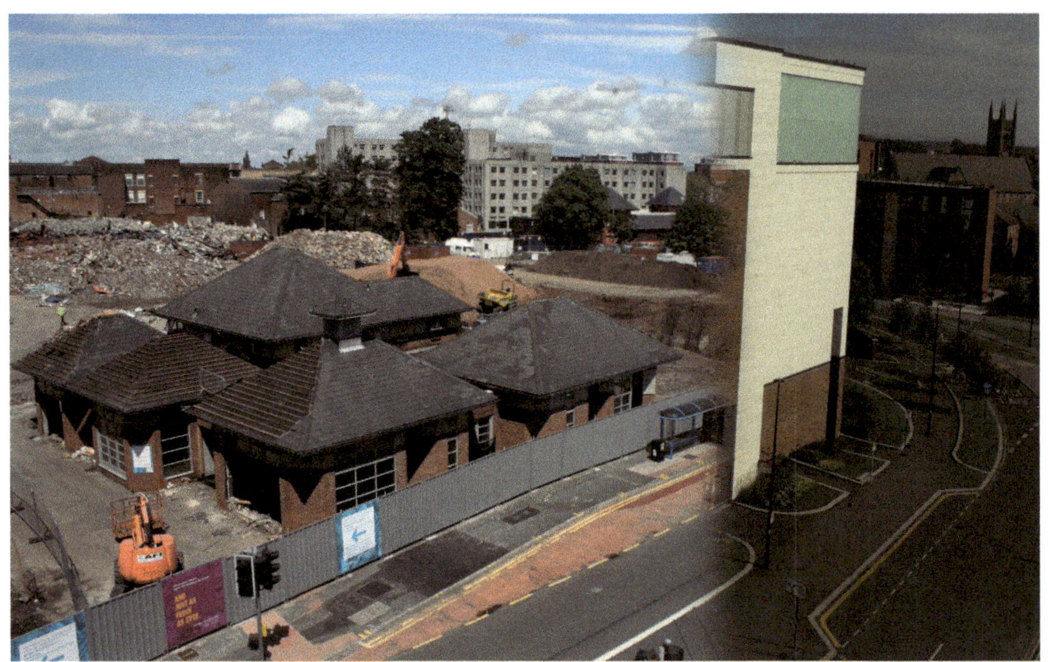

By 2015 the demolition of the original Time Square in the foreground was nearing completion in the view taken from the old Mersey Street car park. New Town House in Buttermarket Street can be seen in the centre background with the tower of St Mary's Church on the far right. The later view of 2022 shows the scale of the new Time Square, dwarfing the buildings on the horizon with only St Mary's surviving as a reference point.

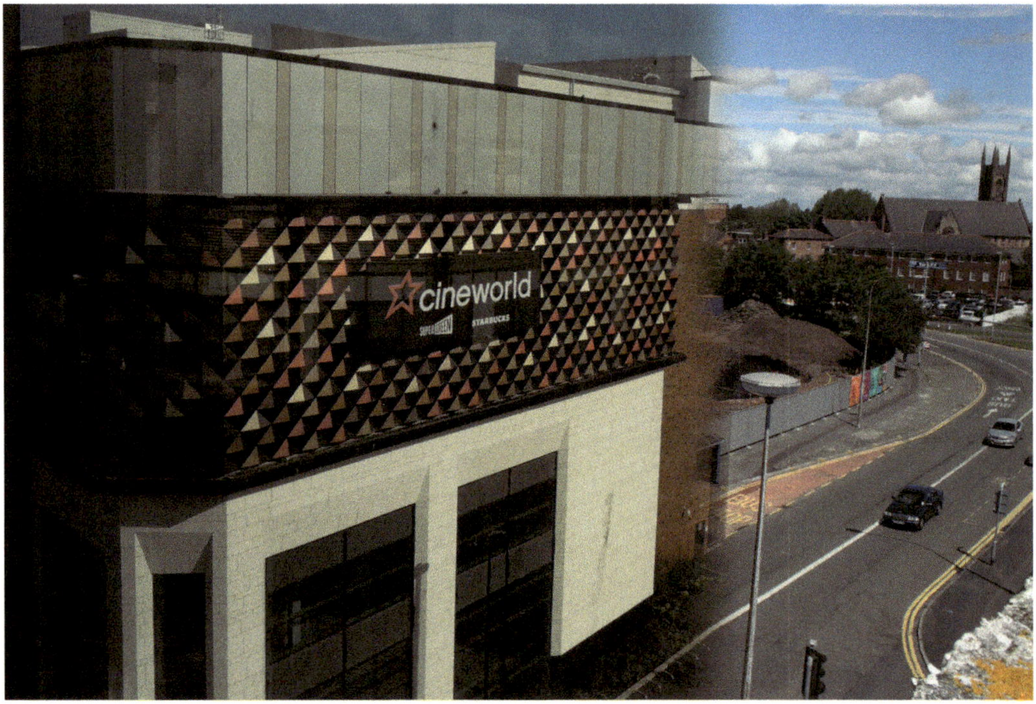

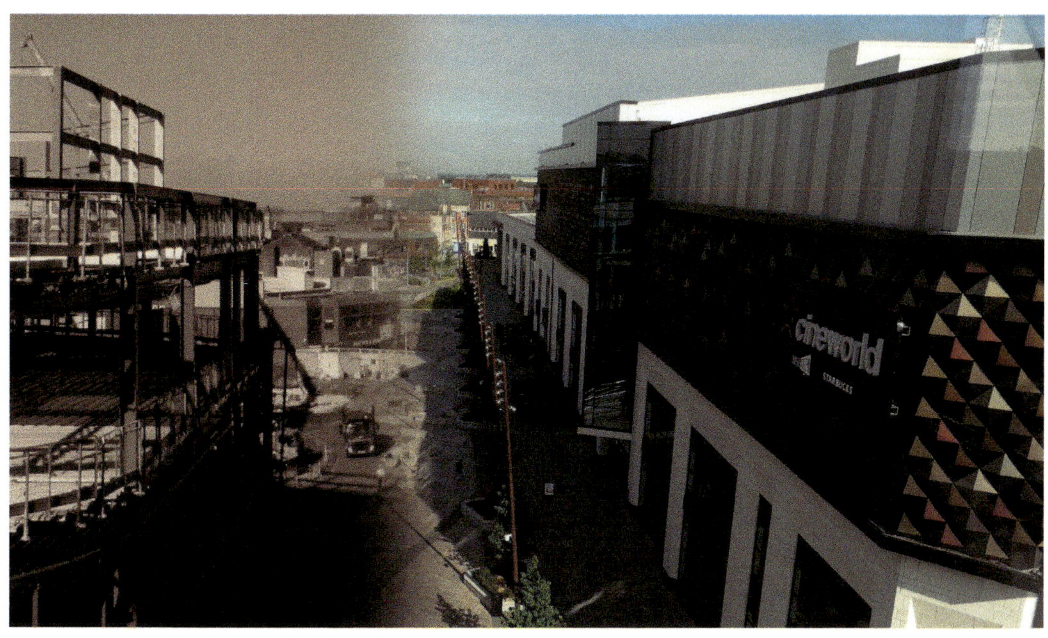

By 2022 Warrington was emerging from the Covid-19 pandemic which had paralysed sections of the national economy, and the newly completed Time Square could finally be appreciated by residents emerging from lockdown restrictions. The apparent chaos of the building site had been transformed into a spacious plaza looking down towards the town centre. However, the post-pandemic recession and global economic uncertainty caused by events in the Ukraine cast a shadow over Time Square's future fortunes.

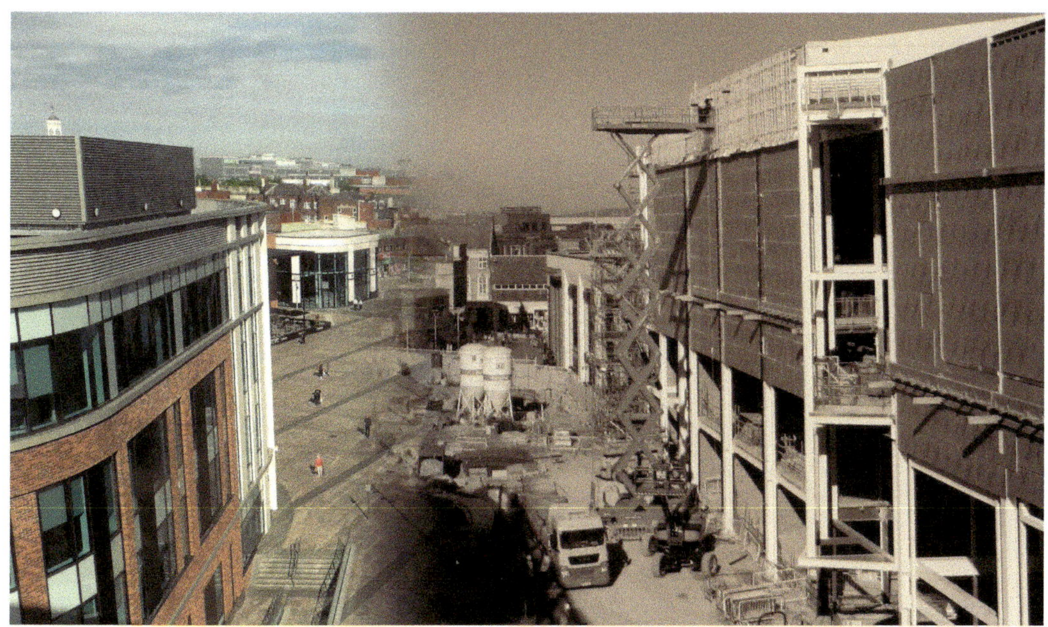

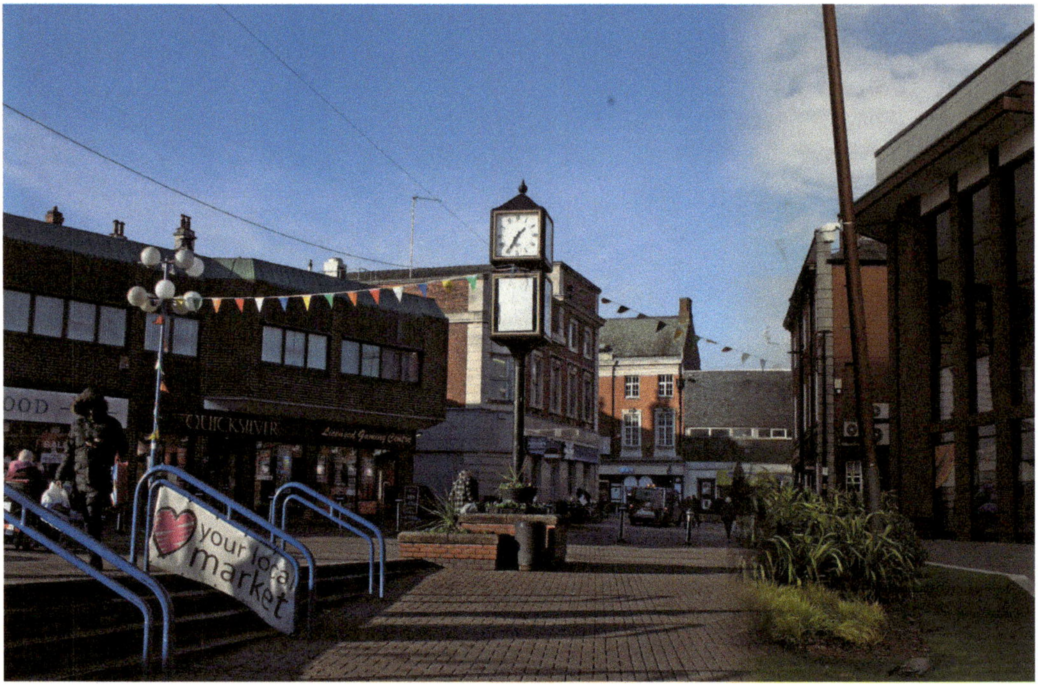

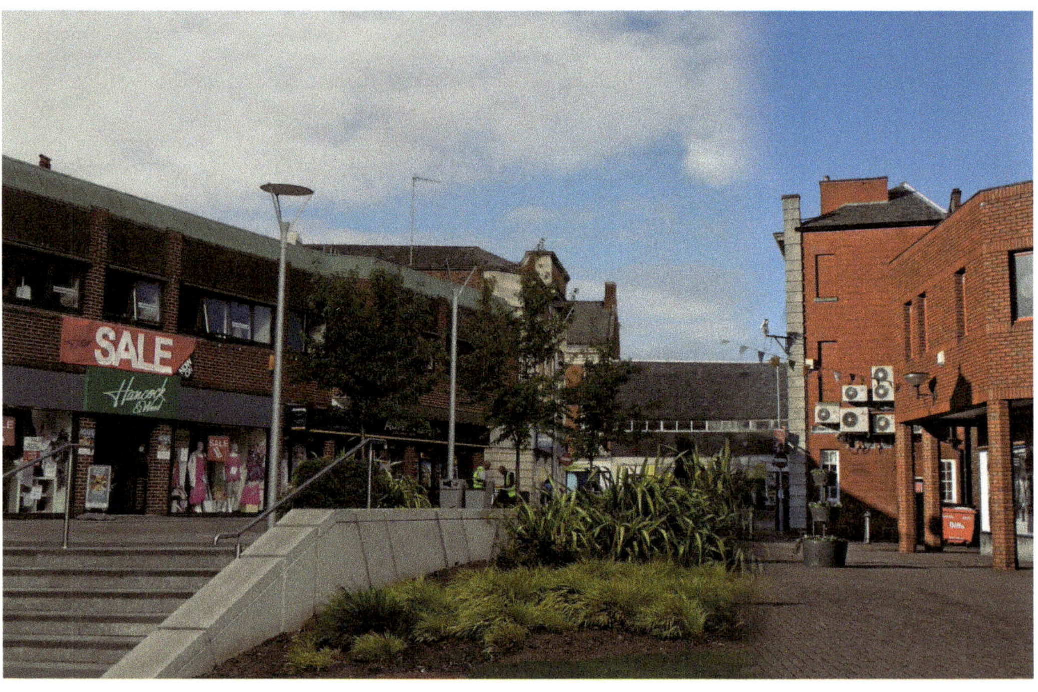

Time had certainly flown in this area looking back towards Buttermarket Street! Massey & Garnett's version of Time Square with its distinctive square clock lasted barely thirty years after its completion in 1986. In September 2017 a temporary market was opened in the building on the right in the first phase of building the newer and larger Time Square but the buildings on the left of both photographs were largely unchanged.

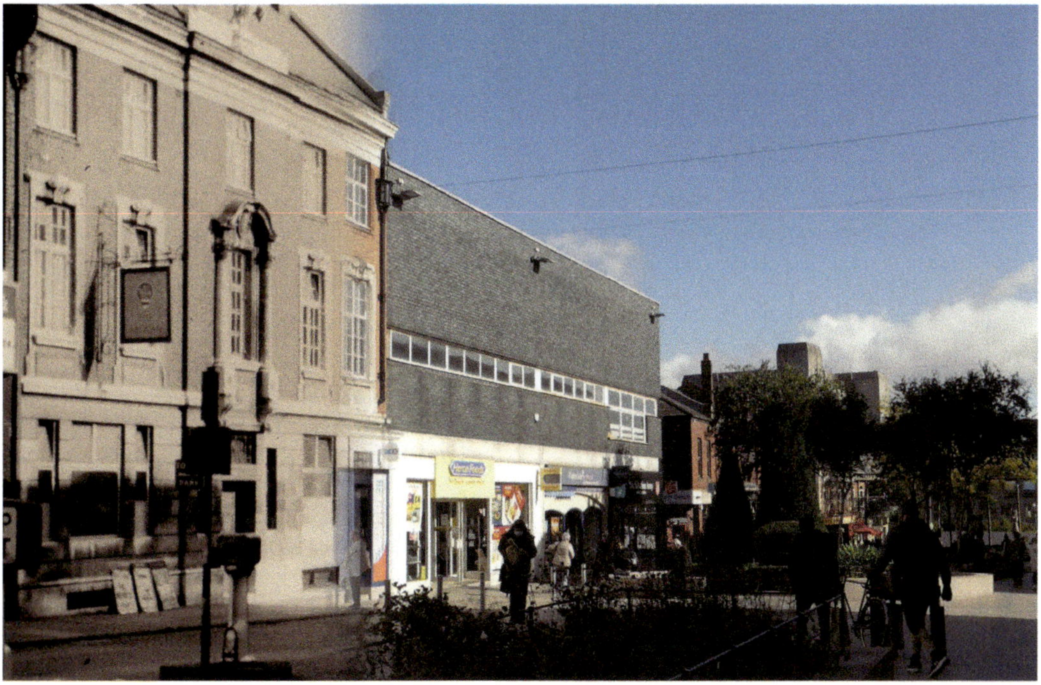

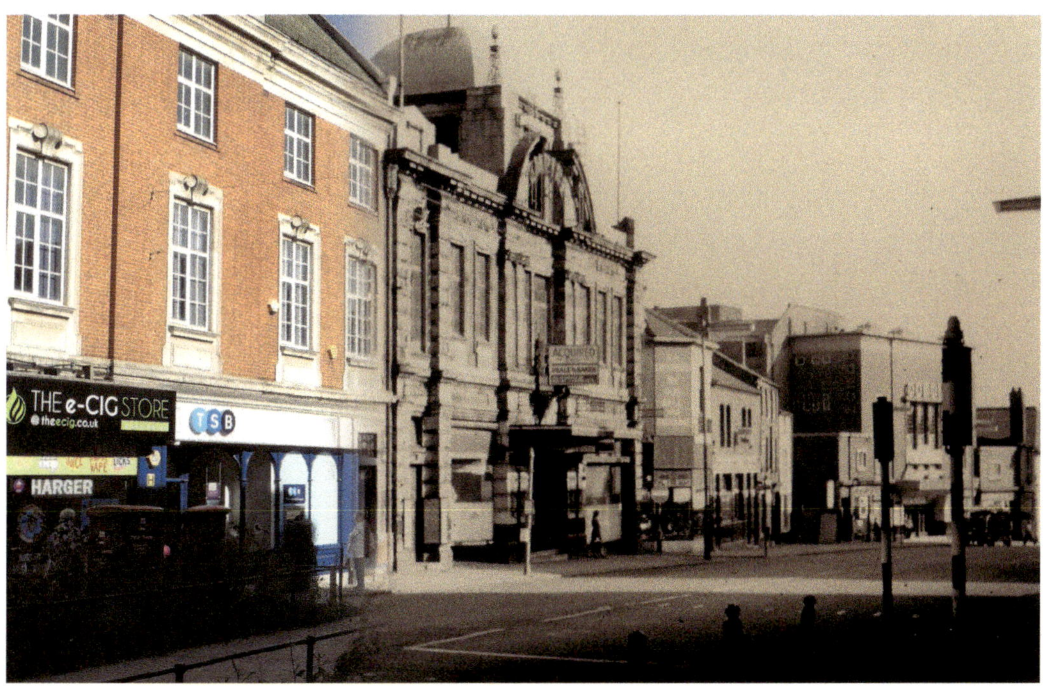

Anyone emerging from Bank Street into Buttermarket Street in 1961 would have seen that the splendidly domed Empire Cinema and Billiard Hall opposite was up for sale. Opened in 1921, its heyday had been during the Second World War when US soldiers stationed at Burtonwood had made this and the neighbouring Pelican Inn one of their favourite haunts. It was demolished in 1961 and replaced by a featureless grim modern retail block first operated by Lipton's supermarket.

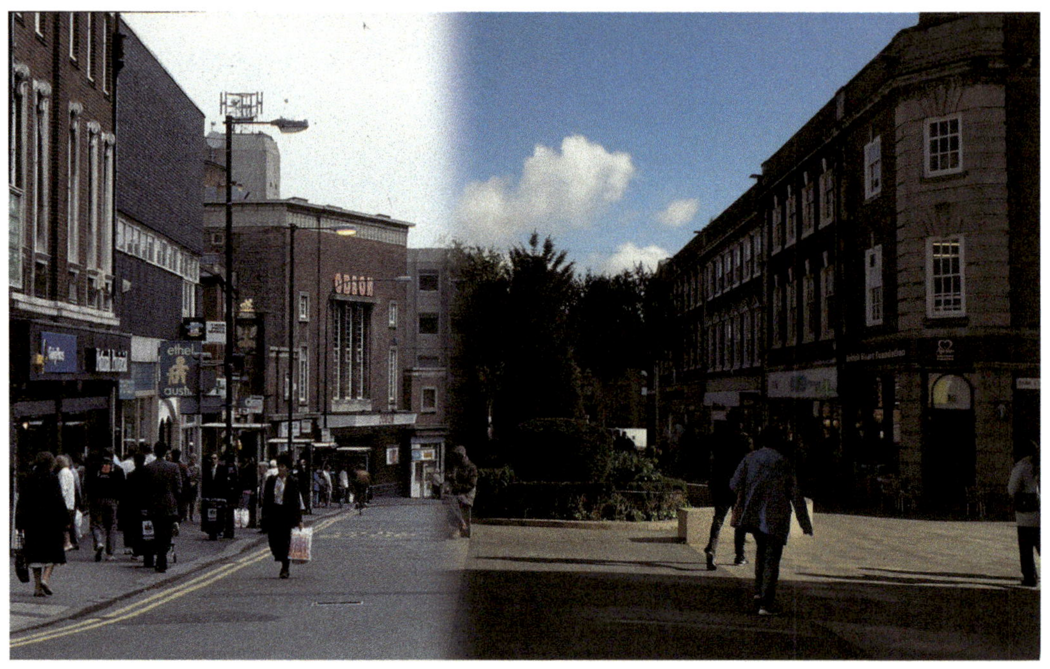

Modern Buttermarket Street is a pedestrianised tree-lined vista but the 1980s view was dominated by New Town House. The former headquarters of Warrington New Town Development Corporation, this uncompromisingly 1970s building emphasised their dominance over local planning but seemed unsympathetic to the surrounding architecture. The nearby art deco-style Odeon cinema was opened in 1937 and survived as the last town centre cinema until 1994 when its operators deemed it could no longer compete with the multi-screen Westbrook cinema.

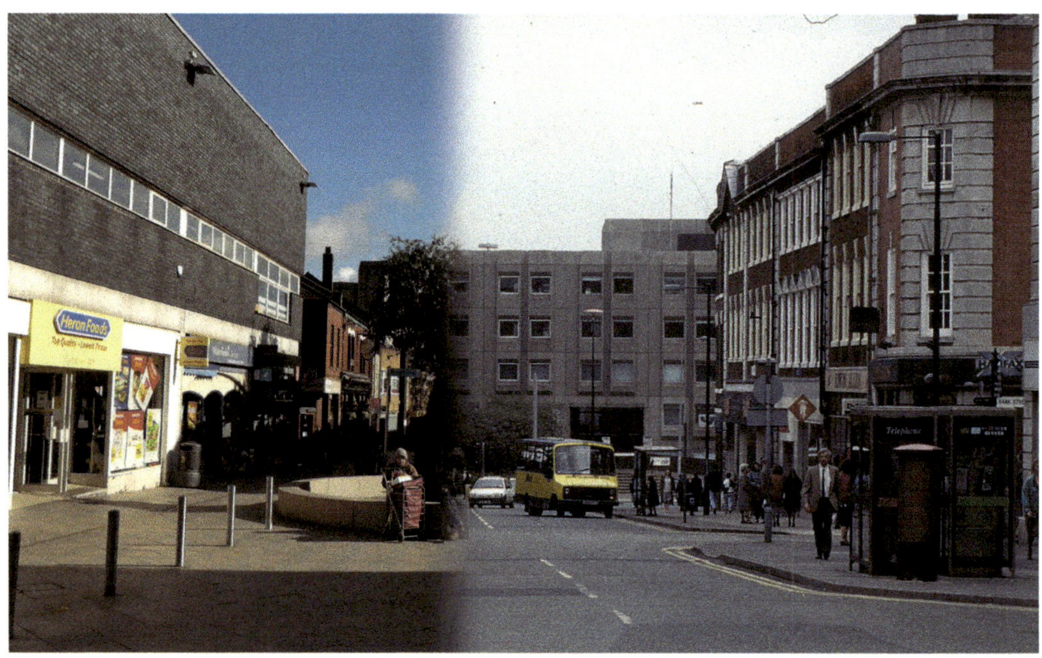

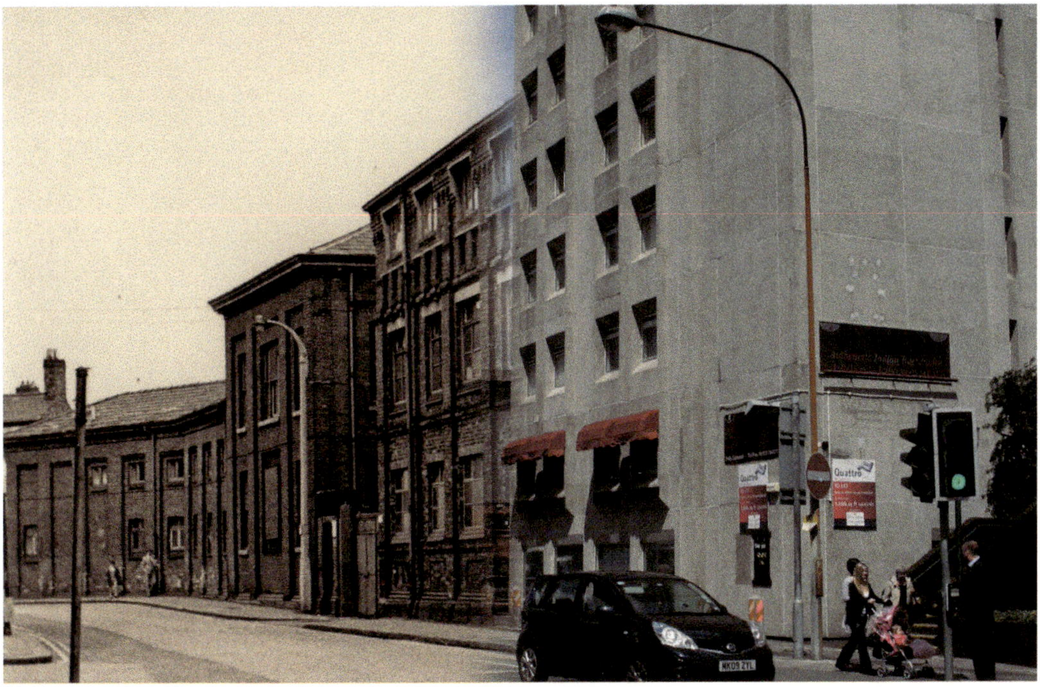

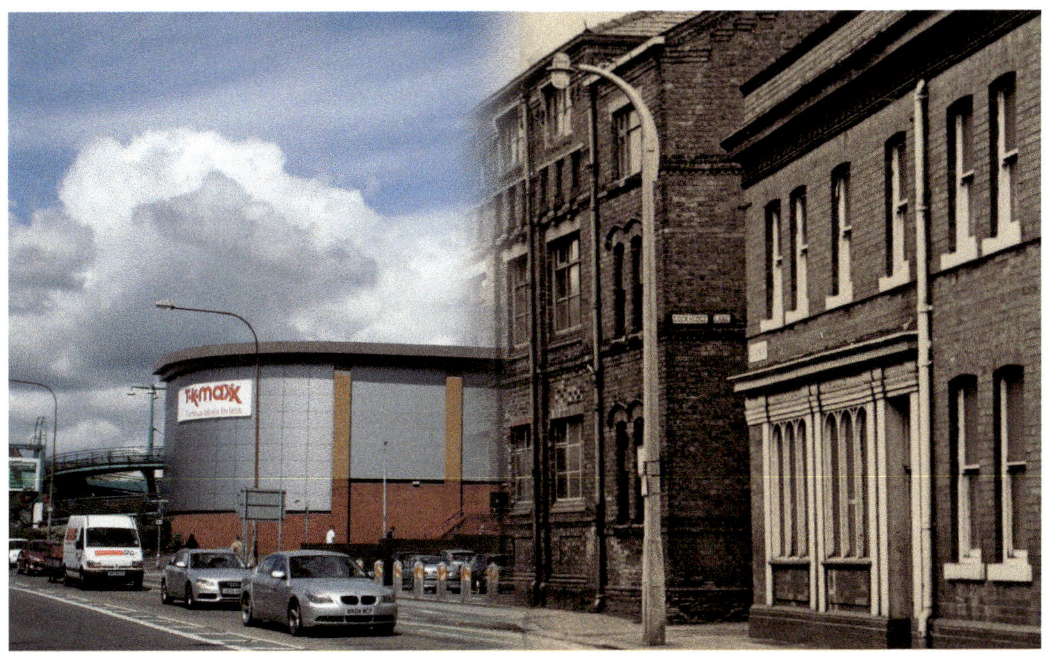

Buttermarket Street's junction with Scotland Road and Cockhedge has changed since the 1980s. Town planners favoured relocating industry away from a town centre while the booming retail sector was looking for prime sites. The Cockhedge cotton mill had ceased to be viable and Peter Stubs File making works (seen on the right of the earlier picture) had relocated. The Cockhedge shopping centre opened in 1984 but in 2022 ambitious redevelopment plans were announced for Cockhedge and neighbouring New Town House.

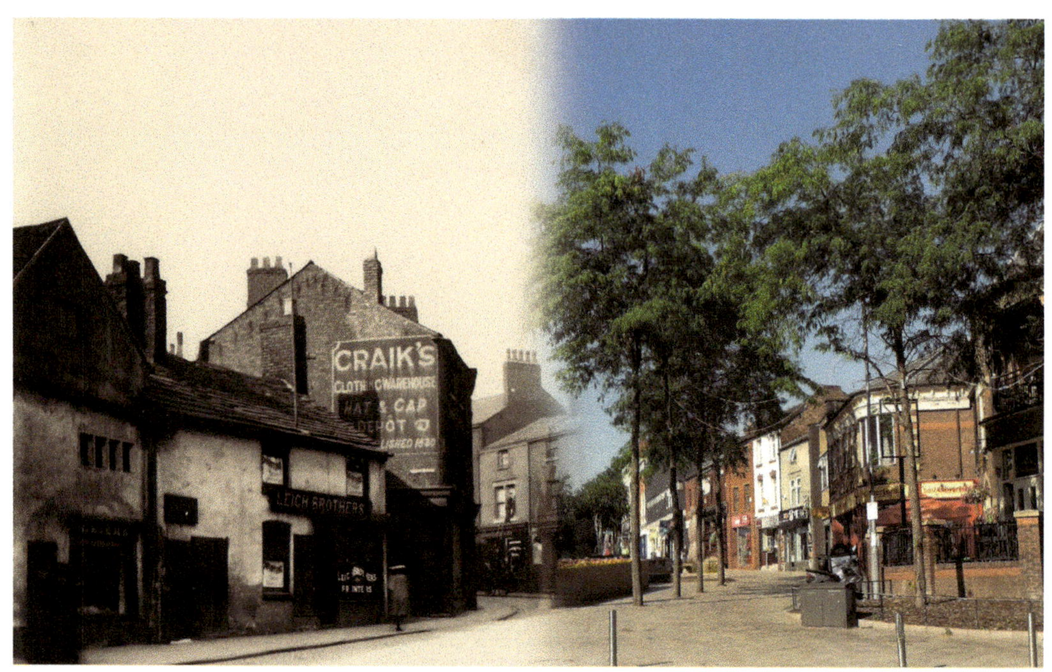

The view up Buttermarket Street from the junction with Scotland Road towards Market Gate has changed drastically since the 1900s and before the road was widened and straightened. On the left-hand side were Leigh Brothers, printers and bookbinders, and Craik's Clothing Warehouse. On the right-hand side were the premises of John Chorley, Iron and Steel merchant, and Reece's Mourning Establishment next to three small premises which would become the site of the Odeon cinema.

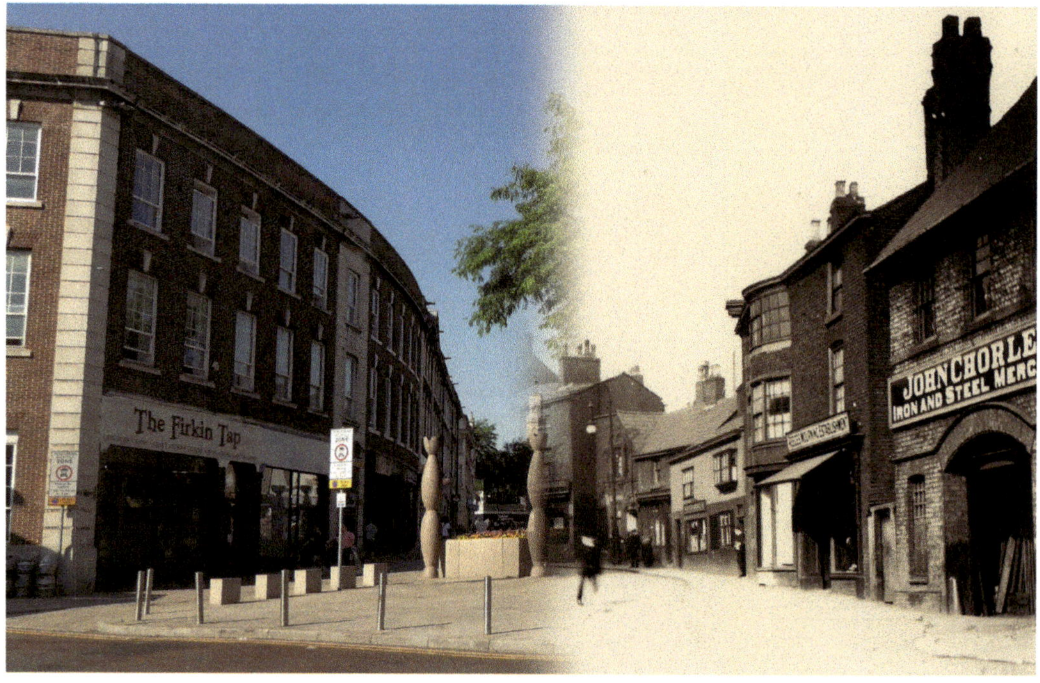

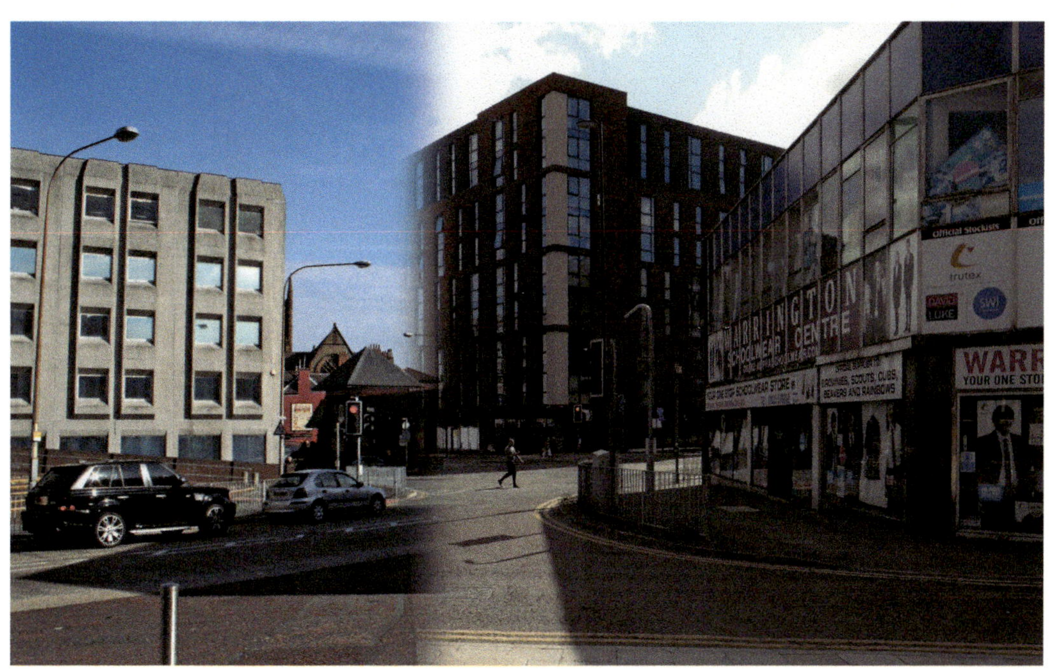

Buttermarket Street was also altered by the creation of a section of the inner ring road called Academy Way in the 1970s. Buildings on either side of its junction with Academy Street were demolished, including the old Salvation Army citadel. Opposite New Town House (to the left of both views) the site was initially occupied by a low-level supermarket block. By September 2022 a new housing development had replaced it, towering over New Town House where demolition had begun.

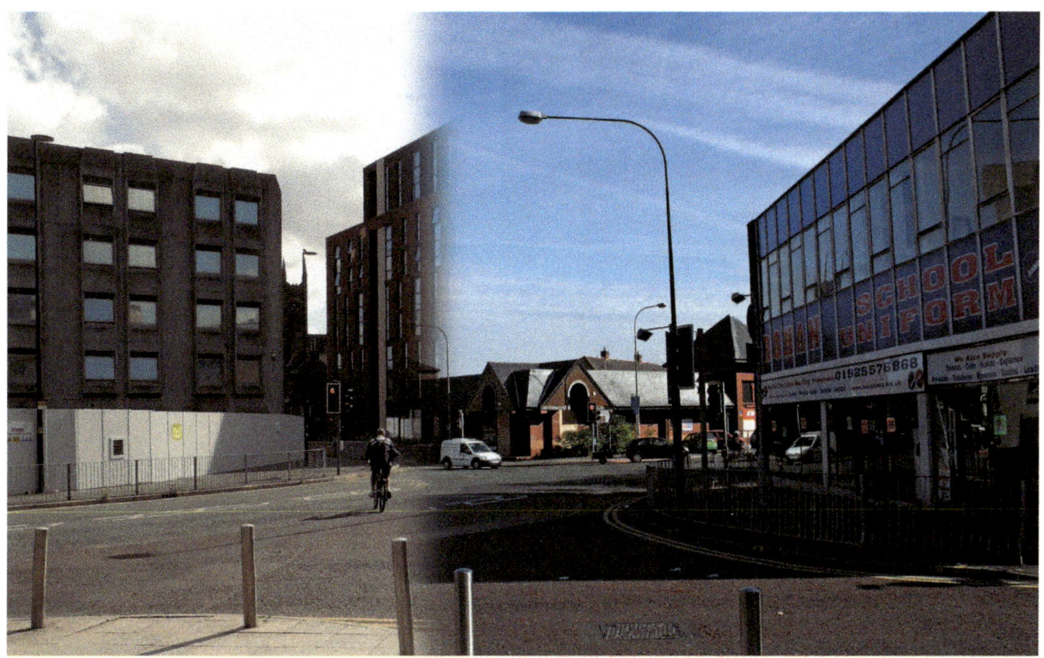

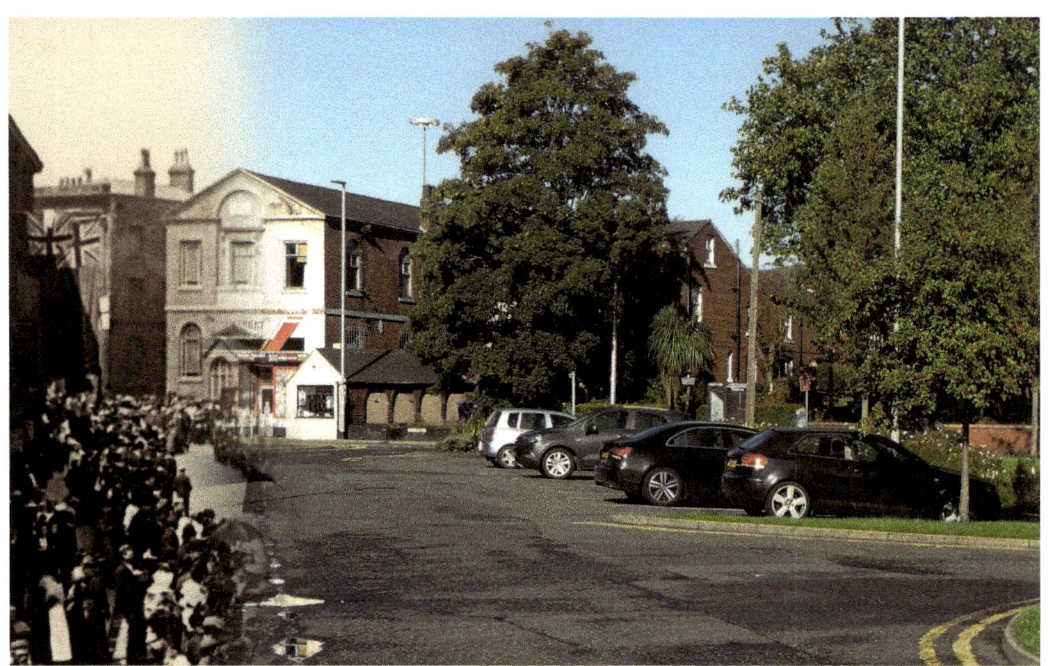

Lower Buttermarket Street beyond St Mary's Church continues along Dial Street to the roundabout at the junction with Mersey and Church Streets. Looking back towards the town a small car park occupies the site of the former Irlam Street Bridewell opened in 1820. This was Warrington's police station, with prison cells and courthouse until the Arpley Street complex opened in 1901. In the background is the white frontage of a former Sunday school and neighbouring Trustees Savings Bank (far left).

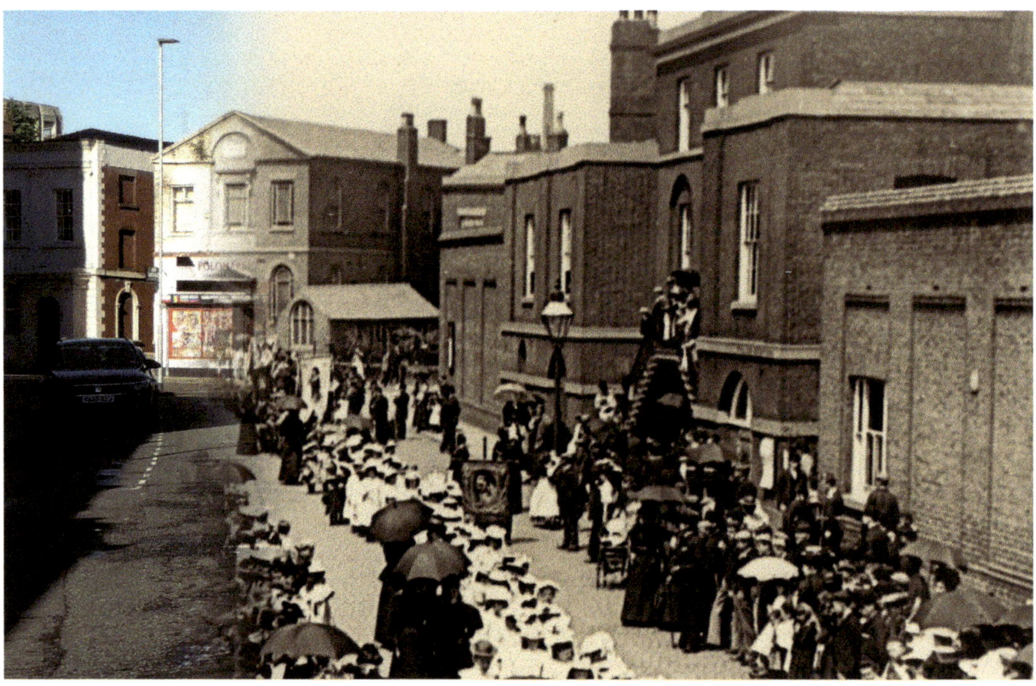

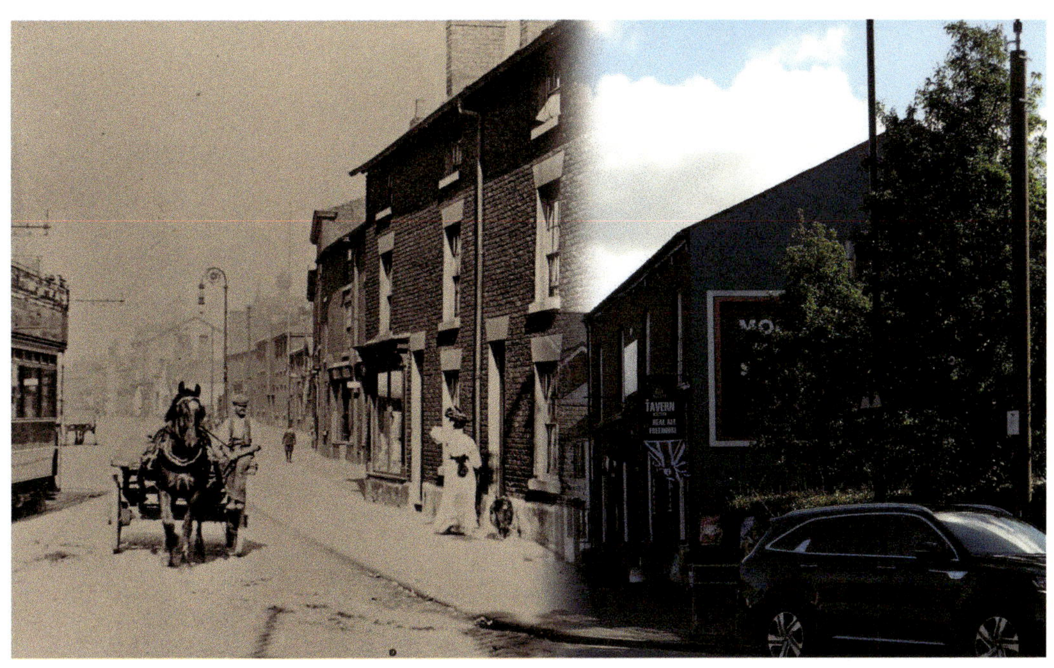

At its southern end Buttermarket Street reaches a junction with Mersey Street (right) and today continues into Church Street across a busy roundabout where few pedestrians venture. Once three small boys could lean casually on a lamp post as only a tram and horse and cart pass leisurely by. Headlines proclaiming 'Another Russian defeat' on the hoardings outside Downs's newsagent date the early view to 1905 rather than Russia's so-called operations in the Ukraine in the later view of 2022.

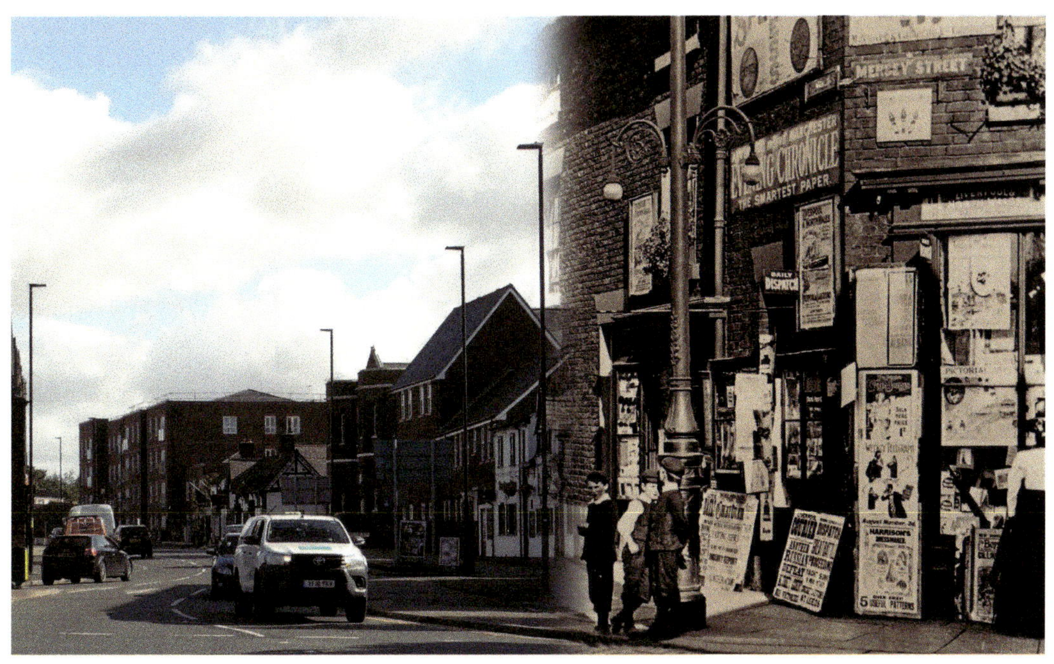

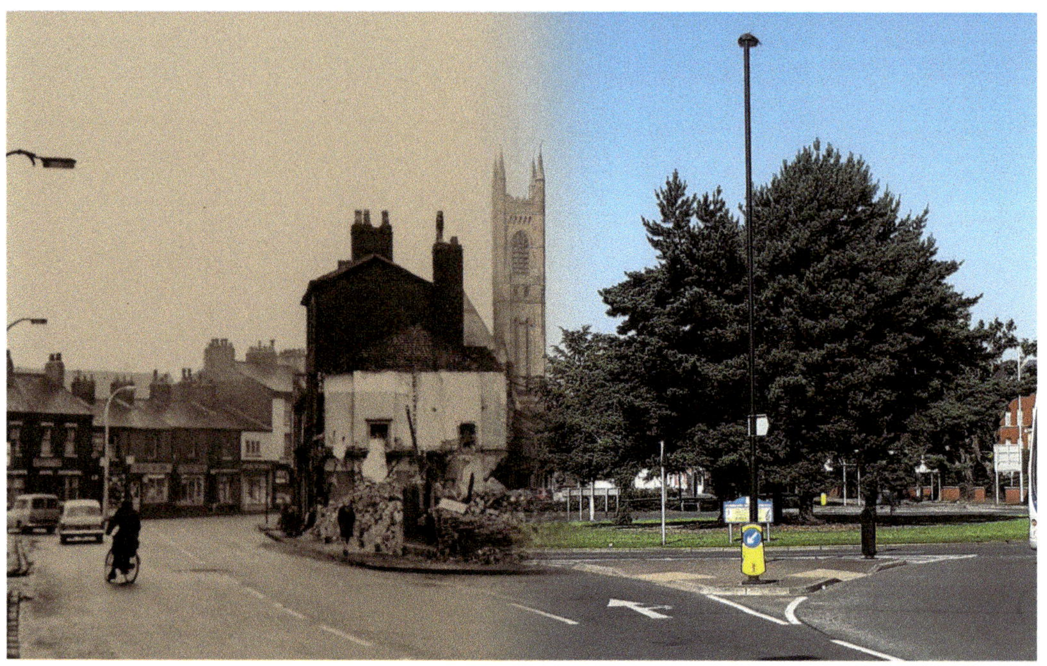

By the late 1970s the town end of Church Street changed dramatically to accommodate the growing volume of traffic. The Co-operative store on the right of the earlier picture and neighbouring premises made way for the new traffic island at the junction of Fennel Street with Mersey Street. St Mary's Church tower in the background still provides a reference point in the changing streetscape with new developments off Buttermarket Street behind.

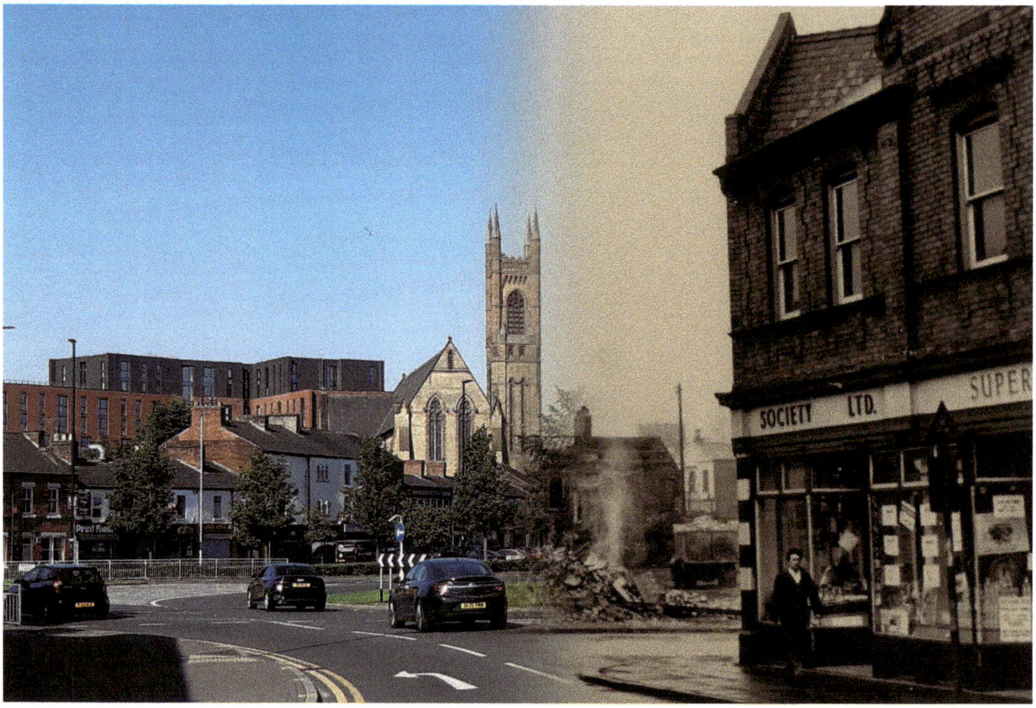

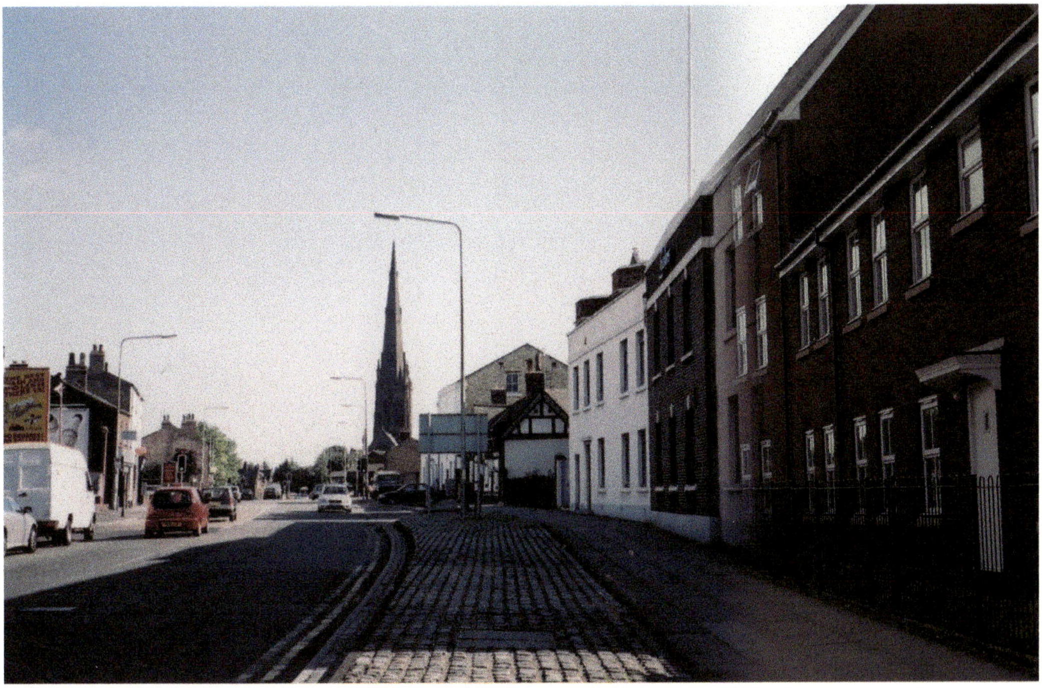

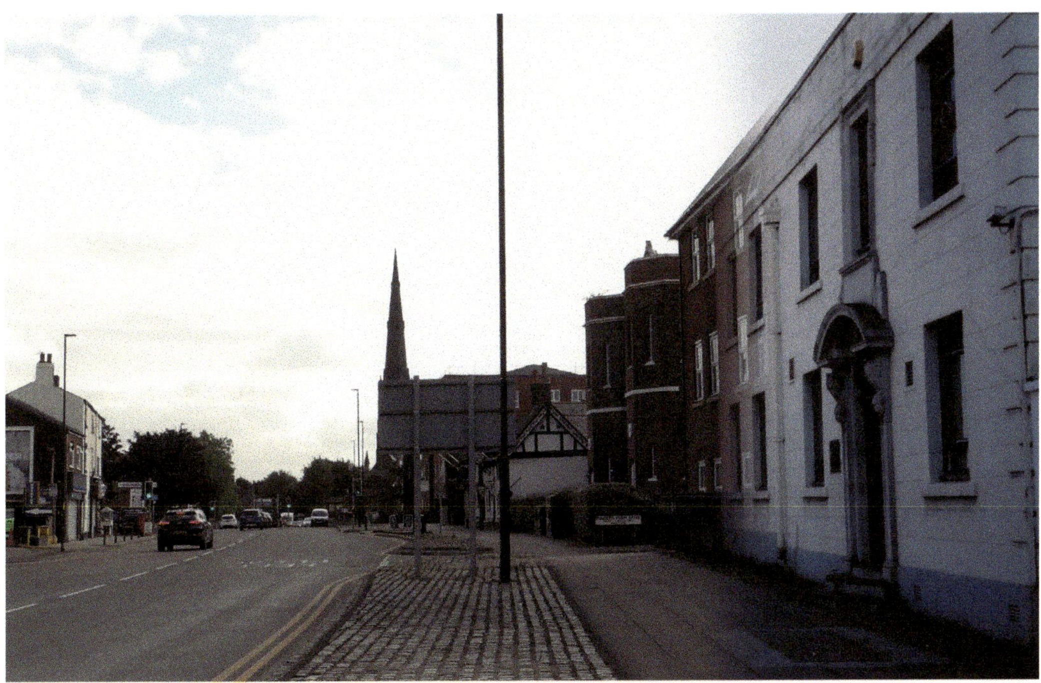

Until the turn of the twenty-first century Lockers wire-weaving works had been a prominent part of the landscape off Church Street. Their white office block on the right of the street was demolished and replaced by more modest housing in the first decade of the new century. Both views reflect the width of Church Street dating from its medieval function as the original site of the town's market. The Parish Church spire remains the street's dominant feature.

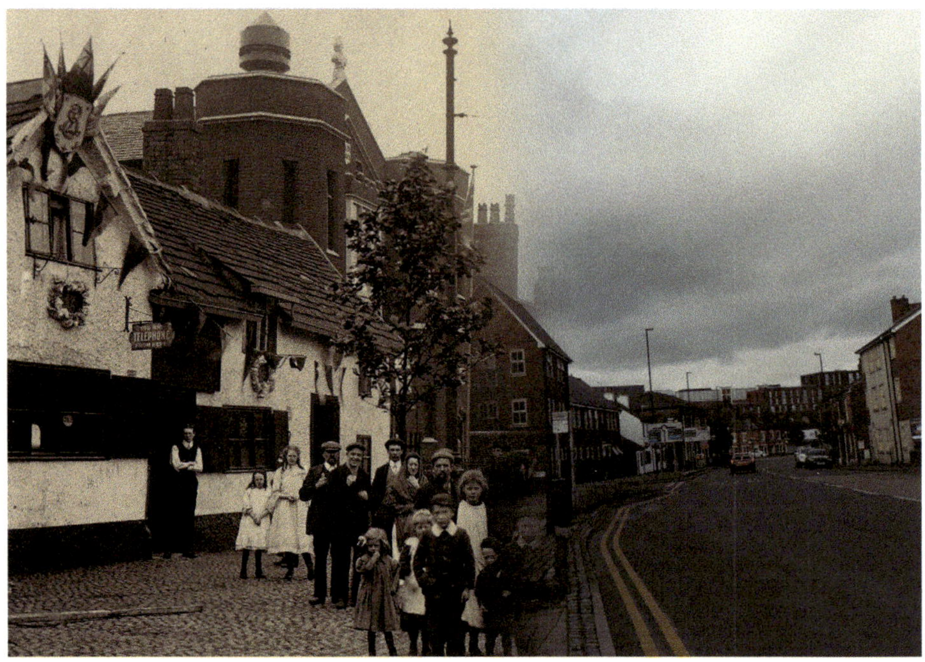

Medieval Church Street was lined with thatched timber-clad cottages but today only three remain with the former Marquis of Granby inn seen on the left. In July 1909 the street was decorated with bunting to welcome King Edward VII on his route to Warrington Town Hall. The curious children were probably pupils of the adjacent National School opened in 1833. Today only the façade of the building remains as the rest was demolished in the 1980s with new apartments created behind.

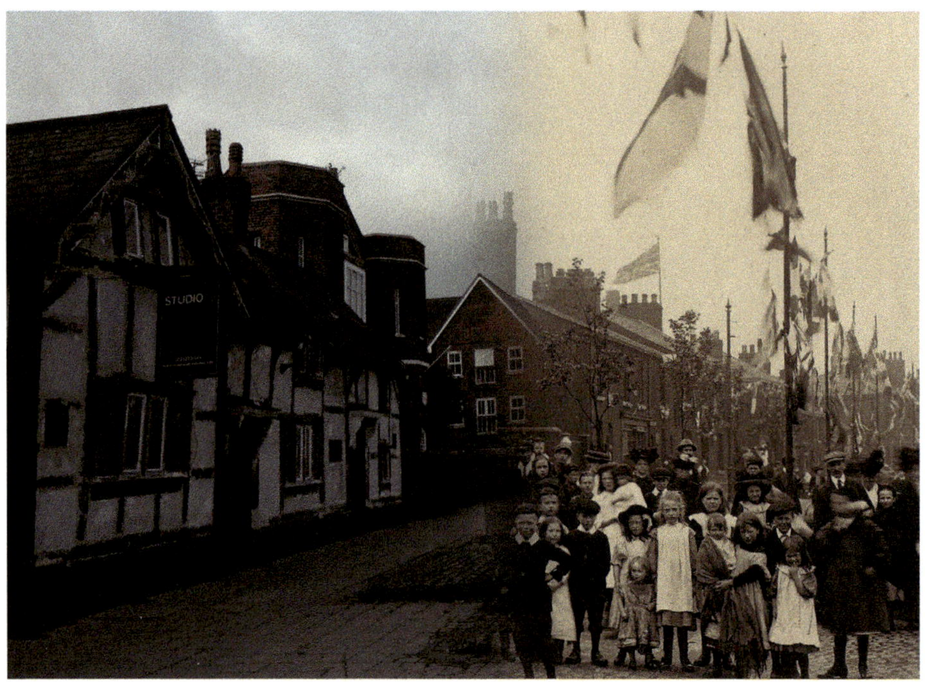

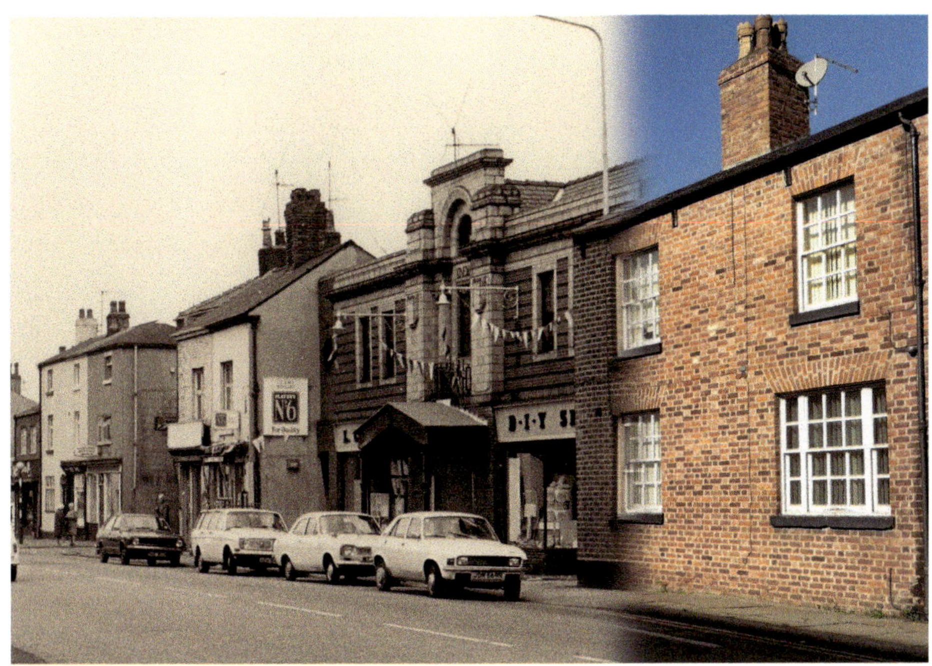

The opposite side of the street has also seen major changes since the 1970s. The red-brick building on the right of both images seems the same but the former General Wolfe pub was completely rebuilt in 1996. To the left was the Star Kinema, one of Warrington's earliest cinemas which opened in January 1914. After its closure in 1956 it later became Catterall's DIY shop before demolition in 1981 and eventual replacement as a care home.

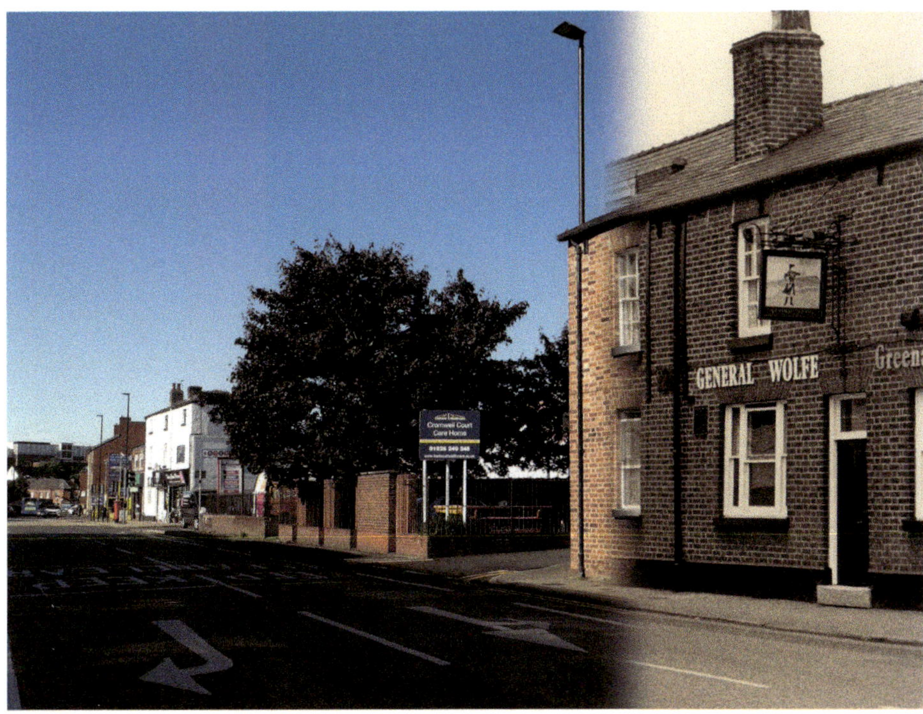

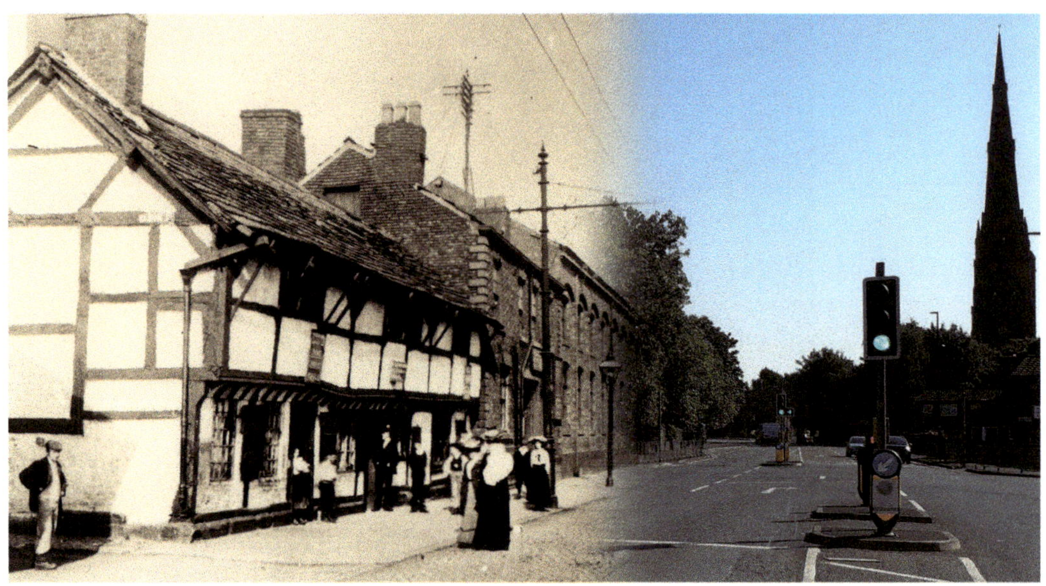

Apart from the Parish Church the only remaining landmark from the early 1900s is the so-called black and white Tudor Cottage. A plaque on its exterior states that Oliver Cromwell stayed there in 1648 during the English Civil Wars but in reality he slept in the neighbouring Spotted Leopard Inn, later the General Wolfe. In the 1900s it was three separate shops standing next to Rylands extensive wireworks which dominated the view from 1810 until the 1980s.

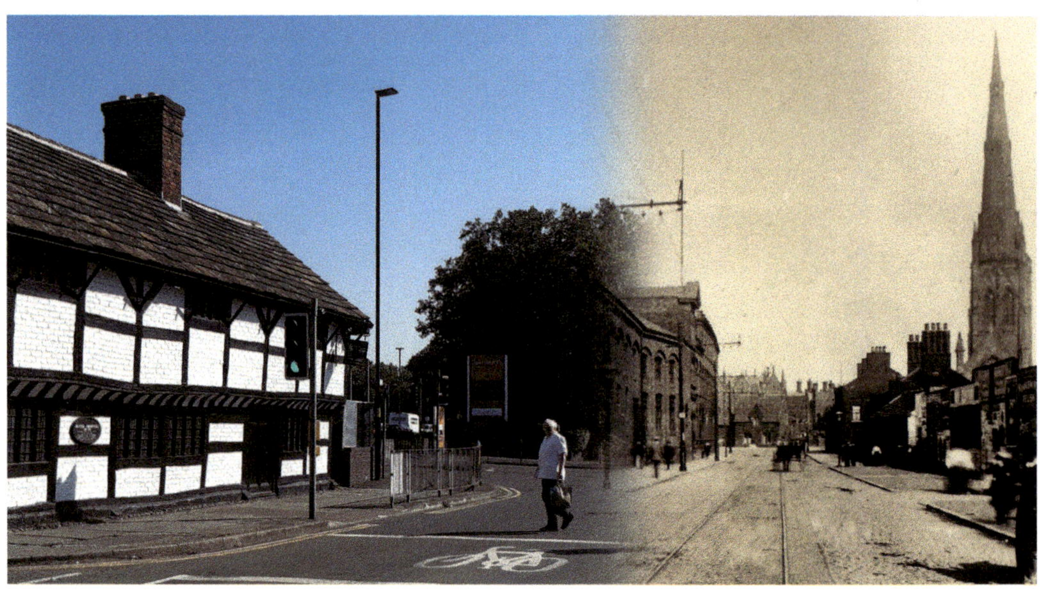

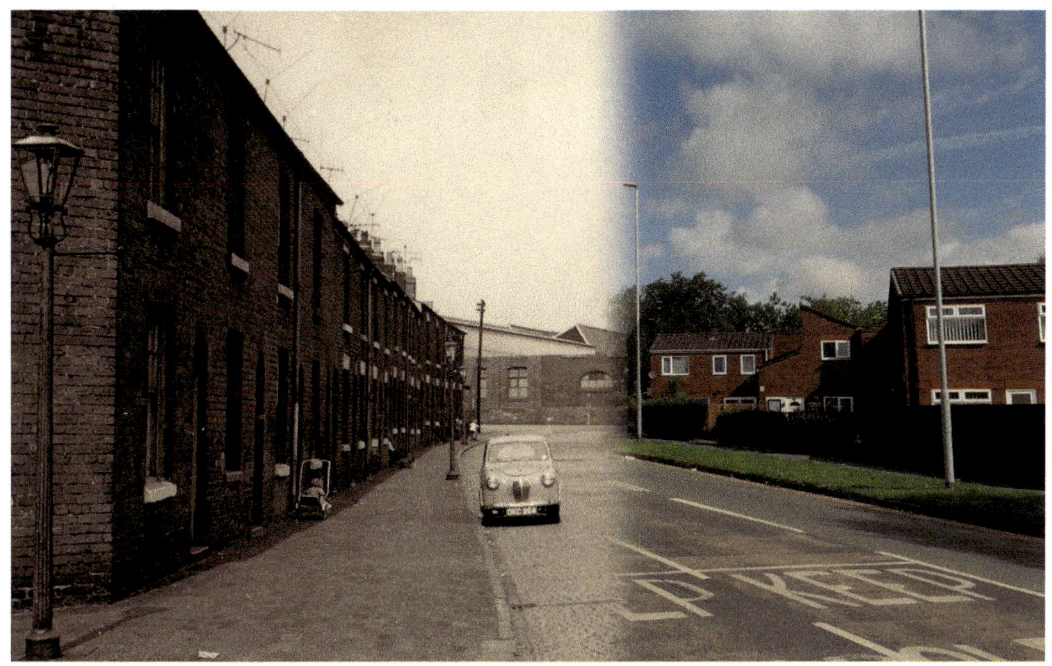

Howley Lane/Farrell Street has changed considerably since the photograph of 1962 recording an era of small terraced houses, gas lamps and cobbled streets with Rylands wireworks in the background on Church Street. As Howley's wireworks and tanneries declined the area was slowly regenerated from the late 1970s and a new community emerged.

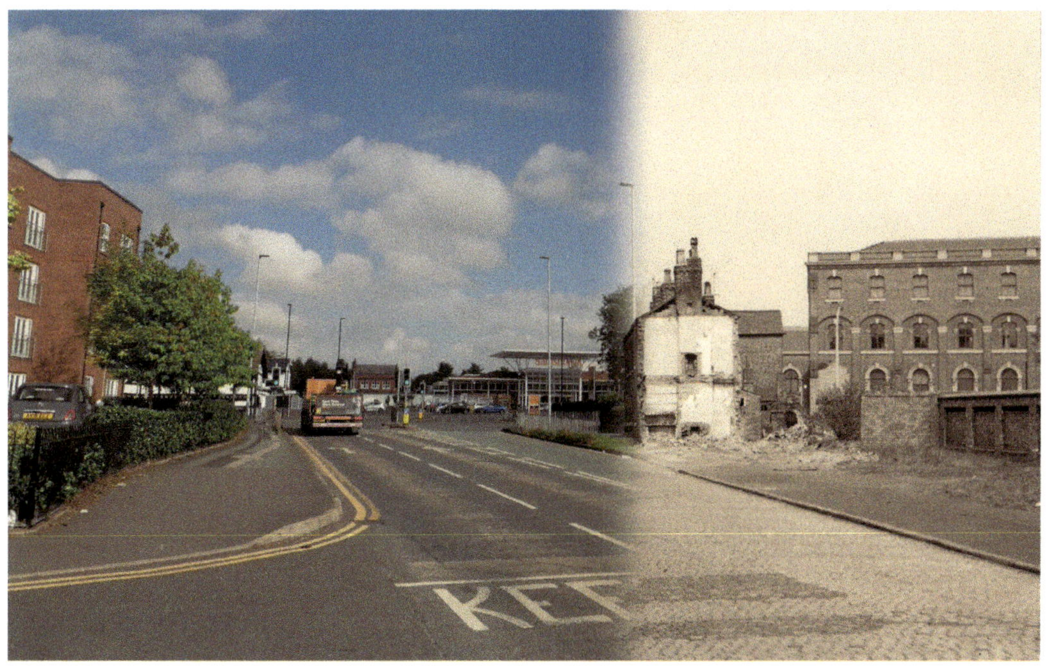

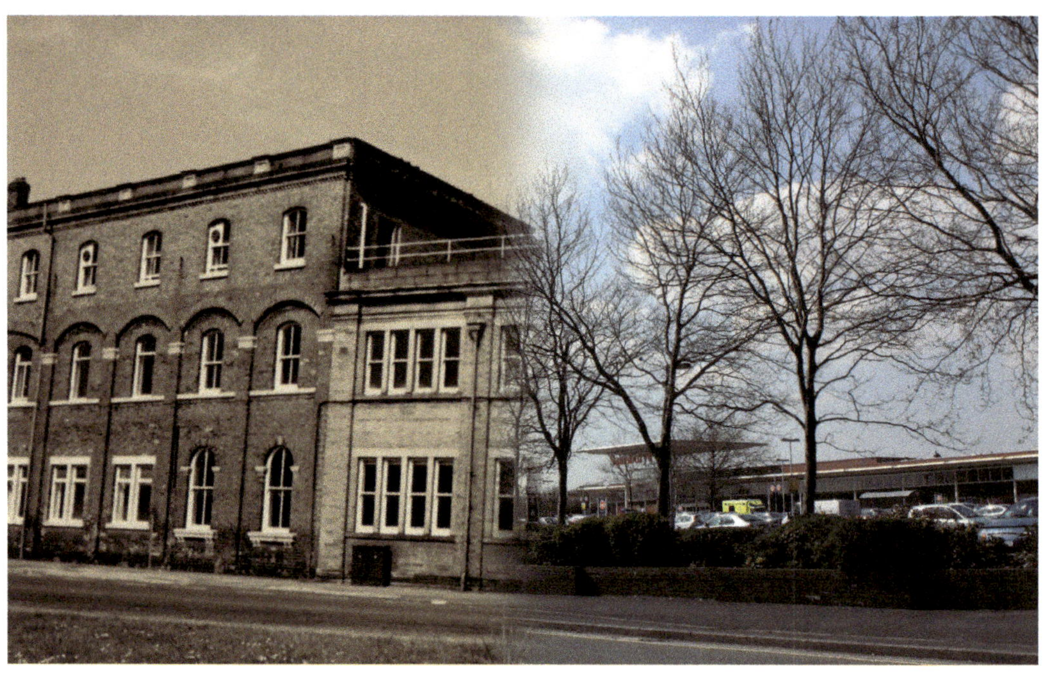

How many shoppers pushing trolleys around Sainsbury's supermarket today realise that they could once have been made from wire produced on the site? Rylands wireworks arrived in Church Street around 1810 and within a century had become major employers exporting their products worldwide. Their impressive office block was demolished with the rest of the works in the early 1980s following a nationwide rationalisation of heavy industries.

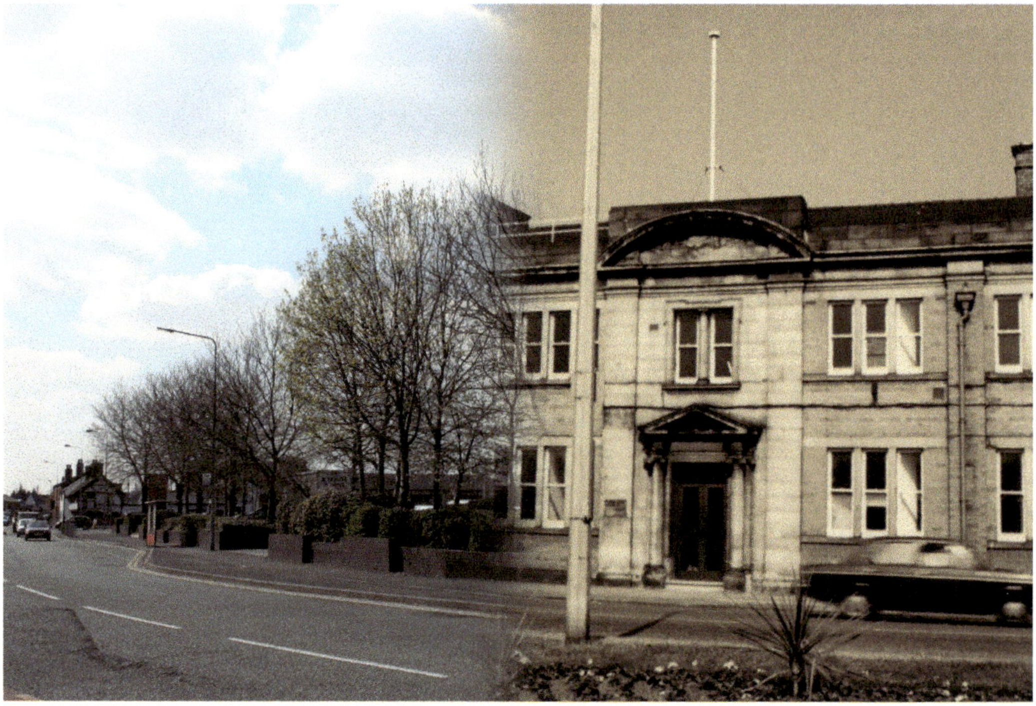

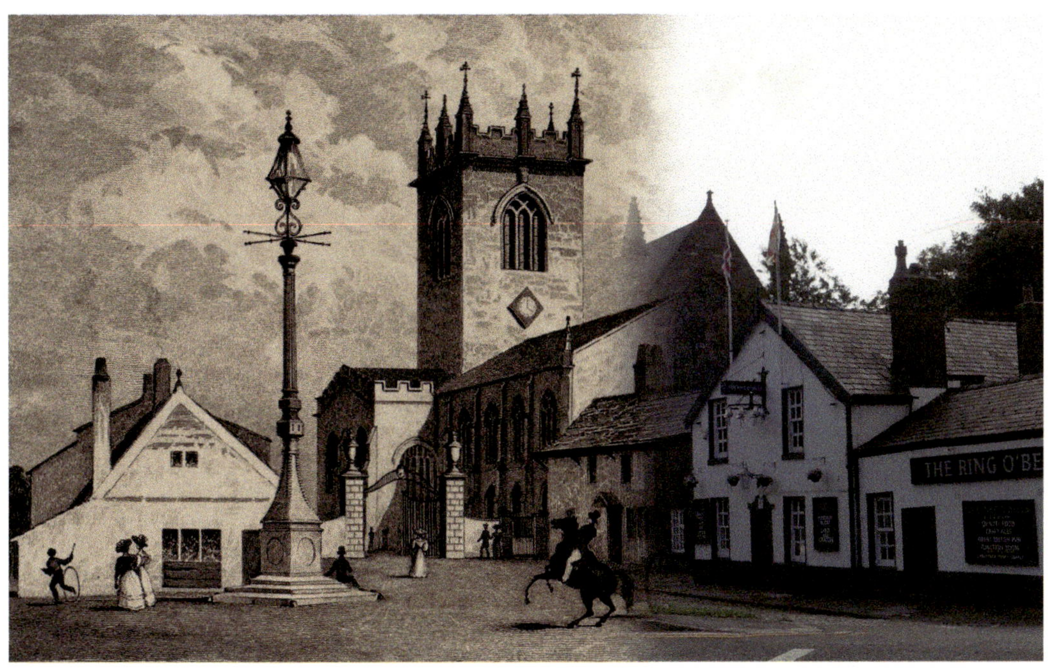

The spire of Warrington's Parish Church is the most visible feature of Warrington's skyline in the surrounding landscape but the building is tucked away on the fringe of the town centre. Dedicated to St Elphin and mentioned in the Domesday Book of 1086, it originated as part of the Lord of the Manor's castle nearby. The 1830s drawing contrasts with the present church which dates from the alterations of the 1850s–60s topped by the third highest parish church spire in England.

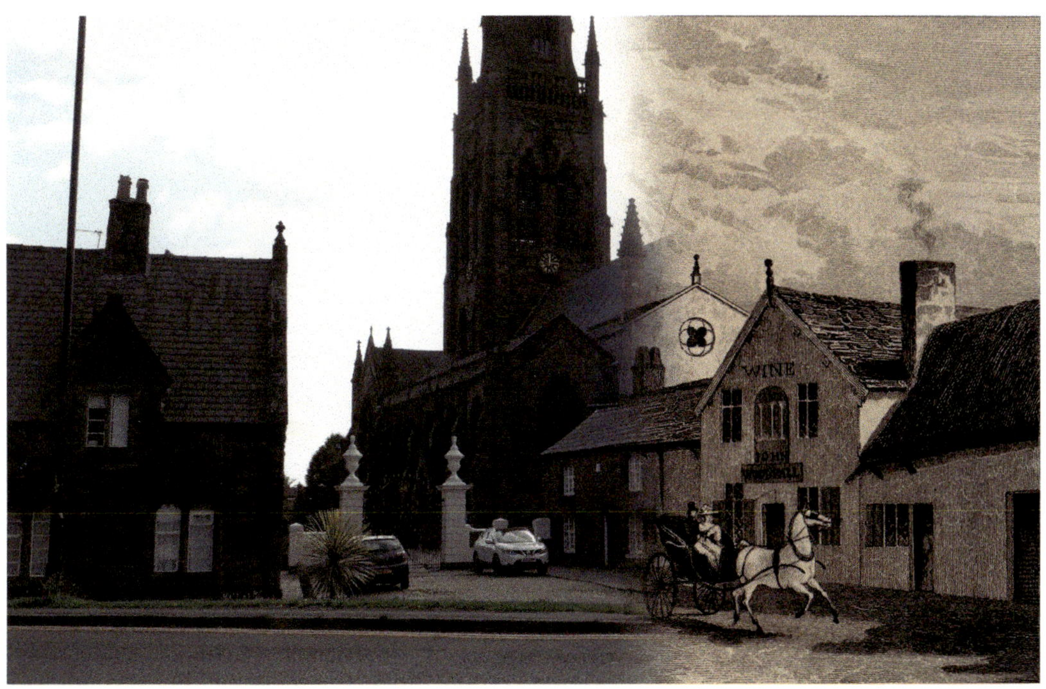

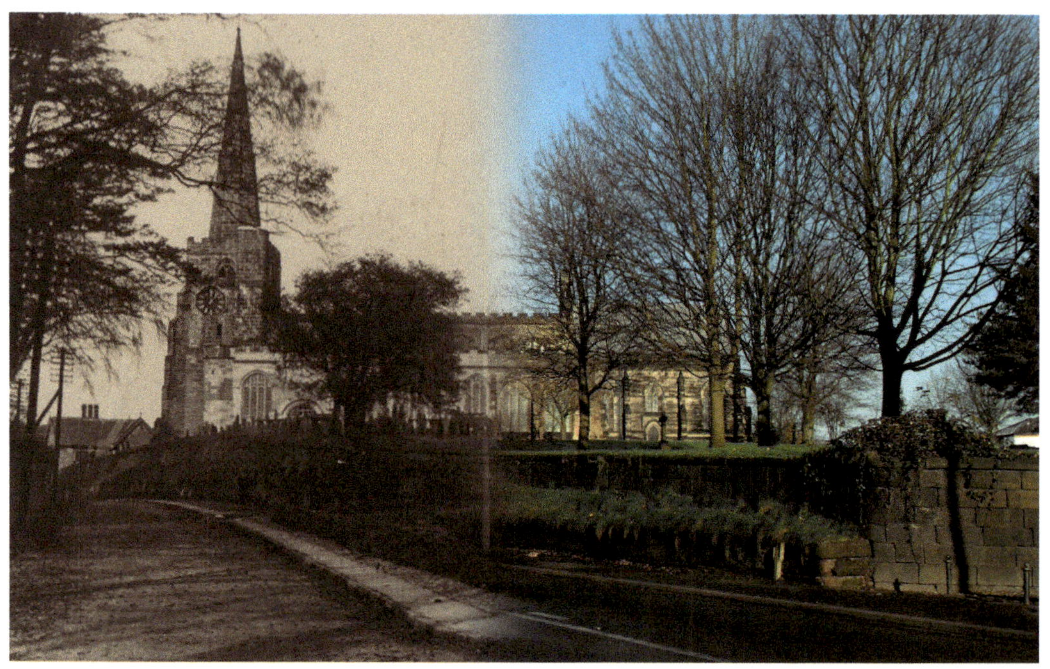

Rivalling Warrington's Parish Church in antiquity is St Oswald's Church at Winwick, which is now at the northern edge of Warrington but for most of its history has been outside the old borough. In the mid-nineteenth century it still stood on a major highway tramped by poor travellers who could pause for refreshment at the drinking fountain before continuing their desperate cross-country search for work. Today most travellers bypass the road in favour of nearby motorway routes.

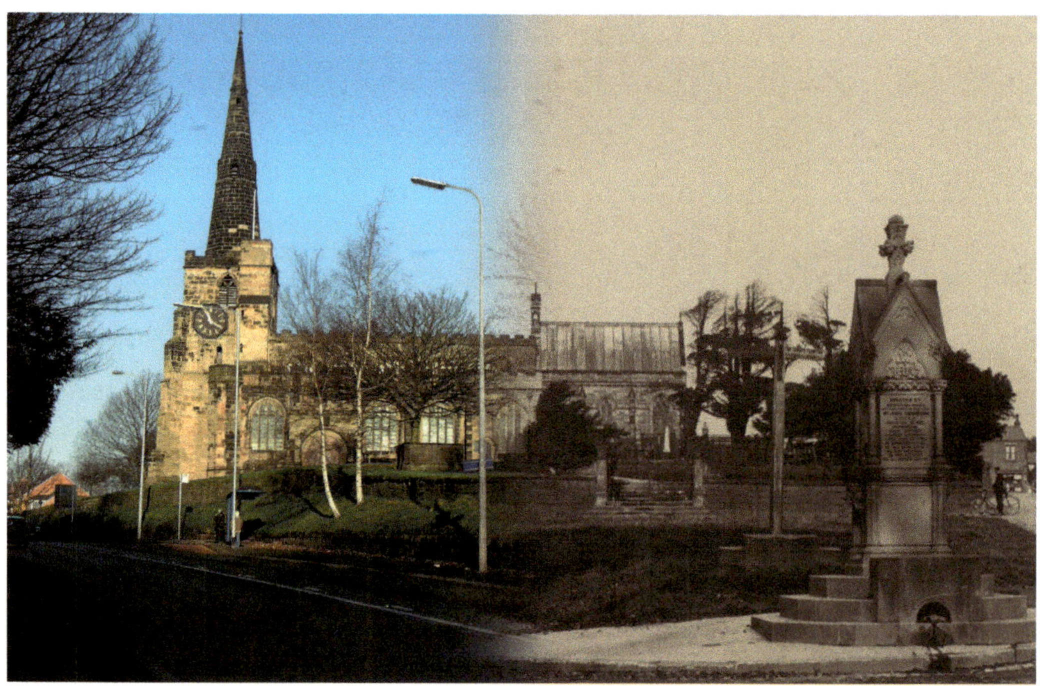

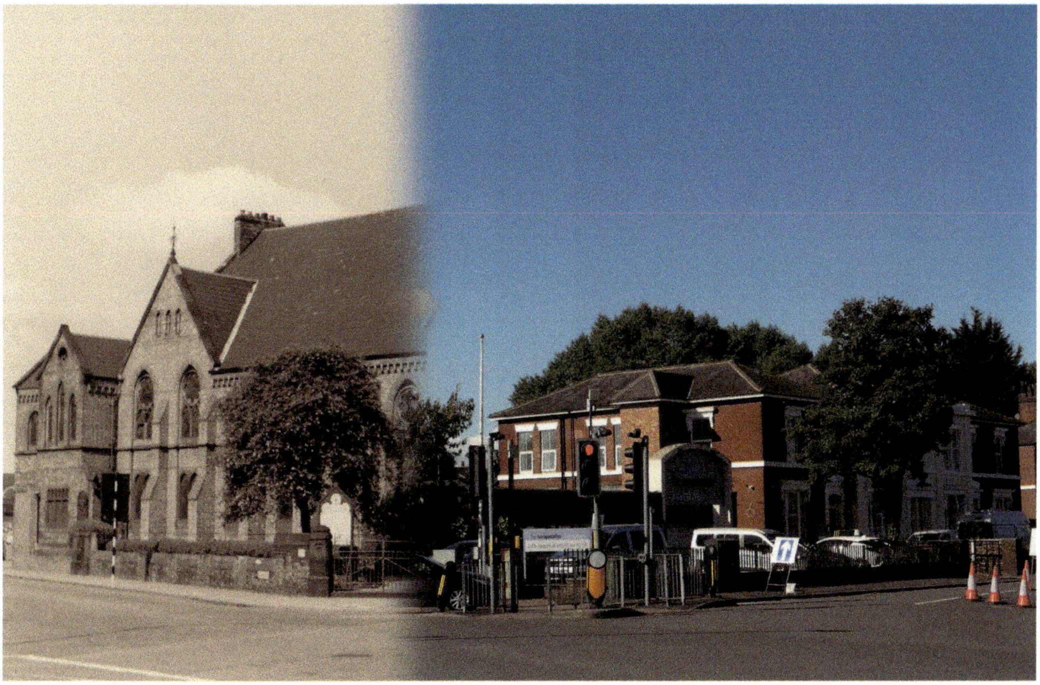

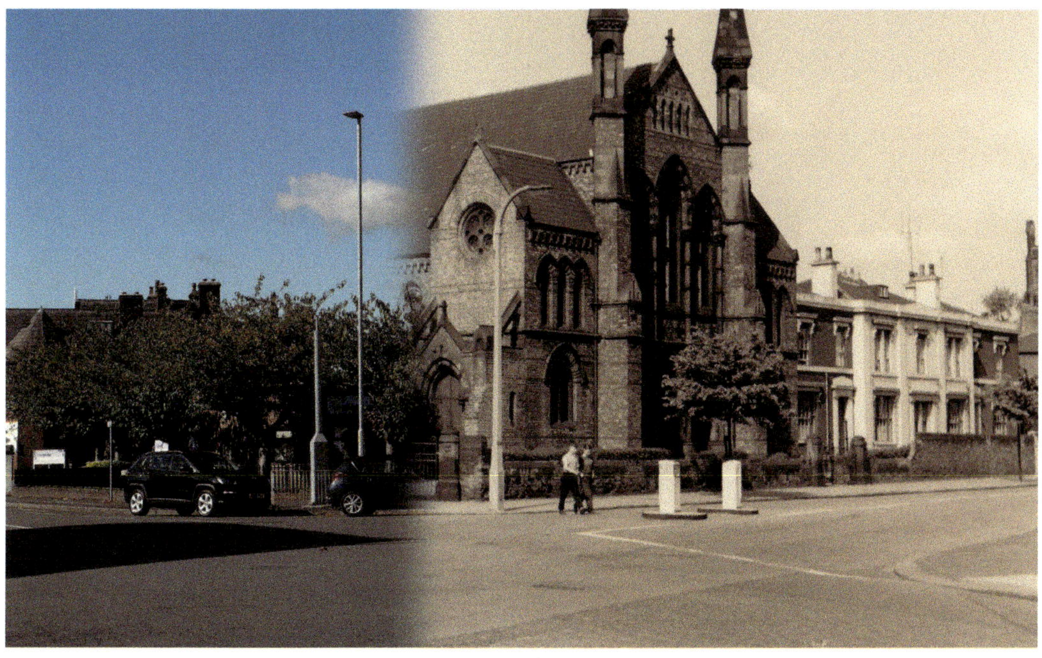

This corner of Bewsey Road and Froghall Lane was once a thriving community with middle-class villas and terraced housing for the employees of numerous local wire, iron and steel works. By the mid-1960s the area's population and its church congregations had declined, leading to the closure and demolition of St Paul's Anglican Church on the far right of the 1960s photograph. The imposing Bewsey Road Methodist chapel with its distinctive pinnacles became the site of a funeral parlour.

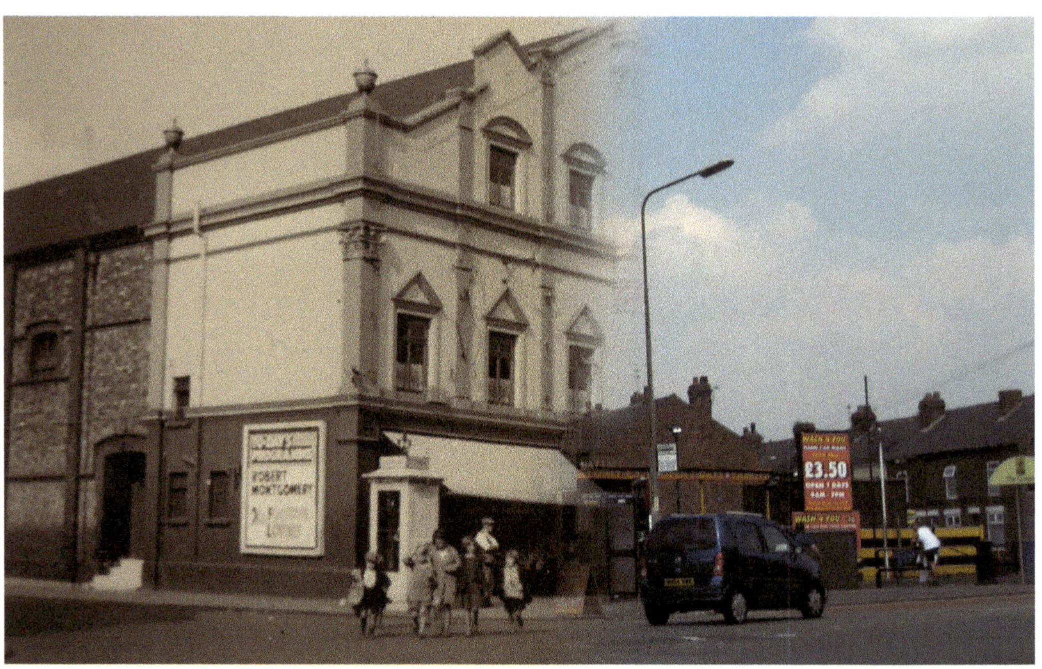

Long before the days of television, the internet and the family car Warringtonians found their entertainment at the movies. The Queens Cinema in Orford Lane was just one of the local picture palaces where people could escape from the reality of daily life. Changing fashions saw cinemas all over the country demolished in the later twentieth century and the Orford Lane site became first a garage and later a car wash.

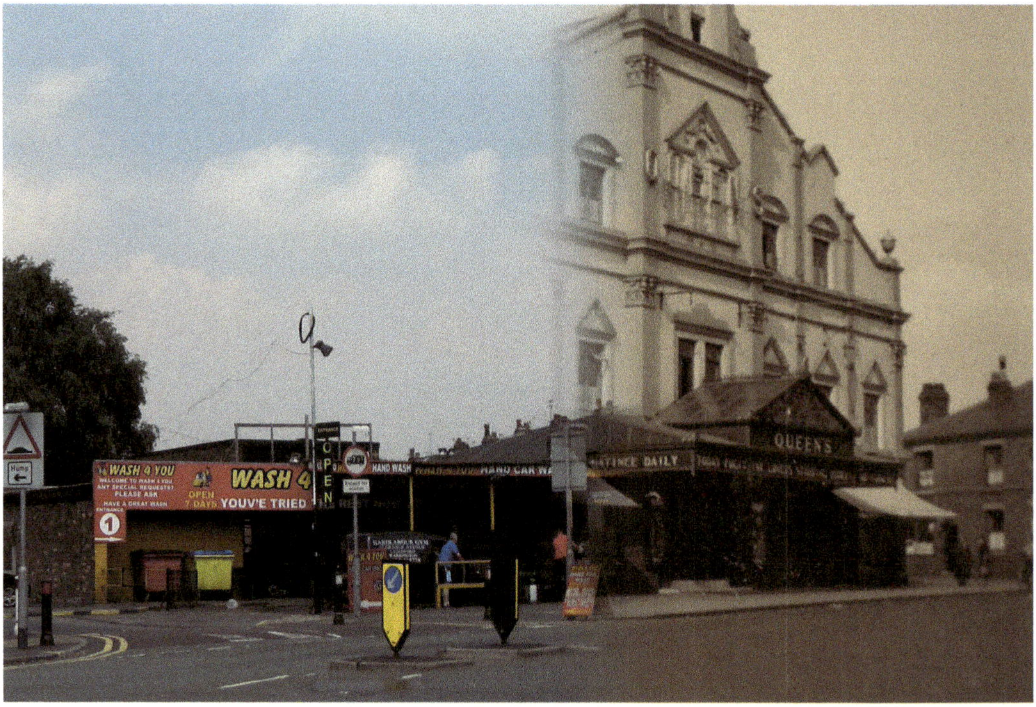

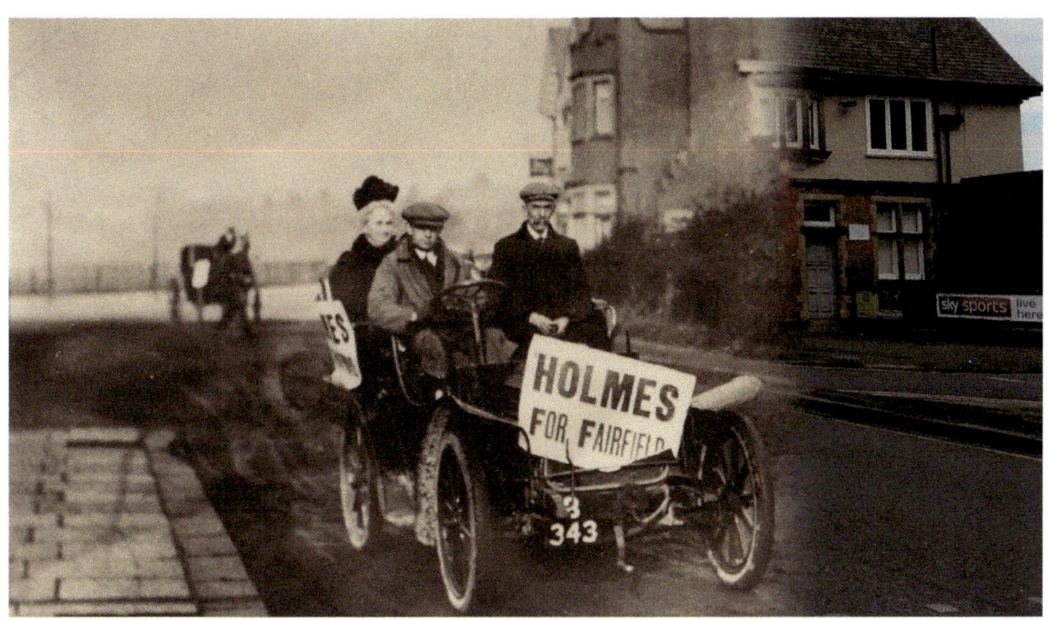

1 November 1909 was a double cause of celebration for Mrs Burrell – she could vote for the first time in local elections ferried by a newfangled horseless carriage. This is now the busy road junction of King Edward Street and Padgate Lane with the public house on the right originally named after the July 1909 visit of King Edward VII and Queen Alexandra. Today's terraced houses and shops had yet to be built.

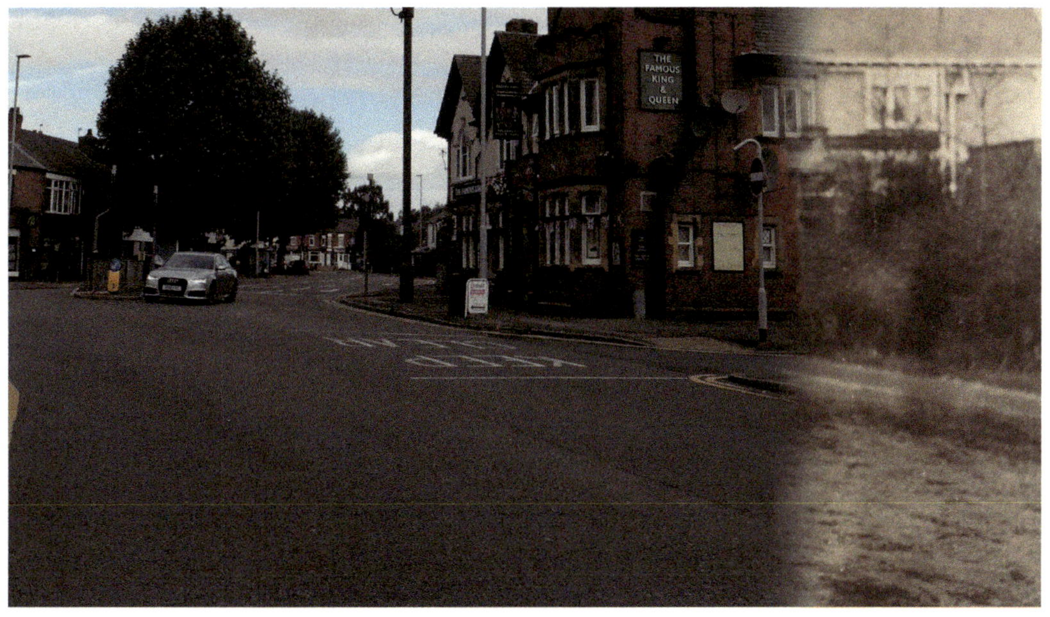

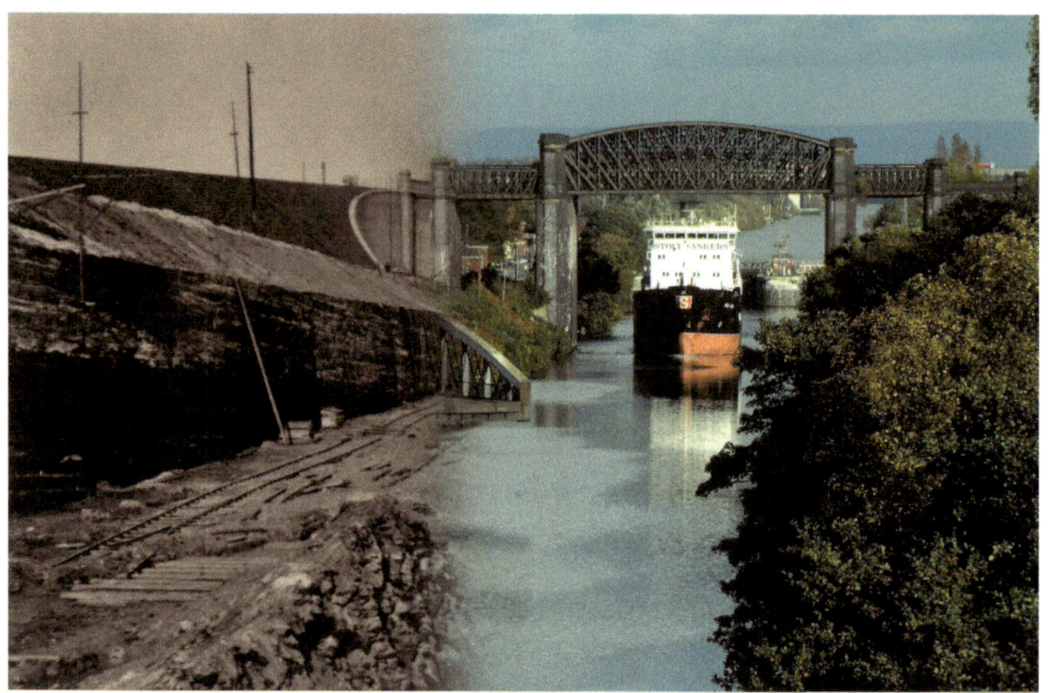

Built between 1885 and 1894, the Manchester Ship Canal was a huge engineering project to enable ocean-going vessels to reach the new inland port of Manchester. Towering above Latchford Locks a railway viaduct carried the now closed London and North Western Railway line. The canal had a dramatic impact on the landscape of South Warrington. Latchford was cut off from Thelwall and Grappenhall and Wilderspool isolated from nearby Stockton Heath while the swing bridge closures caused massive traffic tailbacks.

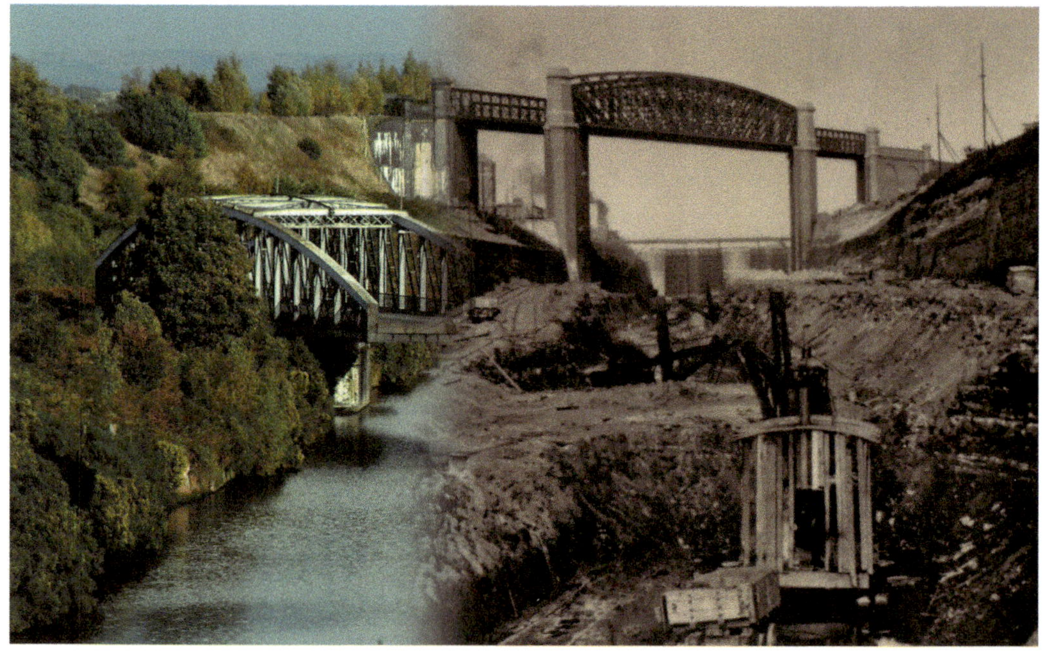

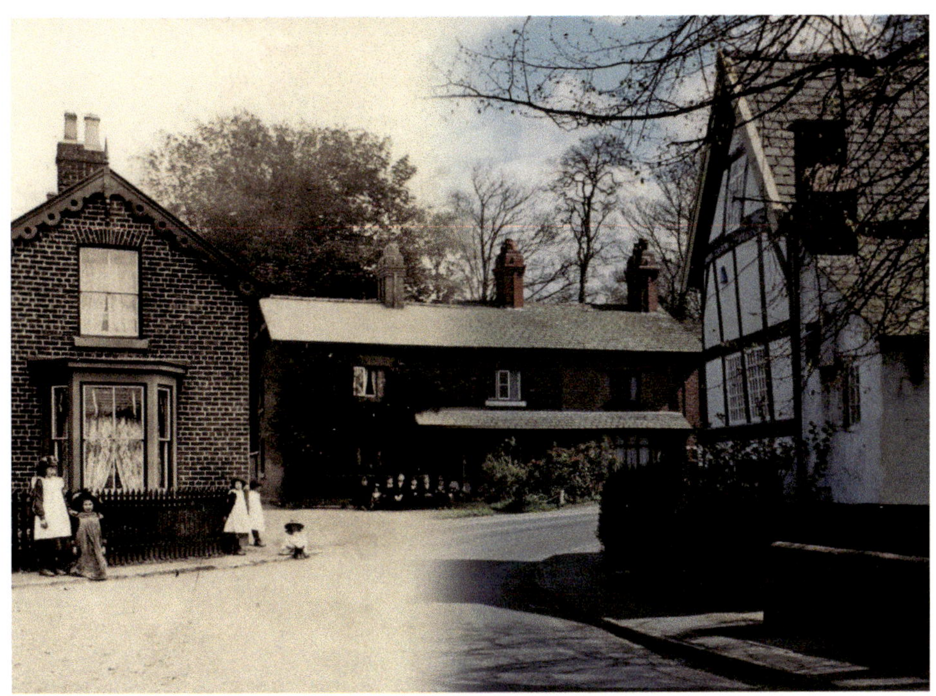

Thelwall's village pub chronicles the history of its village. The Pickering Arms reflects a major local landowner while the inscription on the gable end of the half-timbered building recalls an earlier history: 'In the year 923 King Edward the Elder founded a city here and called it Thelwall.' The settlement was then on a strategic river crossing between the warring kingdoms of Mercia and Northumbria whilst today nearby Thelwall viaduct occupies an equally important site on the national road network.

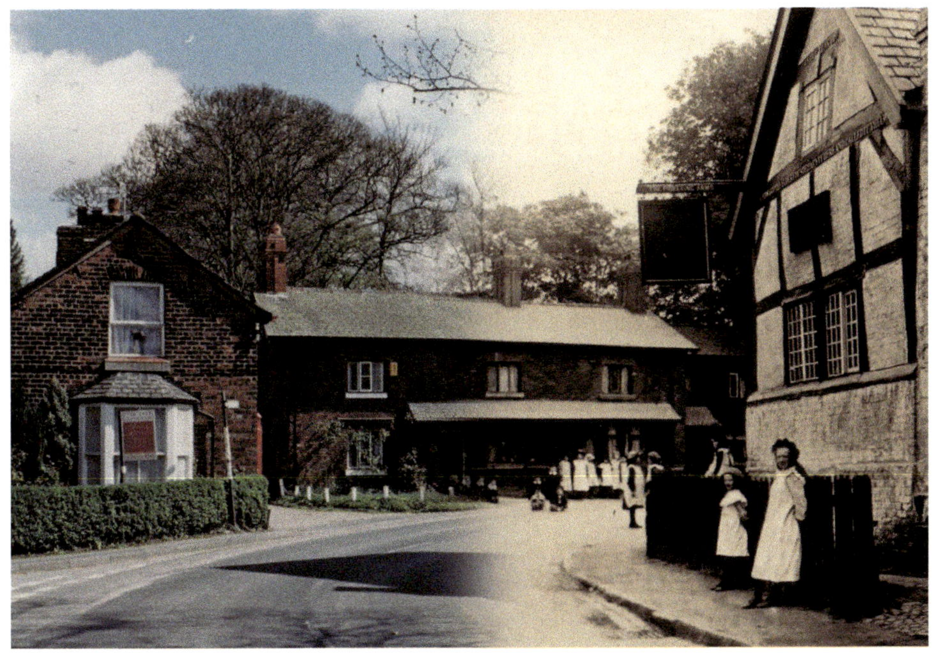

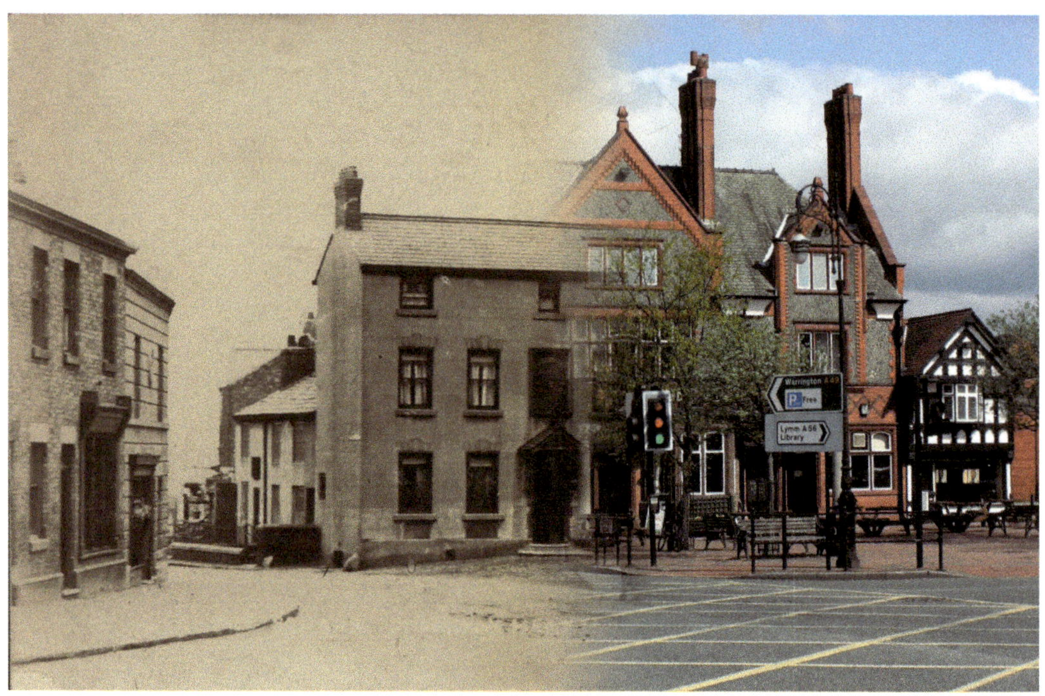

The tranquil sepia scene of Stockton Heath in the early 1900s is barely recognisable as Victoria Square. Renamed in honour of Queen Victoria's Diamond Jubilee of 1897, the area had previously been known to locals as Pigeon Bank. The horse bus was soon replaced by trams, which necessitated the demolition of Beaconsfield Terrace (left). The Old Mulberry Tree Inn (centre) was rebuilt in 1907.

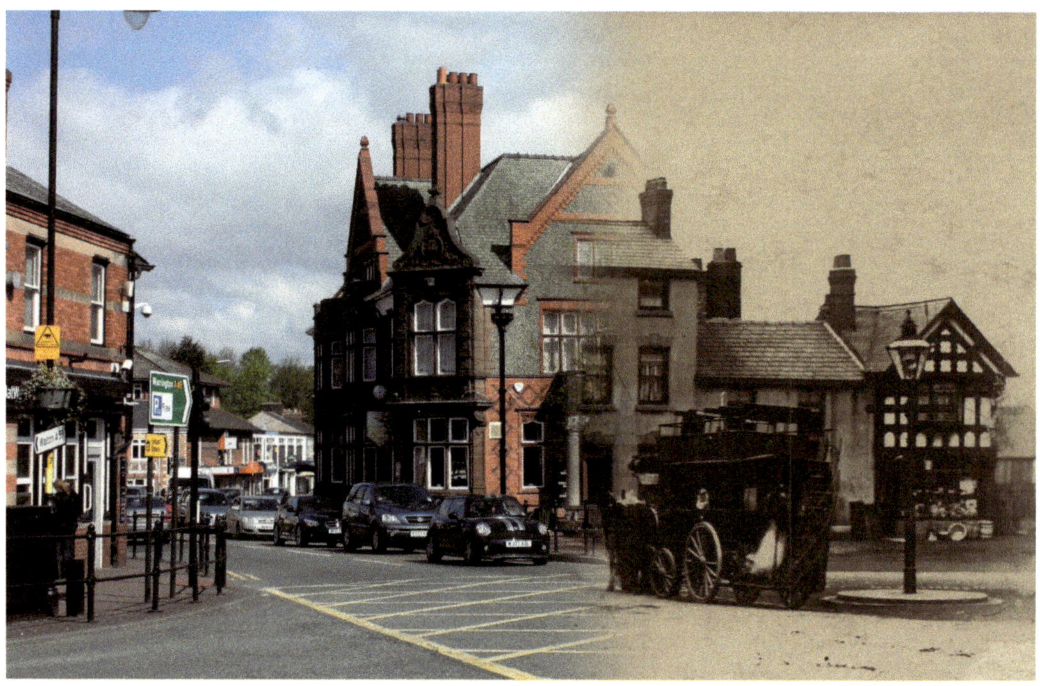

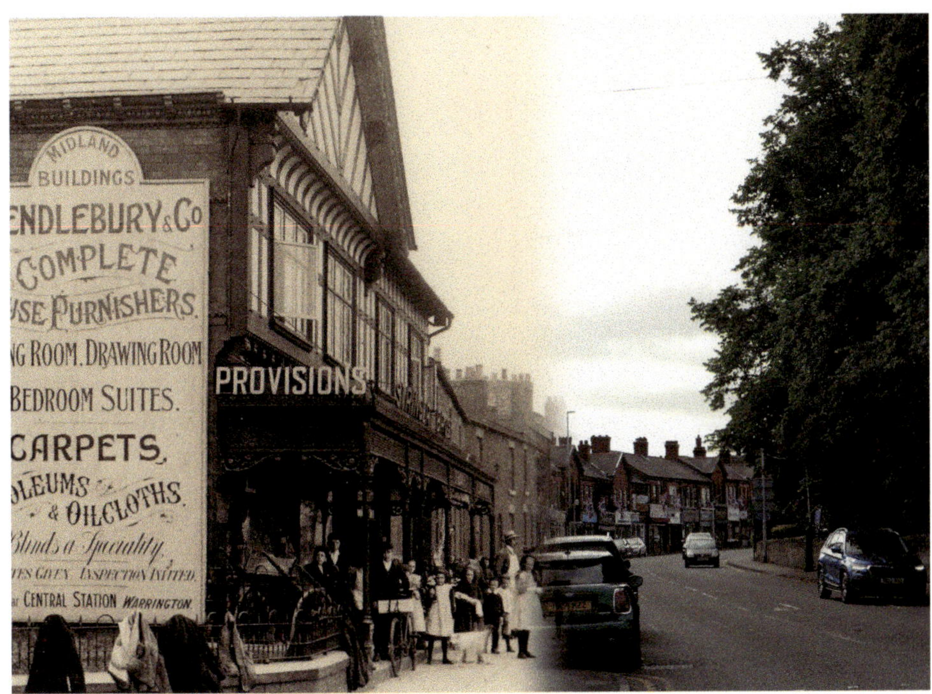

In 1902 Warrington's new tram network reached as far as Wilderspool, leaving Stockton Heath residents using the local horse bus or walking over the swing bridge. The older photograph shows workman laying the tracks which would finally link the village with the town centre. Many of Warrington's middle class began to commute from the suburbs to their offices in town while an increasing volume of traffic clogged up Stockton Heath as the car became king.

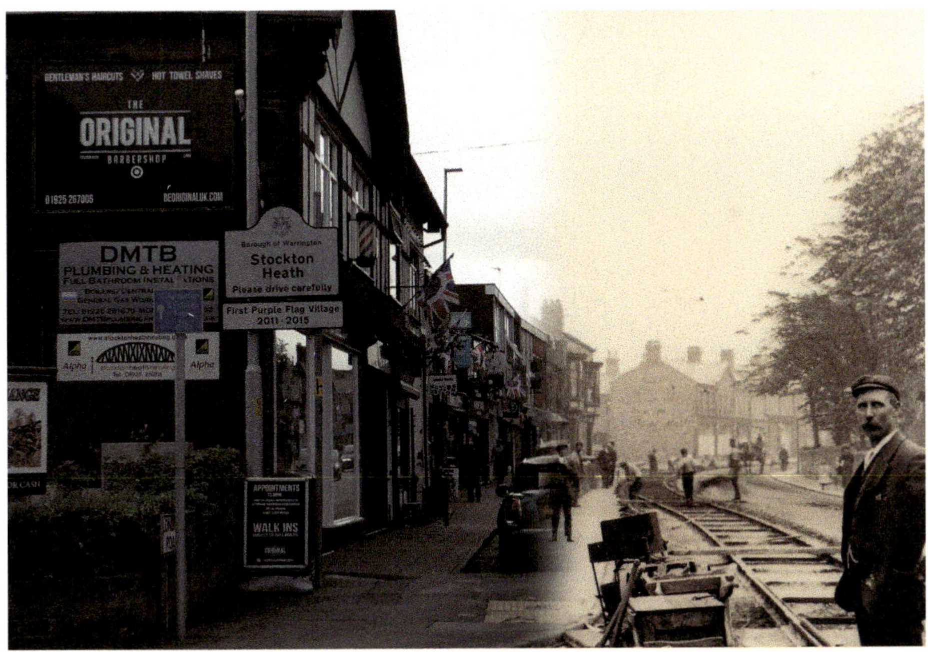

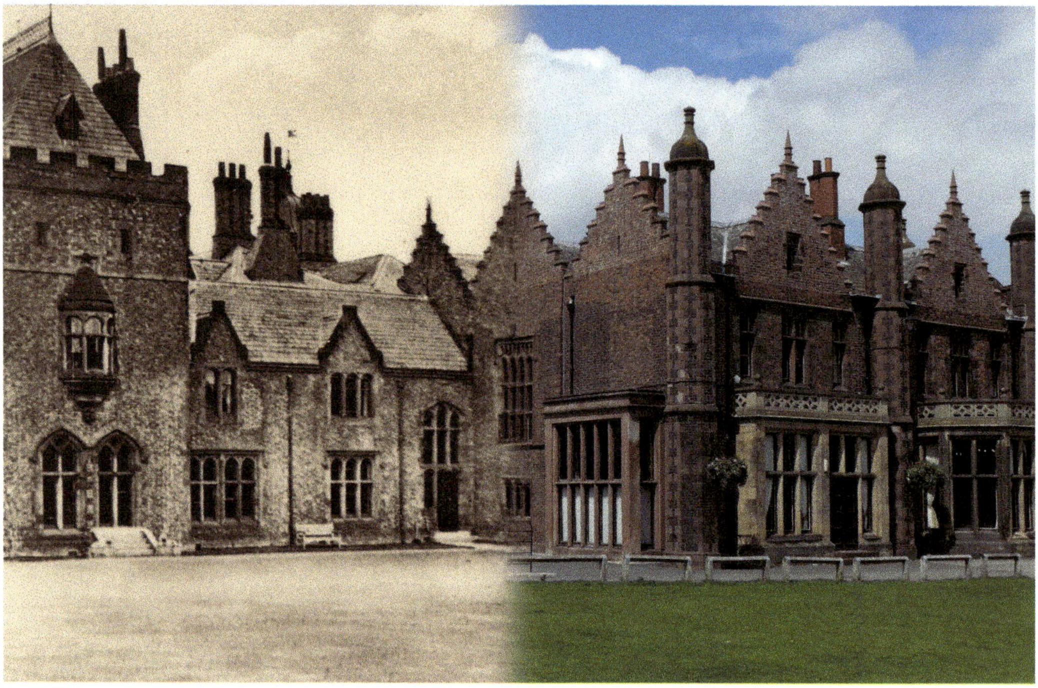

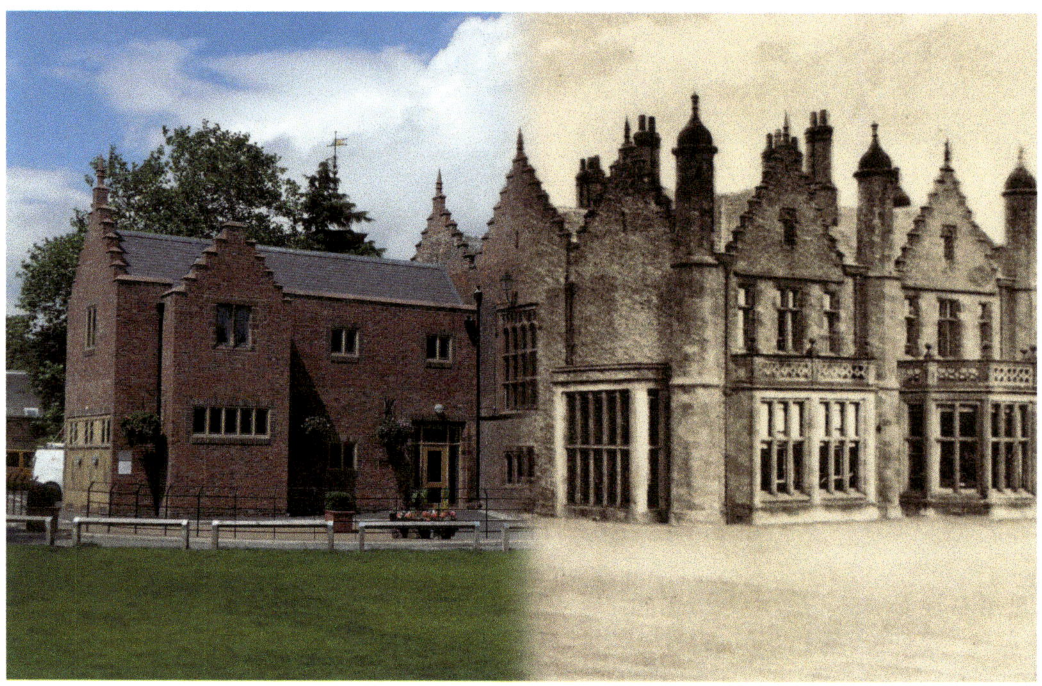

Purchased for the town in 1941, Walton Gardens became a popular local leisure destination but they were originally the private estate of the Greenall brewery dynasty of Wilderspool. The original Elizabethan-style block can be seen on the right of both photographs. In the late 1860s to mid-1870s the hall was extended with a new wing in the popular style imitating a Scottish castle with a square tower which was subsequently demolished and remodelled.

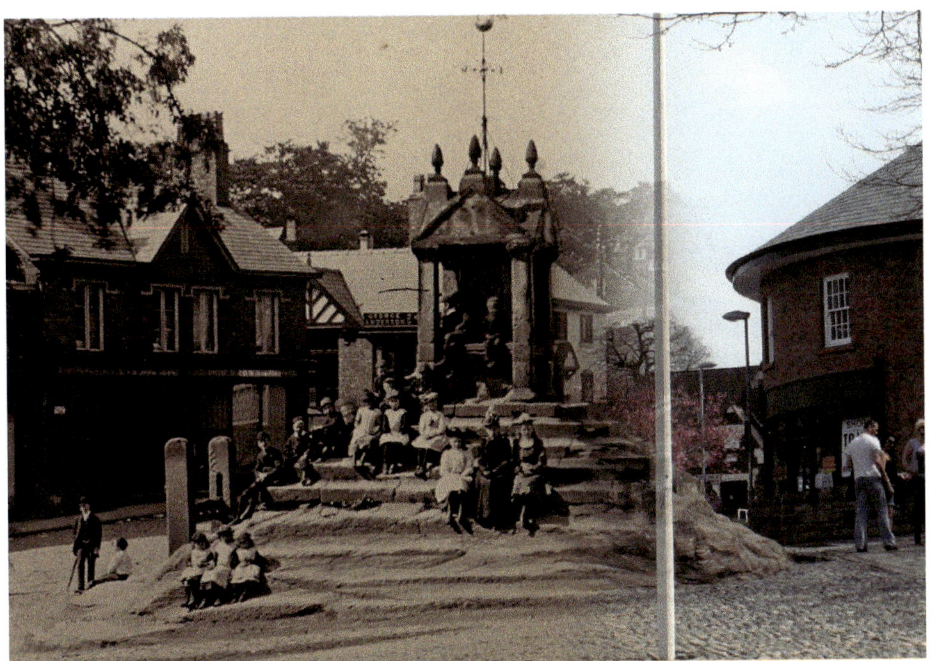

Lymm still retains much of its historic character as a settlement distinct from Warrington and neighbouring commuter towns. Lymm's centrepiece is its ancient cross and village stocks. By the older photograph in the 1890s more shops were appearing around Lymm Cross which was later restored to commemorate Queen Victoria's Diamond Jubilee of 1897 with a symbolic golden crown replacing the old cockerel on the weathervane.

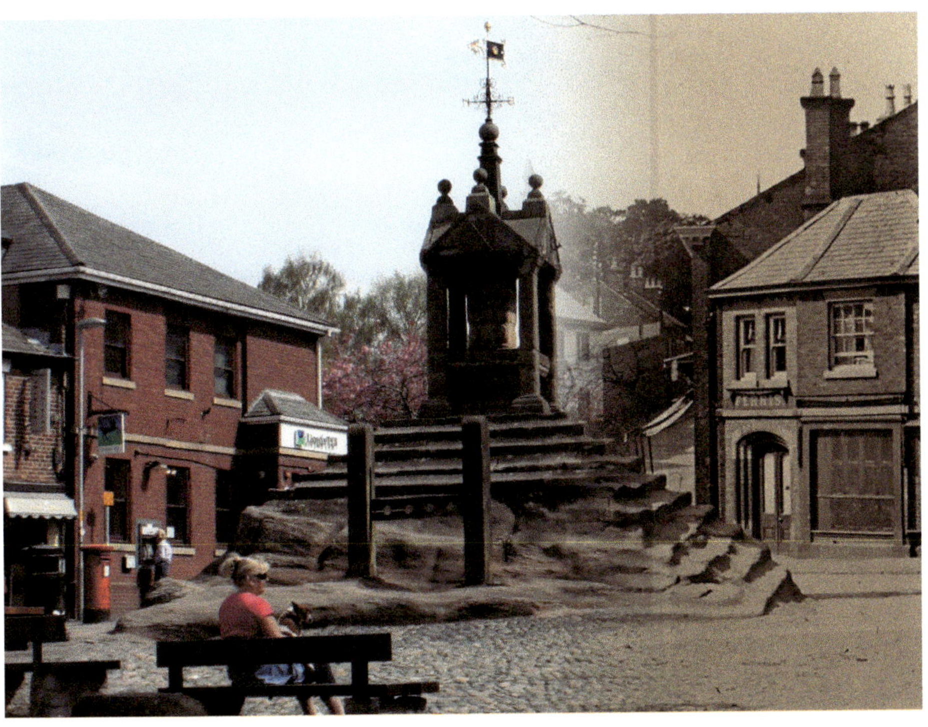

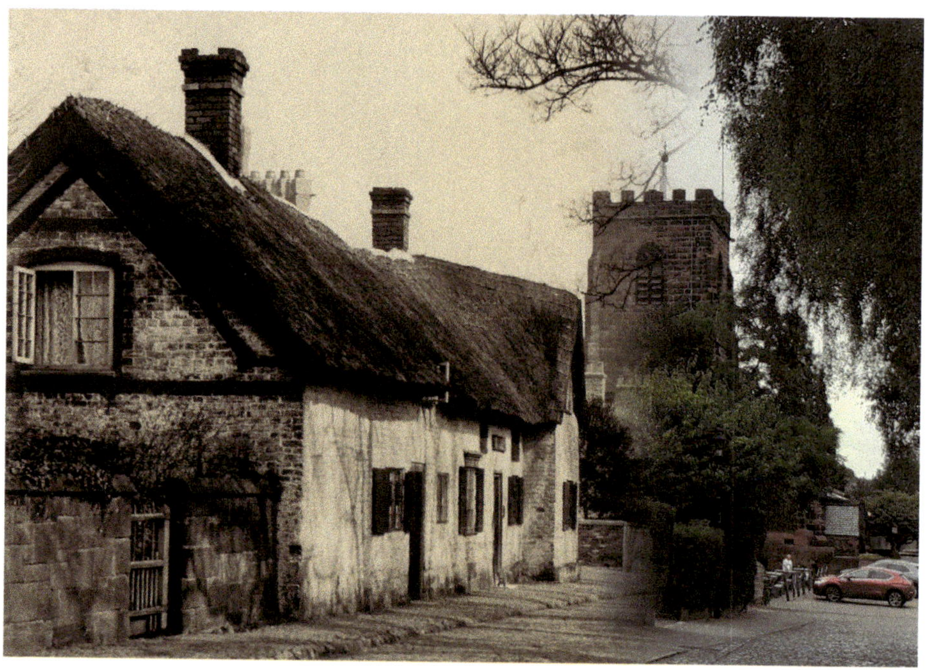

The heart of Grappenhall village, with its cobbled street and parish church of St Wilfrid's, seems to have largely escaped the passage of time. Recorded in the Domesday Book of 1086 as Gropenhale (Grappenhall), this ancient parish also included Latchford before the cutting of the Manchester Ship Canal. St Wilfrid's interior still reflects the village's medieval history with an effigy of a Norman knight whilst a carving on the church tower may have inspired Lewis Carroll's Cheshire Cat.

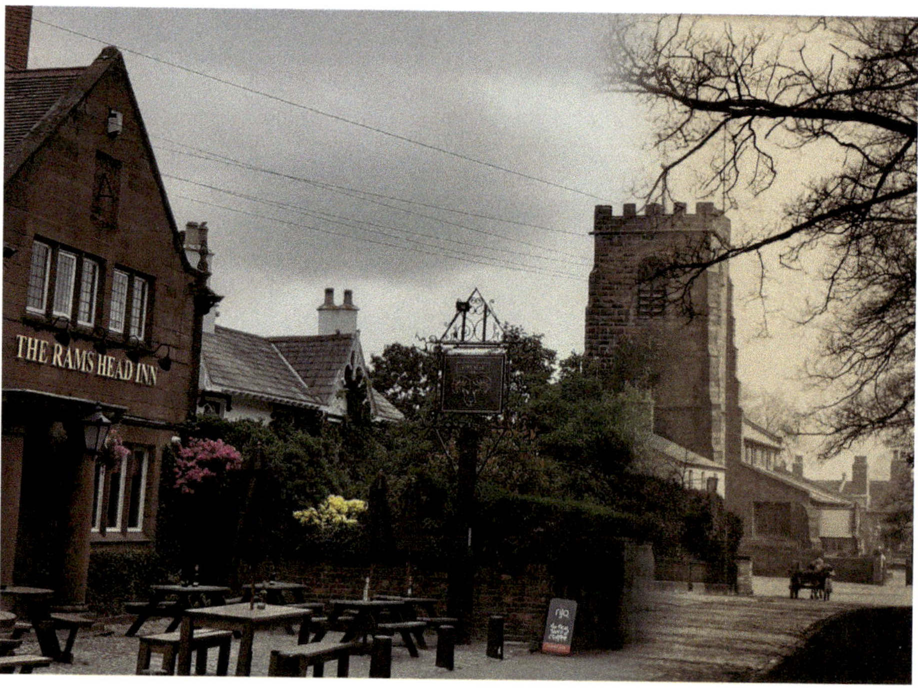

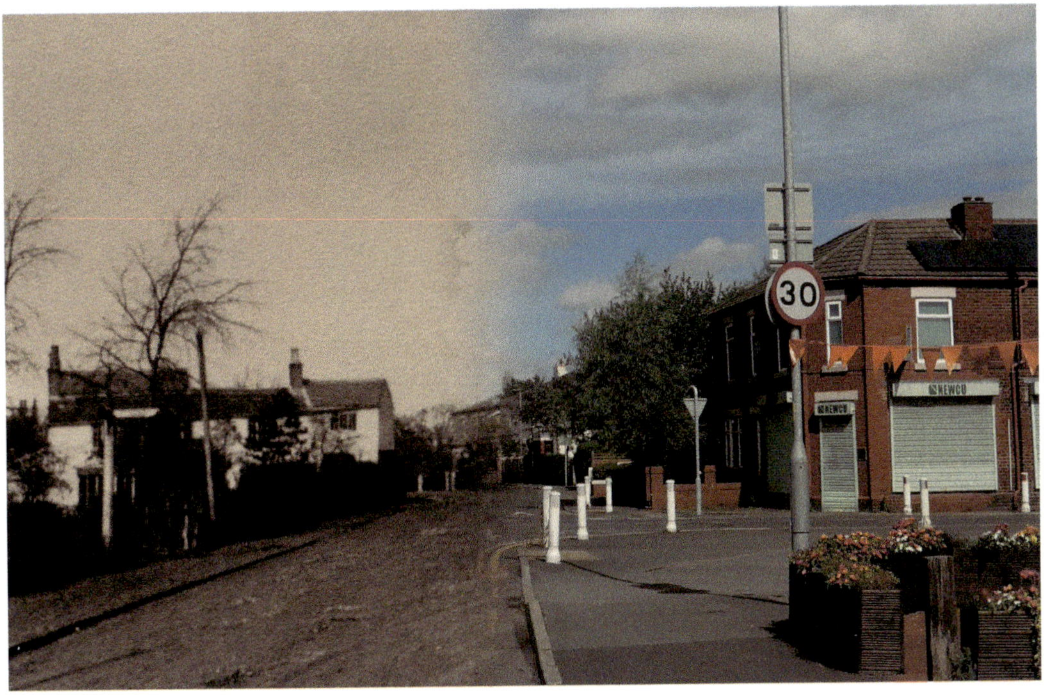

Over a century separates these two views of Fearnhead Cross but this is no longer a sleepy backwater of the town. From April 1939 to 1957 over 300 acres of Padgate farmland to the left of this site were a training camp for RAF recruits. This redundant site would become the focus of an extensive new Padgate district with its focus near Fearnhead Cross complete with shops, library, secondary school and community centre and an important area of modern Warrington.

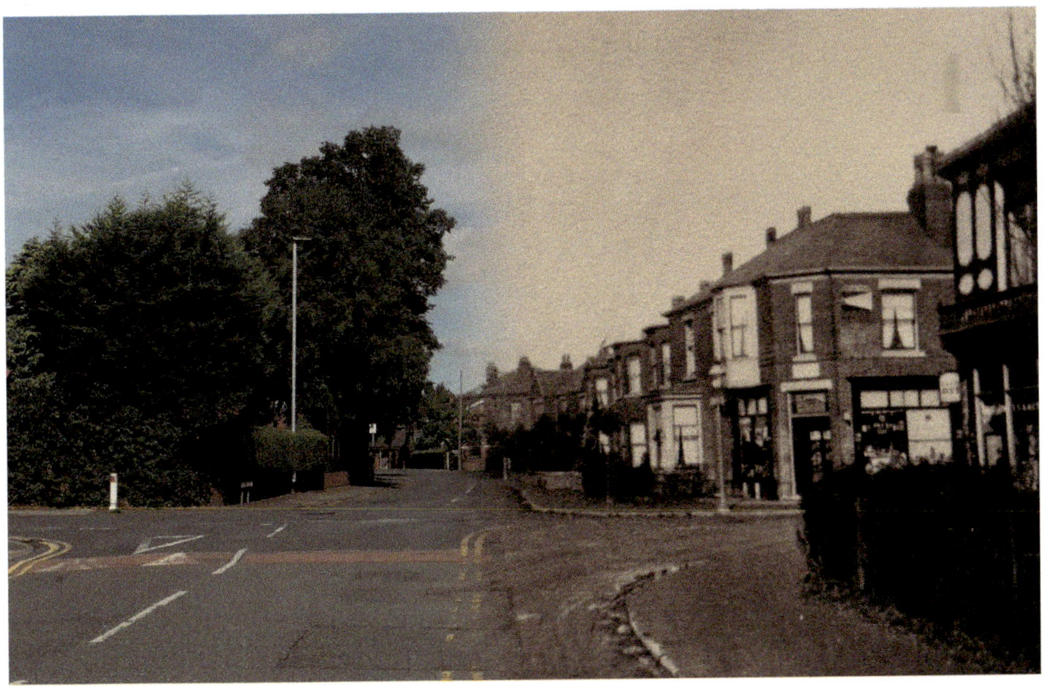

Acknowledgements

This volume has mainly been compiled from the extensive photographic collections of Culture Warrington's Local History Archive.

Acknowledgements are also due to all those who have contributed to the photographic archive and added to our knowledge of Warrington. Particular thanks are owing to all the professional and amateur photographers who have documented the changing face of the town. Every effort has been made to trace the copyright holders but the museum is always interested to learn further details of any of the featured images.

Thanks are also due to the staff of Culture Warrington from the Museum and Archives sections who document the town's history for present and future generations.

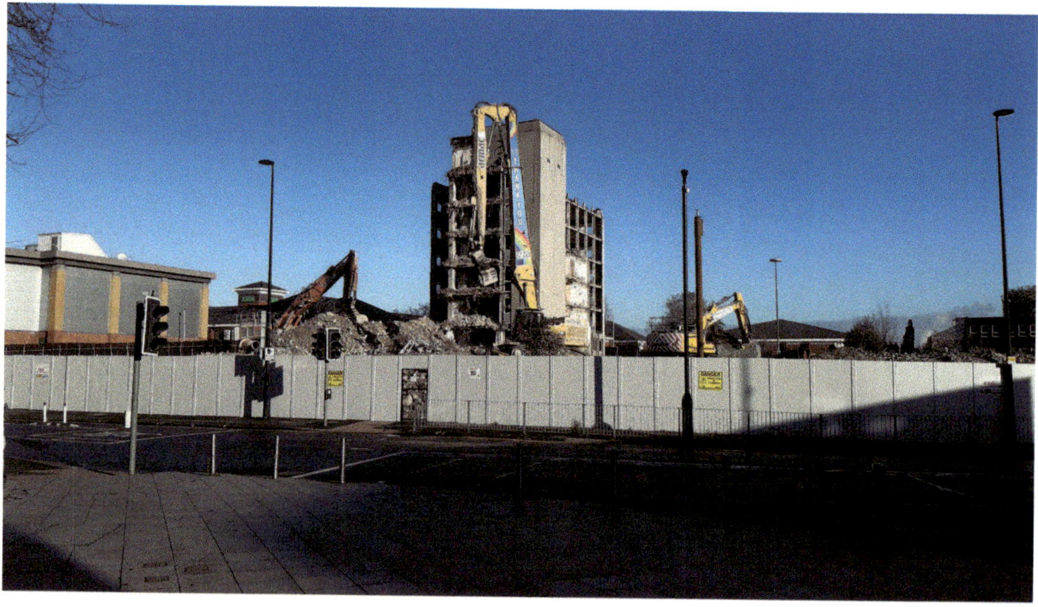

The demolition of New Town House in November 2022 opened up the site for new developments in the Cockhedge area as Warrington's landscape continues to evolve.